Gun Digest

GUIDE TO

CONCEALED CARRY
HANDGUNS

DICK JONES

Published by

Gun Digest® Books, an imprint of F+W Media, Inc.
Krause Publications • 700 East State Street • Iola, WI 54990-0001
715-445-2214 • 888-457-2873
www.krausebooks.com

To order books or other products call toll-free 1-800-258-0929
or visit us online at www.gundigeststore.com

Cover photography by Kris Kandler

ISBN-13: 978-1-4402-4388-2
ISBN-10: 1-4402-4388-3

Cover Design by Dave Hauser
Designed by Jana Tappa
Edited by Chad Love

Printed in China

10 9 8 7 6 5 4 3 2 1

TABLE OF CONTENTS

LIFE AS A CONCEALED CARRY CITIZEN

There are two kinds of people in today's society: those who believe our government and public servants can do the job of keeping us safe, and those who believe they should have the right and ability to protect themselves if faced with predators or aggressors and no law enforcement is present. Both sides of this argument are completely convinced their opinion is correct, and since the late 60s there's been an ongoing war between these two factions.

Those who believe citizens should be passive and allow society to take responsibility for their safety are convinced we're more likely to injure ourselves or worsen the situation if we take responsibility for our safety as individuals. They believe firearms in the hands of individuals create more crime and catastrophe than would be the case if firearms were only in the hands of law enforcement and government entities.

Of course, there are multiple problems with this mindset. To begin with, there are estimated to be well over 300 million firearms in the United States. There's no way to collect all these guns and even if there were, the right of citizens of the United States to own firearms is guaranteed by the Constitution. Even if such laws were passed, criminals who live their lives outside the law wouldn't comply. Furthermore, there's never been an instance where reducing the number of firearms in a country has reduced crime, though there are numerous cases of confiscation of firearms preceding the organization of a totalitarian system of government.

Since all but the most rabid of the anti-firearms faction realize that removal of all citizen-owned firearms is impossible, other approaches at reducing citizens from firearms access have been attempted. Certain classes of guns have been banned for import and manufacture, there have been limits imposed on magazine capacity, guns have been banned from certain areas, and the results of these attempts have had no effect in reducing crime. In fact, it is an almost universal truth that the parts of the country that have the most stringent firearms laws also have the worst rates of crime, indicating that crime isn't related to availability of firearms.

Certainly most of the mass murders that achieve monumental levels of media coverage almost exclusively occur in areas where guns are banned. Situations where firearms are allowed probably don't represent a high-value target for mass murderers, since they seem to have a desire for high body counts in order to make their crimes more notable and memorable. Most of these events are planned and contemplated ahead of time, and planning a mass murder with a high body count where one of the intended victims might have the ability to end the event would be foolish. In fact, there have been multiple events where a well-prepared would-be mass murderer encountered an armed citizen who ended the event early. Those situations don't draw non-stop media coverage and rarely even make national news. When something doesn't happen, there's no story.

Depending on whose numbers you believe, between 180,000 and 2,500,000 people successfully defend themselves with a gun every year. Given the highest number of deaths and comparing them to the lowest number of successful uses of a firearm for defense, for every person that dies from a criminal's gun, there are more than 13 people who successfully defend themselves using a gun for every one that dies from a criminal's gun.

Carrying a gun isn't an unreasonable decision. The odds of needing to use a gun for defense during your lifetime are similar to your house burning down. I assume most homeowners who read this have fire insurance. I have several fire alarms in my house, in spite of having homeowner's insurance and a fire department that's only 4.6 miles and eight minutes away. In fact, recent statistics from our own government have shown that in spite of the fact that firearms sales more than doubled over the last ten years, crime has declined at a remarkable rate for the same period. Indeed, recent times have seen a lot of positive legislation for firearms owners, rolling back much of the draconian Gun Control Act of 1968 which was fueled by a strong liberal shift in national politics and the assassinations of President Kennedy, Bobby Kennedy, and Martin Luther King.

In part, the new public acceptance of firearms ownership has come as a result of the passage of concealed carry legislation in so many states. In almost every state where concealed carry laws have been enacted, crime rates have declined and none have increased. Ordinary citizens who've never had an interest in guns are suddenly realizing the value of having the ability of reasonable self-defense. In teaching the North Carolina Concealed Carry Certification Course, I find that the students in my classes often have no prior connec-tion to firearms ownership. They have decided there's value to the ability to defend themselves and the ones they love. Many want to learn to use firearms without the intention of daily carry and I do everything in my power to convince them to becoming committed, daily carry concealed carry citizens.

I haven't always been a committed concealed carry citizen who carries a gun every day. When I began teaching my certification class, I kept a gun in my kit bag and that bag went everywhere I did between the seats of my truck. During a class, one of my students reminded me that carrying a gun every day isn't something you do simply to save your own life. It's something you do to make sure your life continues so you can continue to be a part of the lives of those you love.

If I lose my life, I'm not the only person affected. The premature end of my life affects everyone who cares about me as well. It affects my wife, my daughters, my grandchildren, all my friends, and the lives of all those people who could be positively affected by my actions. Since I live my life with the intention of others, a lot of individuals would be adversely affected if my life ended today. My responsibility isn't just to me, it's to all those I love, and all who love and care about me.

At that point, I committed myself to daily carry and I carry in every place I possibly can without violating the law. Furthermore, I often avoid locations where I can't carry because I know, based on past mass murder locations, that a "no weapons" sign is a welcome sign for violent crime. In the last calendar year, I carried 354 days. Four of those days I was in Italy and the rest, I was in New York. If I'm pulling out of my driveway and realize I've left my gun, I return and fetch it. As I wrote this book, sitting in my office, my gun was on my person, because it's an integral part of the way I live. My life or the life of someone I love may be ended prematurely, but I'm determined it won't happen because I was too lazy to have my means of defense handy.

While the decision to be a committed concealed carry citizen is an honorable decision to make, it doesn't come without responsibilities. You must know the laws concerning every aspect of concealed carry and the laws concerning the use of deadly force. While citizens who defend themselves are almost never charged with a crime, they are almost always sued by the aggressor if he lives, or by a family member if he doesn't. You need to know that the law relates more to this civil litigation than to the prospects of criminal charges. Try to remember someone who used deadly force in self-defense who was actually convicted. Try to think of a case where a defender was charged. Likely the only situation you'll be able to recall is George Zimmerman, and the police chief of Sanford refused to charge him and lost his job as a result. Later, as everyone knows, Zimmerman was found innocent.

What will almost certainly happen should you use deadly force, whether it's with a handgun or a golf club, is a lawsuit. Part of your responsibility to yourself and those you love is having knowledge of the law that will allow you to be properly prepared for that lawsuit. Know the law and know that your interview after a self-defense event will be public information and what you say in that interview can cause serious issues in a civil trial.

In addition, you have a responsibility of safety to both yourself and everyone around you, from members of your own family to the general public. Safe gun handling is of paramount importance for those who carry every day, and the simplest slip in gun handling discipline can turn into a catastrophic event in seconds.

Not long ago, in Colorado, a two-year-old child unzipped his mother's concealed carry purse and managed to fire her gun, shooting the mother in the head and killing her instantly. The story has created a firestorm on the Internet, with pro-gun people saying she was careless to allow the child to access the gun, and anti-gun forces saying it's just another reason why guns are bad and no one should have one. The morning the story hit, I received an email from my niece. She was considering getting a concealed carry permit and was asking how this could happen and if it could have reasonably been avoided.

As much as I hate to say this, and although I feel sympathy for the family, the only way this could have happened is if the mother made a serious mistake in gun handling. Most of the mistakes we make in life have low levels of consequence; we can make the same mistake a thousand times with no consequences at all, but there's always a chance a simple mistake will be a life-changing one. The mother knew guns; her friends and family said she was safe and careful with guns and knew how to handle them. She normally carried her gun on her, but she received a concealed carry purse for Christmas and the gun was in the purse when the incident happened. She left the child in the shopping cart with the purse and for some reason the child accessed the gun and shot it. She was hit in the head and died instantly.

Her mistake was she left the gun in a position where the child could access it. Perhaps she was distracted. She might have forgotten the gun was in her purse, since she normally carried on her person. She may have thought the zipper on the purse was locked when it wasn't, since many concealed carry purses have locking zippers. Whatever the reason may have been, she made a mistake, because a two-year-old child got his hands on a loaded gun.

She was criticized for the fact she was carrying a gun, but that was not her mistake. Carrying a gun isn't an unreasonable decision. Gun ownership and carrying a gun for personal protection is a right in this country, and a reasonable decision, but constant vigilance regarding safety is paramount. Sadly for one family, a moment of inattention cost a heavy price.

Another reason for having constant control of your firearm is the possibility it might end up in the wrong hands. Most states have laws concerning minors' access to firearms. While you have no legal liability should your firearm be stolen, can you imagine going through the rest of your life knowing your carelessness allowed a gun to be stolen, and that gun later took the life of an innocent person? While those who oppose individuals having guns for self-protection have told the public for years that having a gun is a bad idea because a criminal might take it away from you and use it against you, instances of this actually happening are extremely rare. If you carry a gun, however, you must be constantly vigilant that you maintain control of it.

Yet another responsibility of the concealed carry citizen is the responsibility to be able to effectively use your gun, should the unfortunate occasion arise where it's needed. Buying a gun and taking a certification class is only the beginning. Anyone who carries a gun in public must have the ability to hit the target, because a miss can potentially take the life of an innocent person. In North Carolina, our certification course for obtaining the CCH permit is 30 shots in a target at three, five, and seven yards. I've never had a student who didn't qualify for their permit, though a few have needed to come back for some extra work. This level of competence is far below the level that's responsible for an individual who carries a gun in public. Having said this, consider that in spite of this low level of training and practice, a concealed carry citizen is far less likely to wrongly shoot than a police officer. Remember that we've already discussed the fact we never or almost never hear of a concealed carry citizen wrongly shooting anyone.

Remember that in every state I know of, to use deadly force, you must be in real danger of losing your life, or have fear of great bodily harm or sexual assault. You must literally be frightened for your life. Under these conditions, your performance will suffer. People under stress don't rise to the occasion as happens in the movies; they fall back on the level of training they have. If the threat is a simple one, your level of training will probably suffice, and in fact, it almost always does. While most defensive situations of armed citizens are rarely examples of exemplary marksmanship, they almost always end with a good result, even when the aggressor is armed. In the vast majority of personal defense cases, the mere presence of the gun is enough to end the confrontation. Still, regular practice and learning the right way to operate your defensive gun increases the odds of your success, and perhaps more importantly, they generate confidence, which is a valuable asset when you're under stress.

While this book is about the gun choices you have available to you, the most important choice you make is the choice to take the responsibility of daily concealed carry seriously. When I made the decision to carry a gun on a daily basis, I knew it was a serious undertaking. I wrote down, and now keep in my office, a list of my own responsibilities and convictions.

• It's my belief that I'm responsible for the protection of my own life. I am aware I spend most of my life in places where there are no police there to defend me, and that even if I could call the police before the dangerous event occurred, the event would most likely be over by the time they arrived.

• I believe that by being armed and well trained, I am able and willing to change the outcome should a bad person decide to harm me, someone I love, or an innocent person I don't even know.

• I'm willing to go through the process of having my actions judged by others as to whether I've made the right decision should I have to use deadly force, because I have educated myself on the laws concerning self-defense.

• Every hour of every day, I take the precautions required to keep my firearm out of the hands of someone who would accidentally or intentionally harm someone else.

• I'm fully aware that the consequences of a mistake concerning my decision are life-changing. I'm also aware that a civilian is much less likely – by a substantial margin - to wrongfully shoot or accidently shoot an innocent person than a sworn law enforcement officer.

• I know that even though the anti-gun side warns that the good guy's gun is often taken away and used against him, it almost never happens, but I must maintain control of my gun at all times.

• I've talked to people who faced situations where their lives were threatened. Some of those people were armed and some were not. I prefer the outcomes the armed ones experienced, and this is my motivation to be prepared through daily carry.

• I have seen reports of situations where I honestly feel I could have stopped the killing of innocent people by the mindless murderers who, from time to time, decide they wish to end their lives (whether by going to prison or being killed by police) in a hail of publicity and fame on news shows. In every single case we hear about on the news, a single, well-prepared citizen or police officer could have stopped the carnage, and in every situation where that armed person is there, there is no story to dominate the news for weeks. We simply don't hear about the positive outcomes of firearms ownership, because when the bad guy is stopped, or simply decides to walk away and save his skin, it isn't a national news story. I am resolved to do everything in my power to be sufficiently prepared to prevail should I ever have to face such a situation.

As you make the decision to be a concealed carry citizen, please think about your responsibilities. It isn't something to be taken lightly.

CHAPTER 1

CHOOSING THE RIGHT CONCEALED CARRY GUN

Life is about options. From the time we're capable of making decisions as a child, our quality of life depends on the choices we make. Some of us choose wisely, others choose poorly, and unless we are blessed with random positive circumstances, those who choose wisely generally experience a better quality of life. Unfortunately, in any society there are those who make the choice to prey on others who might have made better choices and have better life circumstances.

Every gun shown here, and hundreds more, are viable choices for daily concealed carry. The object is to choose the gun that fits your lifestyle, carry method, and skill level.

It's because of this unfortunate fact of life that we even have to discuss the idea of concealed carry for personal defense. Some in our society choose to allow sworn law enforcement to be wholly in charge of their safety. If you're reading this book, you've probably made the decision to augment the protection the police can provide, and become an active first responder when it comes to your own personal safety.

As I will point out elsewhere in this book, the most important choice you can make - besides the decision to take some responsibility for your well being - is to be aware of your surroundings. Simple situational awareness will likely be your best defense in staying safe, but even if you do everything right, there's always the chance that at some point you'll find a need for self-defense. Of course, you could learn martial arts or become a master in the art of the blade, but for most people a firearm is the best possible equalizer. In fact, a firearm - and the ability to use it properly - isn't an equalizer; it's a serious advantage in most situations, the mere presence of which normally resolves the issue.

The object of this chapter is to help you make a wise choice in the gun you decide to carry, but no matter which gun you choose, your commitment to learn to use that gun properly and safely is much more important than caliber, magazine capacity, size, or operational design. Well-placed shots from small calibers are infinitely more effective than close misses from major calibers. The importance of the ability to properly operate the gun is only exceeded by the importance of actually having the gun available to you should that unfortunate situation occur.

In firearms choice for the concealed carry citizen, the right answer for each person ranges over a broad spectrum of firearms, and covers caliber, action type, sight options, weight, and size; both in slimness as well as overall profile. All these factors are important parts of the right answer for your needs, but the truth is, what you carry as a concealed defense handgun depends most on where you go and how much of the time you intend to spend with the firearm connected to you.

My recommendation is that concealed carry citizens carry their guns every day and everywhere they're legally allowed to carry. As I said earlier, last year I carried 354 days. I spent four days in Italy and seven in New York. I cannot carry in either of those places, and I felt uncomfortable the whole time. My commitment to concealed carry is that the need to use a firearm for self-defense is about the same as the chance of a house fire in my home. Since I keep insurance on my house all the time, I see it as common sense to carry a gun all the time.

Of course, when you decide to carry a gun every day and everywhere you go, you need to purchase a gun that's easy to hide, comfortable to carry, yet still effective. That balance of weight to power and magazine capacity becomes a serious issue. Power-ful guns are undoubtedly better in a fight, but you must be accurate with the powerful gun, and it must be easy enough to carry that you have it with you all the time. A .22 rimfire in your hand is always better than a .45 on you dresser, unless you're in your bedroom next to the dresser.

Another issue, of course, is reliability. Defensive guns must work when you need them because a gun that doesn't function is the same as not having a gun. One might argue that a gun that's 99 percent reliable is enough, but I'd prefer one that's 99.9 percent reliable, or 100 percent reliable, if possible.

Part of that level of reliability relates to your ability to reliably operate the gun. If you have trouble operating the slide, or the trigger is so heavy you can barely pull it in double-action mode, you have reliability issues. If the two issues listed in the last sentence made you wonder, please consider that many women and older or smaller people simply cannot operate the slide on many small-frame, striker-fired, semi-autos, and those people are the fastest-growing segment of the concealed carry market. I've learned

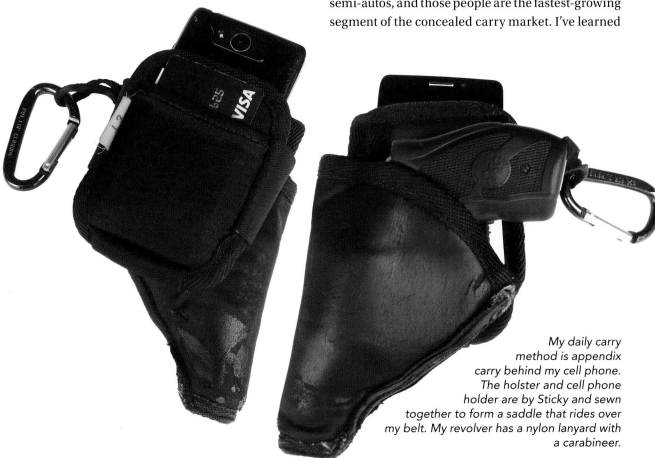

My daily carry method is appendix carry behind my cell phone. The holster and cell phone holder are by Sticky and sewn together to form a saddle that rides over my belt. My revolver has a nylon lanyard with a carabineer.

> "...NO MATTER WHICH GUN YOU CHOOSE, YOUR COMMITMENT TO LEARN TO USE THAT GUN PROPERLY AND SAFELY IS MUCH MORE IMPORTANT THAN CALIBER, MAGAZINE CAPACITY, SIZE, OR OPERATIONAL DESIGN."

this from experience as an instructor, and it would surprise most people to know just how intrusive this problem is.

Accuracy is important as well. While it's true that most defensive situations for civilians occur at very short ranges, there's always the possibility you might need accuracy beyond seven yards. Nothing irritates me more than the phrase "minute of bad guy." I know this statement in a gun review generally says something about the skill of the gun writer rather than the gun being tested, but if a gun is only capable of 12" groups at seven yards, I'm not going to trust my life on it because there are too many guns that are perfectly capable of quarter-sized groups at this distance. Accuracy does matter, and even with the tiny concealed carry sights on some guns, real accuracy is possible. Add a laser that's properly zeroed, and the average 15-ounce carry gun should be capable of quarter-sized groups every time.

Compounding the accuracy issue is the fact that under stress, performance deteriorates at a drastic rate. Police officers, who have no trouble qualifying out to 25 yards, often shoot a full magazine at an assailant under the pressure of a gunfight without a single hit. These are people with regular training schedules and qualifications, who are shooting full-size guns, and get free ammunition for practice. Accuracy does matter, but of course, if you can't shoot, the most accurate gun in the world will only make you slightly better. Generally, guns miss by inches and shooters miss by feet.

Finally, the ability to carry the gun safely might well be the most important factor of all. When you make the conscious decision to take some of the responsibility for you own safety and carry a firearm, you also assume the responsibility of making sure you aren't a safety hazard to yourself or the public. This means your concealed carry choice must be a gun you can reliably carry with no danger of accidental discharge or you failing to hit your target and

harm an innocent bystander. We have enough opponents to the right of individual self-defense as it is. We don't need sloppy gun handling adding to the problem.

So for daily carry, the firearm must be light, concealable, powerful enough to stop a bad guy, accurate enough to hit a bad guy, and as close to perfectly reliable and easy to operate as possible, and certainly as safe as possible. While this sounds like a tall order, I contend that it's not. In writing this book, I've been amazed and heartened by just how many truly excellent guns the modern concealed carry citizen has to choose from. After compiling the list of guns in this book, I know there are at least 30 of them that would suit my needs and do everything I need from a daily carry gun. Some of those guns are semi-autos and some are revolvers. All of them are accurate, lightweight, compact, reliable, powerful, and small enough to hide, even with the way I dress in the deep south in summer.

Which brings us to a vital part of the equation: how you dress has more effect on your needs in a concealed carry gun than almost any other factors. Other than the constraints of feminine style, my summer clothing style is probably the toughest to cover unless you're a flip flops, tank top, and athletic shorts guy, and come to think of it, the un-tucked tank top can hide a pretty big gun. I wear shorts and a tucked-in, short-sleeved shirt in summer. Tucked-in shirts make concealment harder, but I find I can reliably hide a 3" barreled 20-ounce semi-auto or revolver pretty well. Having said this, a 20-ounce gun gets pretty heavy and hot on a North Carolina summer day, so I stay with a two-inch, 13-ounce gun.

I've found many CCH permit holders only intend to carry the firearm in their vehicles when traveling and have it in their home for personal use. For them, the problem is simpler. Of course, if you're planning to never carry the gun on your person, the heavy gun makes more sense. The only time the weight is a prob-

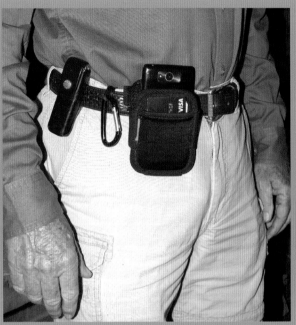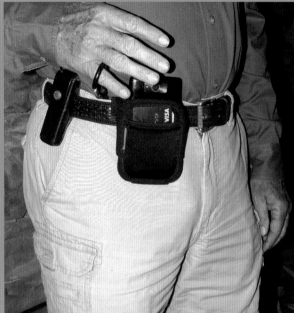

To draw, I hook my pinkie in the carabineer and the gun comes up from below my belt line.

lem is when you transfer the gun from the car to the house. Bigger guns are easier to shoot well, more accurate, have larger capacity, and are generally more power than small ones. Having said this, I strongly recommend carrying seven days a week, 52 weeks a year.

For many who have less shooting experience and choose to carry a firearm for self defense, the decision rests more on ease of operation than any other factor. A long-time shooter won't find a 1911-type autoloader difficult to operate, but to a beginner it's an intimidating gun, indeed.

The issues of level of training have been addressed with the advent of the modern striker-fired autoloader. They're reliable and simple to use, but many contend they're still too complicated for most new shooters to handle in a pinch, and some smaller or older people have issues with operating the slide. Revolvers are simpler to operate and certainly the most reliable firearms in production, but again, people with low hand strength have trouble with the double-action trigger.

In spite of this, I think they're almost always the best choice for people with low training levels, and maybe the best overall gun for concealed carry citizens. Most people who put in some effort can learn to operate the double-action trigger well, and there's no argument that the revolver is the most reliable action type for handguns. Double-action semi-autos offer some advantages of both revolvers and semi-autos, and modern striker-fired pistols are reliable, accurate, and easy to learn to operate.

Another consideration is the magazine safety. Some semi-autos use a magazine safety that disables the gun when the magazine is removed, even though there's a round in the chamber. There are proponents of this arrangement and detractors. The downside is that a gun that loses a magazine is no longer a gun. This also happens to be the upside. I know law enforcement officers who like magazine safeties because if there's a fight with a criminal over the gun and the criminal is losing, the officer can push the magazine button and render the gun useless should the criminal gain control.

Another plus for a concealed carry citizen is the owner can use the feature as an added safety level around children. For instance, a woman might remove the magazine from the gun and carry it with her while her child is in a shopping cart, allowing her to leave her purse behind for short periods. The downside is that without a magazine safety, a semi-automatic is a

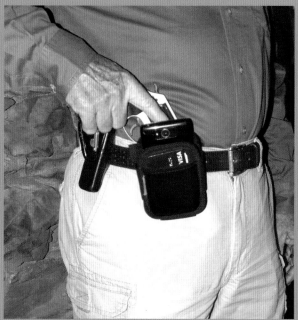

When the gun is clear, I grip the grip and rotate the gun to horizontal. It's faster than most methods where the user can wear a tucked shirt.

functional single shot. Also, some magazine safeties have an adverse effect on triggers and the free drop of a magazine. There are preferences for both systems and it's something to consider.

While I love the 1911 platform, I see them as a poor choice for concealed carry. I hate to put this in print because I know it's worse than making a public statement about how to resolve issues in the Middle East. I know it will make 1911 devotees angry, but a 22-ounce 1911 is as light as you get and this is still a heavy gun.

Furthermore, unless I can carry in a strap-under-the-hammer holster, I don't feel comfortable with a cocked and locked 1911 being banged around in my active daily lifestyle. Tiny 1911s have only slightly more magazine capacity than a small, powerful revolver, and the revolver has fewer safety and reliability issues. Lightweight 1911s can get pretty picky.

The challenges the 1911 faces as a carry gun extend to almost all the single-action, concealed carry, semi-autos as well. The original semi-auto concealed carry guns were designed just after the beginning of the 20th century. They preceded the 1911, and offered only a thumb safety to prevent accidental discharge. There wasn't even an exposed hammer that could be lowered. Most who carried them did so with an empty

chamber for safety, and I believe this was a good idea.

The current crop of single-action-only, concealed carry pistols are much safer than those original guns, but still lack a level of safety I'd prefer. They can be carried with an empty chamber or with the hammer down, but that handicaps them when a fast shot is needed. Most don't even offer the passive grip safety that's an added layer of safety for the 1911.

All guns that are carried with the striker or hammer completely cocked and rely on an external manually-operated safety carry a liability in what happens after the shot is fired. Unless the operator is trained to a level that insures the safety will be activated before the gun is re-holstered, there's considerable opportunity for an accidental discharge during the re-holster.

With any gun, the process of drawing, holstering, and re-holstering, is probably the most dangerous sequence of operation. When law enforcement made the transition from revolvers to semi-automatics, one of the major issues was that officers who'd drawn their guns and taken them off safe were forgetting to make them safe before re-holstering. Remember, this was happening with officers who'd received regular and formal training. The adrenalin shot of a high-risk situation alters judgment and awareness in civilians as well as law enforcement. This issue, as much as any other, was what drove the movement to guns with passive safety systems, and is responsible for the rise of the modern striker-fired pistol, as pioneered by Glock.

The modern striker-fired guns make an excellent choice for the concealed carry citizen. The best of them offer 9mm and even .40 S&W power in a small package that weighs less than 20 ounces in the single-stack versions. They have reasonable magazine capacity in single-stack and very good capacity in double-stack configurations, although the double stacks do become a bit girth-y and exceed the 20-ounce mark. They have excellent safety features, good triggers, more than acceptable accuracy and reliability is quite good. There are a lot of very good guns in this class.

The double/single and double-action-only guns make a viable choice for concealed carry because they can be safely carried with a round in the chamber, hammer down, and offer a very fast first shot unencumbered by the need for carry with an activated safety. They also offer second-strike capability. Walther made this design popular with the iconic PPK, and even James Bond chose one, though I've never been impressed with 007's choices in firearms.

A downside of the double/single actions is they, like 1911s and other single action semi-autos, require the operator to remember and manually make them safe before re-holstering. While de-cocking models address lowering the hammer ,and models that allow a hammer-back safety mode provide for some safety, both require a conscious action on the part of the operator.

Many of the modern internal hammer semi-autos use a double-action-only and I believe this to be a better option for individuals without high levels of training. With double-action-only guns, each shot requires a full double-action pull of the trigger, and the completion of the shot leaves it as safe as it was when removed from the holster.

As a young man who loved guns, I often read gun magazines and fantasized about how it would be exciting to be able to put my preferences and the kind of guns I like in print. In those days, we didn't have the Internet, just the occasional letter to the editor,

and only a handful of those ever made it off the editor's desk. I don't remember how it was to strongly voice your opinion in those days, but I do know that voicing a strong opinion today can get you some powerful criticism. I am, however the author of this book, so I'll allow myself a paragraph to voice my opinion, though I know it will draw some unfriendly fire. Here goes:

I carry a five-shot, two-inch, 13-ounce, .38 Special +P revolver with a Crimson Trace laser grip. Yes, I know, it's less powerful than the 9mm round that many consider the minimum or below for reliable stopping. Yes, capacity is only five rounds. Yes, I know it's an ancient design from 1896, and yes, I know most say such guns aren't accurate.

In its defense, it's light enough that I'm never tempted to leave it on the dresser. It's small enough I can hide it, even while wearing shorts and a lightweight summer shirt tucked in. It's accurate enough that, in order to inspire my students, I always shoot a fly off the target in concealed carry classes if one lands, and yes, I'll take a bet on my ability to do so at five yards, median distance in the North Carolina qualification course. It's powerful enough that I have confidence it would stop a determined attacker, especially with the quality ammunition I carry. And finally, I have 100% confidence that it'll function whether I hold it tight or loose, and that if a round fails to fire, I only have to pull the trigger again. It's also as safe after a round is fired as it was before, and without any conscious action on my part. Feel free to criticize me for my choice, but first make sure your choice will do all this.

Handguns - just like everything else in life - are a compromise. Heavy guns are easier to shoot than light guns in the same caliber and the heavy gun kicks a lot less, but who wants to lug a heavy gun around all the time? The really great part about this discussion is that Americans have the right to buy and carry the gun we choose, and there are so many excellent guns available to choose from. Even better, when we see one we think might be better than the one we have, we can buy it. If you remember nothing else, remember this: you can never have too many guns.

CHOOSING A CALIBER FOR CONCEALED CARRY

Probably the most hotly-discussed topic in concealed carry and personal defense is the argument over what constitutes a proper caliber. We know that no caliber chambered in a regular repeating handgun is capable of always stopping a perpetrator with a single shot. Obviously some calibers are much more effective than others, but there's always a tradeoff in recoil, capacity, and the size of the carry gun. It's a common belief among many that any caliber under .40 is ineffective, and those who carry smaller calibers are constantly bombarded with anecdotes relating the dire consequences of carrying a pipsqueak caliber. Statements about chocolate grips and filed-off front sights abound, but there's really little evidence to prove that bigger calibers are substantially more effective in stopping aggressors than smaller ones.

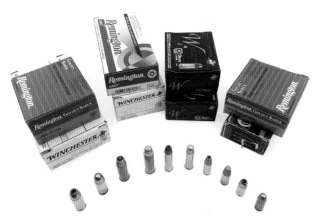

With so many excellent guns in so many good calibers, the choice can be daunting. Often the load chosen has as much effect on success as the caliber.

Bigger guns are better stoppers, but they weigh more and are harder to carry comfortably. Every choice involving concealed carry is a compromise, but modern ammunition makes calibers that were once marginal much more effective.

With the exception of hitting the brain stem or first few inches of the spinal column, handgun calibers incapacitate by causing blood loss. Larger, more powerful calibers are more likely to accomplish this given the same entry location and angle. Ideally, the projectile should penetrate to vital organs or major arteries even if they encounter bone structure. It's a given that the larger the wound channel, the greater chance that wound channel will intercept those large arteries and vital organs, so a combination of penetration and an enlarged wound channel is the criteria for best performance. It's better for the projectile to stay in the perpetrator's body, for two reasons: One, if the projectile doesn't exit, all the energy will be transmitted to the target. Second, since personal defense often happens in populated areas, a projectile that doesn't exit can't do damage to an innocent bystander.

Since the penetration to the spinal column is a major factor in incapacitation, and most defensive situations involve a frontal shot, it would be ideal to somehow push the projectile all the way through the perpetrator with it stopping just short of exiting. Unfortunately, such consistent performance isn't possible because bad guys come in different sizes and wear different kinds of clothing, which can be a factor in penetration, especially if the bad guy is wearing heavy winter clothing.

CONTINUED PRACTICE WITH A GUN LARGER THAN YOU CAN HANDLE OFTEN EXACERBATES THE PROBLEM OF FLINCH.

It's been generally accepted that .38 Special and 9mm are about the minimum in reliable stopping power. In recent years, the performance of .380 ACP has been improved with better bullet design and higher-performance defensive loads. Traditionally, there's always been a school of thought that the .45 ACP is a reliable one-shot stopper. As a young man, I heard stories from World War II veterans about enemy soldiers being hit in the shoulder with a .45 slug and the impact flipping them into a distant foxhole. While early TV shows depicted those who were shot simply freezing in place and dying, later TV shows and movies popularized the concept of bad guys being thrown over cars and across rooms. Neither scenario was realistic. People who are shot react differently, but violent movements come as a reaction from the person who's received a gunshot, not from tremendous energy being released against their body.

The energy of a handgun round is simple physics. If enough energy is released from the muzzle of the handgun to knock the aggressor down, the recoil from that shot will have a similar effect on the person who fires the gun. Even a .500 S&W only deflects my arms when I shoot it. It's quite easy for me to maintain my balance and stay on my feet. A 230-grain .45 ACP round only moves my arms slightly, with most of the movement being absorbed by my arms.

Many who will read this book are already accomplished shooters. Most accomplished shooters can easily handle a full-size .45 or .40 with little adverse effect. That number is reduced, however, when the size and weight of the gun goes from a 39-ounce, full-size gun to a 20-ounce concealed carry pistol. My experience is that even individuals who consider themselves perfectly capable of handling a gun in a caliber that begins with "4" often flinch enough to cause shots below the targeted area, even at close range. Further, continued practice with a gun larger than you can handle often exacerbates the problem of flinch. A shot that hits below the sternum is unlikely to cause massive blood loss, even if it's a fatal shot. Massive blood loss is your best bet for making a determined aggres-

sor cease to fight.

A while back, I had a conversation with the sheriff of a Georgia county who had recently switched his department from the Glock 22 in .40 to the Glock 17 in 9mm. His reason for the switch was that many of his officers were having trouble managing the additional recoil of the .40 S&W round. When the department made the switch, the qualification scores for the department went up substantially. He also made the point that the less expensive 9mm round allowed the department to purchase almost twice as much ammunition for practice at the same budgeting level.

Weight is another problem with large-caliber concealed carry guns. They tend to be heavy. The primary prerequisite to winning a gunfight is to have a gun. Of the guns in calibers that begin with "4", about the lightest models available weigh around 20 ounces empty. Most .38 Special five-shot revolvers weigh in between 11 and 14 ounces, so the average weight reduction is close to 40%, a substantial difference when you carry every day, all day.

Bigger guns are better stoppers, but they weigh more and are harder to carry comfortably. Every choice involving concealed carry is a compromise, but modern ammunition makes calibers that were once marginal much more effective. Or course, in many confrontations between citizens and aggressors, the aggressor doesn't have a gun, and in a large percentage of those cases, the simple presence of the gun is effective for stopping the aggressor, whether that gun is a .500 or a .22.

Even if the citizen has to shoot the aggressor, many bad guys decide to stop simply because they've been shot. While I've never been shot, I have talked to people who have, and they tell me it's not a pleasant experience. Of course, if the aggressor is pumped up with adrenalin, or drugs, or experiencing a psychotic episode, he may not even feel a fatal shot that takes his life within seconds, and this type of aggressor is the only adversary the concealed carry citizen will face who's affected by caliber choice.

This determined attacker has to be physically incapacitated to end the aggression, where the attacker cannot continue due to the level of his injuries. Fortunately, the percentage of determined attackers who persist even though seriously wounded is relatively small. A higher percentage of people simply stop the aggression when they realize they've been shot. Their reaction might come from the level of pain or fear of death and realization that continuing might end their life. This is considered a psychological stop.

Caliber and effectiveness of the round most likely have little to do with what's required to produce a psychological stop. The sound of the gun associated with the pain and perhaps the presence of blood loss, all are likely to contribute to a cessation of aggression in a person predisposed to a psychological stop. In that scenario a .22 rimfire will probably work almost as well as a .44 Magnum.

Unfortunately, there are no in-depth studies that can give us exact information about what the optimum caliber for concealed carry might be. Even if there was, the constraints of each concealed carry citizen's lifestyle would likely be more of an issue than caliber selection. The closest thing to a definitive study is entitled "An Alternate Look at Handgun Stopping Power" by Greg Ellifritz. Ellifritz compiled, over a ten year period, statistics from 1,800 shootings with calibers beginning with .22 rimfire and .25 ACP and topping out with centerfire rifle and shotgun. The results were surprising in some ways and what you'd expect in others.

The criteria involved:
- The percentage of hits that were fatal.
- The average number of rounds before incapacitation.
- The percentage of people who weren't incapacitated.
- The percentage of one shot stops.
- The percentage of aggressors incapacitated by one shot.

The most surprising statistics involved the number of one-shot stops. While rifle and shotgun stops were more successful by an appreciable amount, the one-shot stop rates for handgun calibers from .25

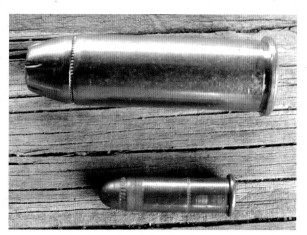

In a situation where the defender doesn't have to fire a shot or in the case of a psychological stop, the little .22 Long Rifle is as effective as a .44 S&W Magnum.

to .44 Magnum were remarkably similar, only varying by a few percentage points. The average number of rounds required to incapacitate aggressors - two shots - was also remarkably similar. This might indicate that caliber makes little difference in the ability to stop aggressors. However, the percentage of people who weren't incapacitated at all was much higher with the smaller calibers, but statistically almost the same for calibers from .38 Special on up to .44 Magnum.

Ellifritz concluded that while it was true that the more powerful the round, the better the chance a determined aggressor could ultimately be stopped, the vast majority of aggressors give up when they know they've been shot. To see the complete study you can go to: http://www.buckeyefirearms.org/alternate-look-handgun-stopping-power.

The point of all this is that any reasonable caliber can stop an aggressor. At the same time, a determined aggressor can continue to fight, even if he's mortally wounded by the largest handgun commercially produced, and even when hit in recommended target areas. It's true that penetration is an important factor, as is the size of the wound channel, but these are issues that only count when the projectile is delivered to the right spot. The best advice is to carry the most powerful caliber and ammunition you - and the gun you commit to carry every day - can handle.

CHAPTER 3

CONCEALED CARRY SIGHT OPTIONS

I was in a local gun shop recently when the discussion turned to the viability of lasers for concealed carry guns. One proponent of the laser explained they were the greatest things since sliced bread, something that could allow any novice to shoot like a professional. The other saw them as the work of the devil, a high-tech contraption that would likely fail at the moment the owner needed it most, leaving the victim standing and staring at a gun that was useless without a laser because it was the only way he could hit a target. Both opinions are wrong.

In really low light or when there's no room for an extended sight picture, nothing beats a laser.

As both a shooting instructor who teaches concealed carry certification and a gun writer, I suffer from a form of double indemnity. For some reason, I seem to get into the center of arguments about what constitutes the best options for concealed carry, and these days this is a hot topic. Besides the normal semi-auto versus revolver and high-capacity versus smaller, thinner gun issues, the discussion often turns to sights. After all, the sights are hopefully the only interface between the defender and the assailant.

Before we get too far into the sight issue though, remember that the average distance for a firearm defense occurrence is less than three yards. It should also be remembered that a full extension of the arms to get a proper sight picture at short distance often puts the gun as close to the assailant as it is to the defender. In really close quarters, extending the arms to get a proper sight picture increases the defender's level of danger because it can put the gun in easy reach of the attacker. In these situations, conventional sights have no value at all, since they can't be safely aligned with the eye.

While this obviously leads to thoughts of lasers, lasers shouldn't be the only viable option available to the concealed carry defender, because lasers are not as effective in bright light conditions. It's true that 70 percent of firearms defensive situations occur in low light, and green lasers are much more effective in bright light, but conventional sights on a defensive gun shouldn't be discounted. Even if your gun has a laser, you should do most of your practice with the iron sights. Lasers are electronic devices, as is the computer I'm writing this on. If your computer never gives you problems, you'll probably never have a problem with a laser sight because they're hundreds of times more reliable than my laptop. Still, there's the potential for the unit to fail or have the light blocked by debris, or for you to fail to properly maintain the batteries.

Considering the less high-tech methods of sighting a defensive handgun, there are compromises to be made. Good sights that are easy to see and maintain an excellent sight picture are always large. Large sights don't generally work well on concealed carry guns because they increase the gun's profile and increase the chance of snagging on clothing or carry devices. Small, easily concealed sights carry well, but are difficult to see in less-than-optimal light conditions.

The most unobtrusive sight system for a small gun is a simple trench milled the length of the slide or topstrap. This is the prevailing system for small revolvers as a rear sight; it's normally paired with a ramp front sight, and it works quite well. In my Concealed Carry Brushup classes, where all the shooting is done at ranges shorter than seven yards, I like to stop the class if a fly or bee lands on a target. I then use my personal carry gun to shoot the fly. If it's less than five yards, I'm almost always successful. Even if I miss at seven yards, the shot is so close the impression remains. You can shoot very well with crude sights if you focus on the front sight and get good sight alignment.

Unfortunately, sometimes point-of-aim and point-of-impact don't agree, and there are few options when this happens with fixed sights. If a gun has fixed sights and doesn't shoot where you point it, you have to decide if you're willing to live with it, but remember; almost all concealed carry defense situations happen within seven yards. There are some excellent small revolvers with adjustable sights

Standard sights on many carry guns involve a simple groove milled across the top of the gun and a ramp front sight at the front. Systems like this are snag-free, a benefit with carry guns that are often in close proximity with clothing.

Fiber optic high-visibility sights gather available light to catch the user's eye. Unfortunately, they do little in really low light situations.

available but they may not fit your requirements for concealability. There are-high visibility options on some small revolvers and they have merit. The hi-vis options offer a gain in visibility, but often there's a slight loss in concealability.

While I don't like white outline or dot sights for competition, I like them for defense guns. Competition is generally done in good light, at targets with excellent contrast. Defensive situations rarely offer these luxuries. Bright white outlines show up in low light and can allow a better sight picture. For guns with dovetailed sight mounting, aftermarket options also include both fiber optic and tritium replacement sights at a very reasonable cost. Fiber optic sights gather light to increase sight visibility.

Tritium sights contain a small amount of tritium. The electrons emitted by the radioactive decay of the tritium cause phosphor to glow, thus providing a long-lasting (several years) and non-battery-powered firearms sight that's visible in dim lighting conditions. Under bright light, white outline, dot sights, and fiber optic sights show brighter than tritium, but under very low light tritium has an advantage, even showing up in total darkness when white or fiber optic sights would be invisible.

Of course, the other options that work really well in low light are laser sighting systems. My reaction when I first saw lasers was skepticism because I imagined they were a total replacement for standard sights. For life and death situations, I don't like total dependence on anything that runs on a battery. I have since changed my mind. While responsible defensive firearms owners need to be able to shoot well with iron sights, a laser offers accurate shooting under the low light that most defensive confrontations involve. They also provide the possibility for accurate shot placement when the defender simply can't align the sights with his eye because doing so gives the assailant too much access to the gun.

A properly aligned laser can provide a greater level of accuracy than most shooters can muster otherwise. They're reliable and operate automatically in many cases. There have been arguments that lasers expose the defender to the assailant, but in a very high percentage of defensive situations, the assailant already knows exactly where his victim is. Another argument is that the defender will learn to rely only on the laser and be confused if it fails to operate. While both are possibilities, the advantages of accurate shot placement under low light, or while the gun is kept close to the shooter, outweigh them. I teach my students to align the laser to shoot just below the point of impact and aim. This prevents them from seeing the laser in practice sessions, yet it's still there if conditions are bad enough they can't get proper sight alignment.

I only carry guns equipped with laser grip sights. They are unobtrusive and have no effect on holsters and carry methods. I use the iron sights in practice and set the laser just under the front sight so I can't see it in practice. In really low light situations and in situations where light is low and the shot is rushed, there is nothing better than a laser.

Laser alignment is simple, though the first time might be a bit tricky. After the laser is installed, and everything is correct and tight, focus on a perfect sight picture and move the laser beam to the point of aim at the desired distance. This can be done without shooting the gun, provided the gun shoots where it's aimed. Then shoot the gun using the laser to confirm the zero. To check the alignment at any time, simply aim at a point on the target and see if the laser co-witnesses it. Another thing to remember with lasers is they normally have a substantial offset from the bore. Properly set, a laser sight on a pistol should intersect with the point of impact at about 25 yards. This will allow accurate shooting beyond that distance yet the difference in point of impact at closer ranges will barely be impacted. With good ammunition and a rest, a carry gun can

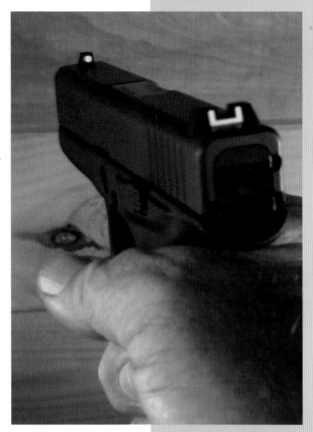

White outline sights offer good visibility even in very low light because they are a bold white shape that catches the eye.

Tritium sights actually glow in the dark, showing up in total darkness. In moderately low light situations they have little advantage if any, over simple white outline sights.

shoot 3" groups at 25 yards using a laser in low light.

There are two primary ways lasers are mounted on handguns. Rail or frame mounts put the laser ahead of the trigger guard, and grip-mounted lasers attach to the gun either as replacement grip panels with the laser and activation button as a part of the grip, or as an over-the-grip unit that wraps around and mounts to polymer-framed integral-grip guns. When choosing either type, make sure the activation button is easy for you to access. I like the button on the front grip strap because activation is almost automatic, though I can consciously relax my middle finger if I want to leave it off. Rear-mounted activation can be problematic for smaller or thinner hands.

Not only are we blessed with the right to own and carry a firearm in the United States, for the most part, we have the right to choose the firearm we buy and how to accessorize it. Ultimately, no one will argue that a better sight system isn't an advantage in a defensive situation. A 27-shot capacity, major-caliber race gun, with a reflex sight would be much better in a gunfight than a small .380, 9mm or .38 Special. A good carbine would be even better, but a race gun or carbine is pretty hard to conceal. The trick is to look at the options, decide where you're willing to trade off and go with what you like.

My solution for sighting options on my carry guns is to train with iron sights and add a laser sight for low-light conditions. The laser adds little weight or bulk, yet it vastly improves my ability to put the projectile where I want under conditions that are less than desirable. I know in bright light and with adequate room, a traditional sight picture of iron sights is faster and more effective than a laser. I also know a laser is a much better sighting system in low light. I firmly believe you need to be able to shoot well with iron sights, but I'm a confirmed laser guy for carry guns.

CHAPTER 4

UNDERSTANDING

At close range and without distractions of sights or sight picture, you can learn a lot about trigger control from firing the gun and concentrating on how the trigger is properly managed.

There are several aspects of shooting a pistol that are critical to getting a good shot. Grip is certainly important, both in shooting accurately and quickly. Sight picture is obviously important, but the biggest impediment for most shooters is trigger management. In an ideal world, the trigger would operate automatically when the gun was perfectly aligned with the target. Even if we could somehow manage this kind of technology, I suspect the human brain would somehow manage to muck up the process, as it often does with the mechanical linkage to finger relationship we currently use.

An accurate shot requires the trigger to be activated without moving the gun off target. At first glance, this seems easy. It would appear that all the shooter has to do is to make the gun go off with the trigger finger while not disturbing the aim with hand movement. While this is a part of the equation in extreme accuracy shots, close-distance shooting doesn't require this much precision. Many pistol shooters have trouble keeping their shots in a four-inch circle at five yards with guns that shoot quarter sized groups. How could this happen?

The largest part of the problem comes from the shooter trying to manage the recoil before the shot actually happens, resulting in the gun moving drastically. Even worse is the tendency to violently push the gun away in fear of the shot, an involuntary habit called "flinch". Flinch makes firing a good shot almost impossible because no matter how well you hold the gun up to the time of the flinch, it will be moved off target before the shot is fired and you won't see the movement. Once this involuntary habit is firmly entrenched, it's difficult to shake.

Practicing with a rimfire pistol helps, because the human mind fears its quieter report and light recoil less, but ultimately the shooter must learn to control the trigger to get over flinch. There are several methods of doing this, but the shooter needs to understand that he has a problem before he can correct it. The tried-and-true method for this is to fire mixed real and dummy ammunition. If you fully expect the gun to fire and it doesn't, you can see the severity of your recoil anticipation. With a dummy round in the chamber, the shooter lines up the sights and breaks the trigger, expecting the gun to fire. The gun doesn't fire and the shooter anticipates the recoil and noise, pushing the gun down and forward. Since the gun didn't fire, the shooter feels and sees the muzzle dip. Now the shooter can see why the shots have been going low and left or right.

The natural tendency for new shooters is to pull the trigger until the gun fires, then instantly release. It seems logical to think there's no reason to continue to pull after the gun fires, so the shooter develops the habit of slapping the trigger, moving the gun a little in the process, and then jerking it down in a flinch. Our brains cause both voluntary and involuntary movements. Involuntary movements occur when we jump at the sound of a backfiring truck or other unexpected noise. Involuntary movements also occur when we know something is going to happen, but we fear the result. Flinch comes from this involuntary movement, and the brain quickly connects it to the pull of the trigger. Even if you can slap the trigger without moving the gun, the sudden movement will likely trigger your flinch reflex.

A better method is to pull the trigger through the cycle and pin it to the rear for a short time. In learning this method, it's good to hold the trigger down through the recoil process until the gun settles down again. Focusing on pinning the trigger keeps your mind off the recoil and often pays the added benefit of reducing flinch. With most guns, there's an audible and tactile click when the trigger resets. If you don't feel and hear that reset, you didn't pin the trigger. The best analogy is to think of popping an inflated balloon on the floor by stepping on it while holding a full cup of coffee. If you stomp the balloon, you'll spill the coffee. If you lift your foot, place it on the balloon and slowly lower your foot to the floor, pinning the balloon until it pops, you won't spill the coffee.

All this is easy to understand and easy to do in an unhurried fashion, but becomes a little harder when you're under pressure and need to do it fast. In order to consistently manage the trigger properly, you must unlearn your old habit so thoroughly that you can manage the trigger properly even when you're not thinking about the trigger. Once you learn proper trigger management when shooting slowly, you can speed up the process. The best shooters who are blindingly fast will tell you they pull the trigger all the way back, even though they're shooting almost as fast as the gun will cycle.

At the same time this is happening, they're beginning the effort to pull the gun back into alignment with the target as soon as the shot is released. While it's true that even the best and most accurate shooters often dip the gun when they experience a misfire, the dip you see from an accurate shooter is the result of managing recoil that never happens. The trick is to begin recoil management after the shot has left the barrel and not before. This precise timing and precision trigger control is what allows very fast shooters like Jerry Miculek to be both fast and accurate at the same time.

Another important aspect of this is different kinds of triggers require a different kind of trigger pull. Properly controlling the single or double-stage trigger of a match pistol requires a completely different technique from pulling the trigger of a double-action revolver. Generally, triggers either require a short movement with a distinct break, or a long movement with the resistance spread out over a much longer distance. The two actions have nothing in common except they both make a gun fire. They're as different as pushing an elevator button is to changing gears in a manual transmission car. Both actions make something happen, but they require an entirely different kind of movement. The single-action trigger is

a button, while the double-action pull of a revolver is a lever.

The button trigger requires sensitive feel and control to make the gun fire when the operator wants it to fire. For this kind of control, the tip of the finger is used because it's more sensitive and allows the shooter to isolate the movement of the index finger from the rest of his hand. Precision shooters often exaggerate this, making sure only the tip of the index finger touches the gun. The amount of pressure to break the trigger is generally light, so the tip of the finger can easily generate enough pressure.

Trying to use just the fingertip on a lever trigger will only result in frustration. It's like trying to lift a heavy weight with your arm straight out from your body. If you pull the heavy weight in close to your body, it has less apparent weight. To manage a double-action revolver trigger, you must push much more finger through the trigger guard and shorten the lever of your finger for more pressure and control. Instead of the pad of the index finger, the middle of the second joint should contact the trigger. This doubles your leverage, and it allows you to manage backlash, the term for the unrestricted movement that occurs after a trigger breaks. Backlash is particularly troublesome with double-action revolvers because all the pressure required to rotate the cylinder and cock the hammer is being provided by the operator. If there's travel after that resistance is suddenly gone, the gun often jumps and causes an inaccurate shot.

Having said all this, there are a lot of different styles of triggers on modern guns and there's a lot of misunderstanding of how those triggers work and how they should be described. Gathering the information for this book made it patently obvious to me that most copy writers for websites (and many gun writers, for that matter) don't understand or haven't put much thought into how triggers work and how they should be described.

In single-action mode with a revolver, the pad of the finger provides the most efficient management of a light and precise trigger. The index finger isn't in contact with the gun anywhere except the control surface of the trigger.

SINGLE ACTION (SA)

A single-action trigger does just that. It allows the sear to move away from an obstructing engagement of a cocked hammer or striker, and allows the gun to fire. Other than most revolvers and some semi-auto handguns, almost all guns use a single-action trigger. It's the simplest form of trigger and is therefore primarily used to define revolvers that aren't mechanically designed for the trigger system to rotate the cylinder and cock the hammer spring.

Large double action guns like this require the shooter to rotate their hand around the grip in order to get more control of a long, heavy trigger stroke.

DOUBLE ACTION (DA)

There was no designation of single action until the term was required when double-action firearms appeared on the scene. Technically, double-action revolver triggers complete five functions. First, the early movement begins the cocking stroke and disengages the bolt that locks the cylinder into position. Next, the cylinder begins to rotate to bring the incoming chamber into alignment. Further into the cycle, the retraction of the bolt is released to allow it to drop into position. Finally, the rotation of the cylinder is complete, allowing the bolt to drop in and lock the cylinder and the last movement of the trigger allows the hammer to drop.

The considerable effort required to get all this work done creates enough resistance that most revolvers have no external, operator actuated safety. The resistance of the trigger provides enough resistance for safe carry and concealment, making the gun and the operation of the gun simpler.

On a good gun, the only part of the double-action pull the operator feels is the compression of the hammer spring. Double-action semi-autos function the same way as revolvers except there's no locking and unlocking and no rotation of the cylinder. They're true double actions on the first shot with most reverting to the slide of the gun performing the cocking stroke after the first shot. This can be disconcerting because the first trigger pull is a totally different pull from the second. Many double-action semi-autos provide for de-cocking through use of a decocker/safety that drops the hammer and blocks the striker when it's engaged. Others allow the operator to put the gun on safe and block the cocked hammer providing a single-action trigger pull on the next shot.

DOUBLE-ACTION-ONLY (DAO)

Most double-action revolvers and semi-autos have exposed hammers that can be manually cocked to provide a single-action precision pull of the trigger when more accuracy is needed. Since revolvers used in defensive situations are almost exclusively used in double-action-only, some guns are designed to work as double-action-only. This allows a cleaner design with less chance of the hammer snagging on clothing or gear on a revolver. Concealed carry citizens should concentrate on double-action shooting. Once mastered, it's so close in accuracy to single action that there's little reason to take the additional time to manually cock the hammer.

Double-action-only guns require getting enough finger on the trigger for good leverage and strength. This reduces the twitch most shooters experience when the trigger breaks.

DOUBLE-ACTION-ONLY, SEMI-AUTOS (DAO)

A semi-auto double-action-only adds the benefit of eliminating the chance of the operator re-holstering the gun with the hammer cocked with a light single-action trigger pull being the only thing that keeps the gun from firing again. When police departments transitioned from revolvers to semi-autos, this was a major issue. Officers were used to double-action revolvers that can be re-holstered with impunity. The semi-autos most departments chose in those days required engaging the safety before re-holstering, and officers who were pumped up with adrenalin from a gunfight simply forgot to put the safety back on, resulting in accidental discharges.

Double-action-only small: Smaller double-action-only guns allow getting a lot of finger onto the trigger, allowing the shooter leverage and control.

SINGLE-STAGE TRIGGER (SS)

A single-stage trigger is a single-action trigger with no take-up before encountering the resistance that has to be overcome to fire the gun. Normally found on precision handguns, or as the single-action pull of a revolver, it's designed to be activated with a minimum amount of effort. When the finger contacts a single-stage trigger, there's no movement until the gun fires. There's resistance on contact, and as pressure increases the resistance breaks, and the gun fires. Rapid, insensitive contact with a light single-stage trigger will often cause the gun to fire before the operator intends, and before it's pointed at the target. A single-stage trigger can be operated rapidly with precise accuracy, but the operator has to be familiar with the level where it breaks, and use the most sensitive part of his finger to prevent inadvertently firing before he's ready. Single-action, single-stage triggers are most commonly found on competitive and hunting handguns.

This kind of light trigger doesn't work well for service and defensive firearms because under the stress of a dangerous situation, the consequences of firing the shot before you're ready are much more serious than lost points in a competitive event. Light triggers on competition guns are fine, but they have no utility on defensive firearms. Single-stage triggers are applicable to defensive use, but they must have a reasonably high breaking pressure, probably five pounds as a minimum. Really light, single-stage triggers on defensive firearms are asking for trouble.

TWO-STAGE TRIGGER (2S)

Another version of the single-action trigger is the two-stage single-action trigger. The 1911 trigger is two-stage, single-action because when the finger first contacts the trigger, there's a slight rearward movement of the trigger that requires only very light pressure before the resistance of the second, firing stage as the trigger is engaged. Two-stage triggers allow the shooter tactile contact with the trigger before the initiation of the pressure that will eventually fire the gun. Two-stage triggers are common on service-level firearms.

Two-stage triggers will allow rapid-sequence firing because the trigger only has to be reset to the second stage, allowing the operator to pin the trigger and then release until the reset is felt or heard. The firing sequence then begins without the interruption of the first stage.

Most semi-autos like the 1911 have a two-stage single- action trigger. This means the trigger has a short distance of free travel before engaging the sear. This kind of trigger is very precise and can be managed with the pad of the finger.

STRIKER-FIRED TWO-STAGE (SF2S)

While many striker-fired guns are described as double action, most are a long-cycle, two-stage, with the first stage being a fairly long stroke that's followed by an easily discerned second stage of resistance that actually fires the gun. Guns like Glock, Springfield Armory XD series, and S&W M&Ps use this system. The long stroke decreases the chances of an accidental discharge and is assisted with blades or hinges in the trigger that require full finger contact, adding an additional level of safety. Some of these trigger types, like Glock, use the long stroke to complete the cocking cycle of the striker and some don't. For the sake of accuracy, a correct description of this type of trigger would be a striker-fired two-stage. Many guns using this system also incorporate an external, manually-operated safety for another level of safety.

Most striker-fired pistols have a two-stage system with a long takeup and a resistance point just before the gun fires. The best technique is to use more finger than would be used with a single- action trigger, but less than a double-action-only trigger.

STRIKER-FIRED, DOUBLE ACTION (SFDA)

Some striker-fired semi-autos use a long, smooth pull similar to a double-action pull. Though this isn't really like the true double-only pull of many guns, we'll use the term striker-fired, double-action only. These guns rely on the long distance the trigger must be moved as the safety system. Many of these also incorporate an external, manually operated safety for another level of safety. With some of these guns the trigger pull actually is a double-action pull that provides all the energy to cock the hammer. This is an added benefit because it allows restrike capability in the event of a misfired round. There are some who discount the value of restrike capability, but a second strike often fires a round that didn't fire the first time, and most shooters could do the second trigger pull while moving the hand into position for a tap/rack to recycle the gun without a loss of time.

When the buzzer sounds at a match or an assailant comes across the room for you, the skills you've cultivated in the quiet of your living room dry-firing, or on the range by yourself tend to go out the window unless you've developed the skills to control the trigger without conscious thought. Managing the trigger has to become second nature, done without thinking about the process, and this requires repetition, especially if you've spent years mismanaging the trigger. Learn to manage the trigger system of the gun you carry and your chances of success are greatly enhanced.

CHAPTER 5

DO DAILY CARRY GUNS NEED TO BE HIGH-CAPACITY?

Unlike police, civilians never intentionally move toward an assailant. In most cases, by the time deadly force becomes an unwanted option the civilian has retreated. Civilians very rarely confront multiple assailants, and most of our encounters are at less than three yards, with 2.3 being the average number of shots fired. Our situations and requirements in our defensive firearm are completely different from the needs of a sworn police officer, whose job is to intervene with criminal activity rather than simply defend against it. So why do so many citizens choose to arm themselves with handguns that are more suited to police work than to their daily lives and requirements for personal defense?

"...WHY DO SO MANY CITIZENS CHOOSE TO ARM THEMSELVES WITH HANDGUNS THAT ARE MORE SUITED TO POLICE WORK THAN TO THEIR DAILY LIVES AND REQUIREMENTS FOR PERSONAL DEFENSE?"

A slim gun with extra magazines might be the solution. Galco's Miami Classic rig balances out the shoulder system with extra magazines.

Those of us who make the commitment to be capable of defending ourselves, rather than relying on society and hoping for the best, almost always choose a handgun as our primary choice. This is because carrying a handgun makes more sense than toting a tactical shotgun or carbine. We know this choice is a compromise. A shotgun or rifle is almost always more effective in a fight than a handgun. We choose the handgun because we balance the threat against the convenience. Police carry handguns rather than shotguns or carbines for the same reasons. Since our needs are different than the needs of sworn officers, doesn't it make sense for civilians to arm themselves with firearms that match their needs rather than the needs of police officers?

In our shooting classes, we advocate our students choose firearms more in line with their lifestyles and the possible situations they might face. We don't advocate carrying large capacity, full-sized firearms, unless the person is exposed to a very high risk. We recommend our students choose a firearm that will interfere less with their daily lives, but still up to the potential threats they may face.

In recent years, there have been several excellent choices in slim, concealable semi-auto carry guns. Guns like the S&W Shield and Springfield XDs offer a smaller and less burdensome choice. They come in the same calibers as their larger, double-stack, service counterparts, with a reduction of about half the magazine capacity. They're reliable, and have similar triggers and sights as their larger counterparts. They're harder to shoot well, but far easier to conceal and comfortable to carry.

But for many of our female students, operating the slide of the compact semi-autos is a difficult task. In a situation where a malfunction occurs, it would be a daunting task for them to get the gun cleared and running again during a life threatening situation. Modern semi-autos are very reliable, but they do malfunction for various reasons, and under pressure individuals without extensive training can have trouble getting the gun going again. Let's face it: most civilians train very little. Having said that, these guns are very good and offer a viable option with power, concealability, and capability for a fast reload.

The smaller subcompacts are probably the smallest compromise of size and power. For women and others with weak hands, their small size can make them even more difficult to operate. The standard chambering of .380 is generally considered borderline, but when concealability is the primary issue, they're very good. Again, they generally have a ca-

pacity of six or seven shots and can be quickly reloaded.

Our number one choice - and the gun both my wife and I carry – is a compact five-shot revolver.

The modern five-shot, compact revolver is lightweight, sometimes weighing less than a loaded spare magazine for a full-size gun. Guns that are unobtrusive are more likely to be with you, and guns that carry like a boat anchor are more likely to be left at home. A .25 ACP in your hand is more effective than a .44 magnum at home. Small guns are much easier to conceal than big ones, and the five-shot revolver is only slightly harder to conceal than the subcompact .380s.

The modern compact revolver is quite accurate out to ten yards, three yards beyond the distance considered critical when facing an assailant who doesn't have a gun. Remember; the average self-defense shooting confrontation occurs at less than three yards. Adding a laser sighting device aids in accuracy, and 70 percent of all defensive shooting situations happen in low-light conditions. While there are more powerful firearms available, modern defensive ammunition in .38 Special +P and .357 Magnum are viable stoppers. Compact revolvers are among the most reliable repeating firearms in history, and if a round doesn't fire, you simply pull the trigger again.

I doubt there are many who read this who have more experience in daily carry of a firearm than Chris Cerino. You may know Chris from Top Shot, or from Gun Talk and Guns and Gear on TV. Chris has spent his entire adult life as a sworn officer; as a park ranger, a police officer, and a Federal Air Marshal and Air Marshal Trainer. Chris' life has been spent carrying a gun

Regular practice and knowing your gun is reliable and capable of doing the job are an asset that I believe exceeds the comfort of a big magazine.

and assessing threat. He's spent the last 12 years of his life teaching other law officers, military, and civilians how to shoot. His everyday carry gun is a S&W 642 five-shot .38 Special revolver.

In writing this, there's no doubt there are many who'll scoff and say five or six shots from a small mid-caliber revolver or semi-automatic is hardly sufficient to stop a determined assailant, and that only a large-caliber, large-capacity semi-auto is a reliable defense firearm. Few of those would argue a shotgun wouldn't do a better job than the handgun, but of course it isn't convenient to carry a shotgun everywhere.

Police officers, whose lives are on the line every day, are willing to compromise and carry a double-stack full-sized semi-auto instead of a shotgun or carbine. Doesn't it make sense for an ordinary citizen who lives a peaceful life to compromise down to a smaller, less obtrusive gun with less magazine capacity?

CHAPTER 6

LETHALITY AND THE CONCEALED CARRY HANDGUN

The object of carrying a firearm as a matter of daily routine is based on the conviction that you have the right to defend your life or the life of someone else. While it's certainly true that the presence of a firearm can

Even a big-bore handgun won't always stop an aggressor with one shot if the bad guy is hopped up on drugs or adrenaline.

When this decision has to be made, the object is to stop the aggressor quickly before he can harm you or someone else. Until technology develops Star Trek-style "phasers" that can be set to "stun", this means imparting enough damage to the perpetrator to cause him to cease aggressive activity. Some individuals cease aggression when confronted with a firearm. Some give up when shot, no matter how serious or trivial the wound. Unfortunately, some aggressors don't stop until they're physically unable to continue.

When I was growing up, I got the impression that any time someone was shot, they simply froze and fell down, incapacitated. On television, Matt Dillon almost always shot the bad guy in the stomach and the bad guy would grasp the wound, look stunned, and fall dead. Sometimes the person who was shot would survive, but they almost always fell to the ground and became immobile. In later TV shows and movies, the gunshot victim would be thrown across the room or spin around as if hit by a baseball bat and fall. Apparently the modern prop guns are much more powerful than the ones Matt Dillon and The Rifleman, Lucas McCain, had access to.

The fact is that the only certain way to make the aggressor stop immediately is to disrupt the central nervous system. A shot to the brain stem will cause instant incapacitation because it interrupts the ability to breathe and control voluntary movement. A shot that severs the spinal cord above the base of the neck will prevent voluntary movement of the arms and legs. While a shot fired to any other part of the body other than the central nervous system can cause the assailant

Bullet design is obviously an issue as is velocity and mass. The lightweight, 150 grain solid copper hollow point on the right will generate a much larger wound channel than the slow and non-expanding standard .240 grain bullet. Such projectiles can make even older calibers like .44 Special formidable stoppers.

to cease aggression, there's no certainty that it will.

Loss of blood will also incapacitate an assailant, but the result will not be instant. The body contains about five liters of blood and a person must lose about two liters before losing consciousness. Severing the aorta will cause the assailant to bleed out in the shortest possible time, but will still allow voluntary action for at least five seconds. Any deer hunter can tell you a heart-shot deer can run a hundred yards. An aggressor with his heart shot out can still have time to kill you and others in your family.

Wounds to major arteries can cause death, but it won't be instant.

Having said this, a high percentage of humans cease aggression after receiving a single gunshot, even if it's not a fatal wound. The cessation of aggression isn't because the body is incapable, but because the mental and physical shock of the gunshot effectively takes the fight out of the aggressor. Individuals with their systems pumped full of adrenalin or drugs are much less likely to give up when dealt a lethal blow. The problem is you can't count on the cessation of aggressive behavior after one shot.

The old argument was that high-velocity handgun rounds could produce hydrostatic shock that would affect neural function, effectively stopping the assailant instantly. The first mention of pressure waves and the human body that I could find in the scientific literature was presented by E. Harvey Newton and his research group at Princeton University in 1947. Under the theory of hydrostatic shock, a high velocity bullet created hydraulic shock waves in the body, and these shock waves did collateral damage to organs not directly contacted by the wound channel.

While the concept of hydrostatic shock is generally accepted, there are detractors. My personal opinion, based on multiple post-mortems of whitetail deer and feral pigs, supports hydrostatic shock as a factor, but the example of the deer who runs off after his heart has been turned to jelly illustrates that hydrostatic shock isn't something that will always provide the stoppage of a drug-crazed assailant.

Compounding the problem for the concealed carry citizen is the fact that few handguns suitable for daily carry produce enough velocity to produce the level of hydrostatic shock the experts agree will sufficiently and consistently cause enough neural disruption to produce hydrostatic shock, much less instantly stop an assailant. Studies show some evidence that hydrostatic shock does produce results, but not consistently enough to count on. With sufficient penetration, there can be neural effects from gunshot wounds from handguns, but there's no certainty of instant stoppage, and instant stoppage is the desired effect.

The upshot of all this is there's simply no way to instantly stop an assailant other than hitting the brain stem or spinal column. Even a shot to the lobes of the brain doesn't always produce an instant or even fatal result. Having said this, it would require skills very few possess to accurately place such a shot, much less do it under the stressful conditions of self-defense.

Faced with these facts, it becomes obvious that there's no magic formula for instant incapacitation other than a feat of almost superhuman marksman-

ship. The brain stem or that tiny section of spinal cord is simply too small a target to be considered a good choice.

The military and law enforcement choose to put their emphasis on a less difficult target area, from the base of the neck across the chest down to the base of the sternum. Within this area are the heart and lungs as well as the spinal column. Any shot from an adequately-powered firearm delivered in this area is likely to be lethal and also likely to deliver enough punch to take the fight out of all but the most determined attacker. About the same size as the A zone on most competitive shooting targets, this area is well within the capabilities of a practiced shooter at the distances where most civilian defense situations occur.

While most vulnerable organs are centrally located in an area large enough for an accurate shot to find them, they're fairly well protected by the skeletal system. For a straight-on shot, the sternum protects the spinal column and much of the heart, which also happens to be the best target. Like much of creation, the human body is well-designed to protect the most vital areas. Certainly there are many handgun calibers capable of penetrating the sternum, but the sternum is capable of protecting vital organs against smaller, less effective calibers.

According to military studies, the third-most-likely target to disable an assailant is the pelvic girdle or the hips. Breaking a hip will certainly prevent your enemy from walking, but it won't stop him from using a firearm. For that reason and because the likelihood the shot won't actually stop the bad guy by breaking his hip, it's suggested that targeting the pelvic area isn't a good idea.

Almost anyone can manage a level of proficiency that will allow hitting the targeted chest area from normal defensive distances. In teaching the North Carolina Concealed Carry Certification, I've learned almost everyone can keep 90% of their shots in an eight-inch area at seven yards. Of course, this is shooting in good light conditions, with plenty of time, and under no stress other than the normal stress beginning shooters have when shooting for

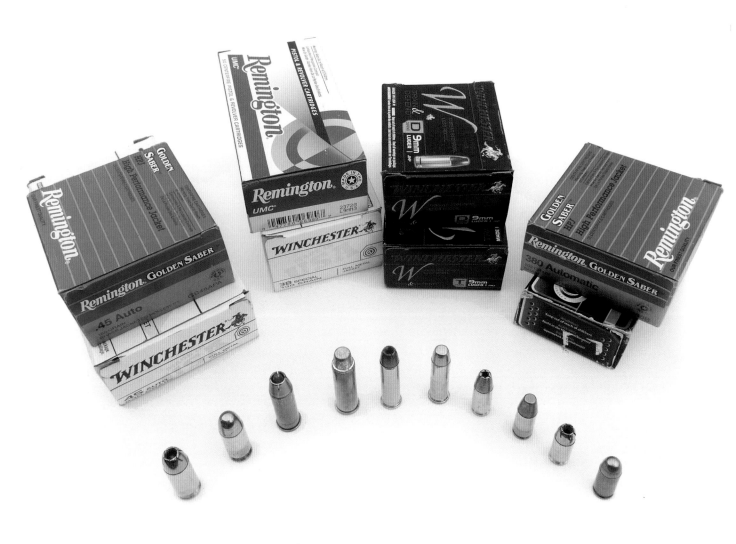

Modern ammunition is much more effective than it was just a few years ago, but ultimately, there is no substitute for shot placement.

record for the first time in their lives.

In order to perform reasonably well under difficult conditions, most people need to be able to perform very well under optimum conditions. It's not at all unusual for a police/criminal gunfight to involve several shots fired with no one getting hit and police generally spend more time in training than civilians. The best preparation for the armed citizen is to train enough to be confident and comfortable with their carry gun and choose a gun with reasonable stopping power while being small and light enough that it'll be comfortable to carry every day.

To review all this, we know the only area that's certain to instantly stop an assailant is too small to target under almost any imaginable set of circumstances. We also know the second choice is large enough for a person of average expertise to hit, but that area is fairly well protected by bone structure. Based on this information, the well-prepared armed citizen should focus on carry and gun handling skills, marksmanship, and carrying a firearm with enough power to penetrate the sternum. Under these circumstances, it's reasonable to say the concealed carry citizen is properly prepared.

THE MIAMI FBI SHOOTOUT

Probably the best ever example of just how much it takes to stop a person charged up on adrenalin happened on April 11, 1986, in Miami, FL, when seven FBI agents cornered two career robbers, William Matix and Michael Platt. Matix was an ex-Army MP. Platt was ex-Army Special Forces. They were armed with a Ruger Mini-14 5.56mm, a shotgun, and two S&W .357 magnums. Matix was shot six times; in the right forearm, in the head, the neck, and three shots in the face, shattering his cheeks, jawbone, and spinal column. Platt was shot 12 times. The first shot went through the upper right arm. This 9mm round penetrated his right lung, collapsed it, and stopped less than two inches from his heart. His chest cavity filled with 1.3 liters of blood. He was then hit in the right thigh and left foot. Platt was hit a fourth time, breaking his forearm. He dropped his gun and was shot a fifth time, the bullet penetrating the right upper arm, armpit, torso, and stopping below the shoulder blade.

Platt recovered his gun and shot back, wounding one agent and hitting another in the neck, incapacitating him. Platt charged an FBI car, though wounded in the leg, foot, and twice in the chest, and shot another officer dead through the chest, shot another in the groin, and killed another agent with two rounds to the head. As he entered their car to get away, still another agent fired five times from a pump shotgun hitting Platt in both feet. Platt attempted to start the car as another wounded agent staggered up to the car and fired six rounds from his .357. The first two missed. The third, fourth, and fifth hit Platt in the face, shattering his cheeks, jawbone, and spinal column. The sixth penetrated Platt's chest to the spine, killing him.

The fight lasted four minutes and saw 145 shots fired. Two agents and the two suspects were killed. Only one of the seven agents and two suspects involved in the gunfight emerged unharmed. Adrenalin provided the suspects with superhuman endurance. Neither suspect had any drugs in his system, according to autopsies.

After reading this, it becomes apparent that it's impossible to be certain of stopping a bad guy. It's also a fact that no matter how safe your vehicle is and how good a driver you are, it's possible you won't survive your next trip to the grocery store. You can increase your odds by driving a huge vehicle and wearing a crash helmet, but even this won't completely assure you can't get hurt. The upshot is that you prepare the best you can in relation to the chances of threat and live with the uncertainty that life always provides.

CHAPTER 7

REVOLVER VERSUS SEMI-AUTO

The revolver versus semi-auto discussion has raged for years across the counters of gun shops, at gun clubs, and between friends. Of course, there's been no actual comprehensive answer to the question of which is ultimately better, and there probably never will because it depends on the intended use and user. The semi-auto certainly has been winning if we use sales numbers as points, and I suspect the trend will continue to push the revolver further into obscurity as time marches on.

Modern semi-auto pistols are remarkable pieces of technology. The modern striker-fired pistol has internal safety features that were unheard of a few years ago. It's remarkably reliable and accurate and most have very good trigger systems. Modern striker-fired guns have passive safety features that make safe operation possible with a much lower level of training than was required for semi-autos of one generation back.

Semi-auto pistols have a tremendous advantage over revolvers when it comes to the loading and unloading cycle. There are no loose rounds, no multiple actions other than drop one magazine, insert another magazine, continue shooting. Most semi-autos also give the shooter a visual indication the gun is empty by locking the slide back on the last round. With the revolver the drill is much more complicated: Operate cylinder release, push out cylinder, eject spent cases, acquire speed loader or loose rounds, stuff the chambers full, swing the cylinder back in and resume shooting. The revolver's manual at arms is infinitely more complicated and a lot of things can go wrong, like failure to drop all the empty cases on ejection, or the shooter dropping a live round during the reloading process.

Furthermore, double-action revolvers require learning to shoot well with a long and heavy trigger pull. In addition to their slow loading times, they have a lower capacity to begin with, putting the revolver guy at a distinct disadvantage in a prolonged gunfight. If it sounds like I'm getting ready to relegate revolvers to the same category as belt pagers and butter churns, I'm not. I carry a revolver in spite of the fact that I have access to almost any imaginable carry gun and as I write this many of the best ones are currently in my gun safe.

To justify why I don't believe the revolver is ready for the scrap heap requires revisiting the history of revolvers and semi-autos. The original repeating firearm was the revolver. There were earlier versions of repeaters, but the Colt revolver was the first commercially successful design. It revolutionized the firearms world and literally did win the west. In the long struggle between the Texicans and the Comanche Indians, the Walker Colt in the hands of Texas Rangers tipped the scales in favor of the settlers.

The revolver continued to be the handgun of choice in most of the world until the adoption of the Mauser Broomhandle, the P08 Luger, and America's own 1911. All these guns were only possible after the advent of smokeless powder, because black powder would have rendered them inoperable after only a few rounds. For military applications, the same feature that originally made the revolver a success – superior firepower – also pushed the semi-autos to the forefront. The ability to reload a semi-auto and get it back into the fight in a hurry is invaluable in battle.

Since the military had much more need for extended firepower than law enforcement, law enforcement stayed with the revolver. Their reason for not adopting the newer technology involved more than just budget levels and sentimental attachment to wheel guns. Law enforcement officials realized that training their officers for safe use of semi-autos in the fields, or perhaps streets, would be much more complicated.

At this time, officers were almost universally using double-action Colt or Smith & Wesson revolvers as duty guns. Operation of these guns was simple and the guns were inherently safe. While loading the gun was more complicated than installing a magazine and racking the slide, once the revolver was loaded you didn't have to remember to engage the safety. This also meant that if the officer drew the gun and fired it in a confrontation, the gun could simply be re-holstered with no other action required. Since the hammer stayed down with the gun in a safe condition at the completion of each shot, there was no need to drop the hammer or put the gun on safe. In fact, revolvers don't even have a safety because they don't need it. The average double-action trigger pull of a revolver is far too heavy to accidently trip it re-holstering, even if the officer was clumsy and got his finger in the way.

Another plus for revolvers was that there was no need to teach officers to clear malfunctions because they didn't happen. Well-maintained revolvers almost never fail, and poorly maintained revolvers rarely fail. If the gun didn't shoot, the officer simply pulled the trigger again and another round was rotated into position while the hammer was being cocked. If a department changed from S&W to Colt or vice versa, the only operational difference was to pull or push the cylinder latch. All other operations were identical.

It was true that the capacity of revolvers was lower

Revolver or semi-auto? There are advantages to both systems but both also have disadvantages. Consider how you live, practice, and react, then choose the right gun for you.

and reloading was much slower, but it was extremely rare for officers to engage in extended gunfights in those days. There simply wasn't enough impetus to make the change. Fifty years after the military adopted the semi-auto, the police were still happily toting their wheel guns.

At some point, it became obvious that maybe law enforcement should become more progressive. Departments began looking at semi-autos to replace the ancient revolvers, and met with limited success. Most departments began by switching to the 1911. This seemed to make sense because the reliable and formidable 1911 had certainly been a proven performer for the military. However, when the implementation began there were immediate issues with training. Officers had difficulty qualifying with the heavy-recoiling .45 round, and the operational sequences were much more complicated. Of course, there's always resistance to change, and many officers didn't like the idea of giving up guns that had proven both adequate and reliable.

Some of the most problematic issues involved safety. In order to achieve reasonably short times for getting off the first shot, officers had to carry the 1911 cocked and locked, a condition known in shooting circles as "Condition One". Condition One means the gun is loaded,

with a round in the chamber, the hammer cocked, and the safety on. This made many departments nervous, and their reservations were well founded, as the number of accidental discharges increased at serious levels. You can be pretty sloppy with your trigger finger drawing a double-action revolver because it takes a long and heavy stroke of the trigger for the gun to fire. Officers simply weren't used to the light triggers that break at much lighter weight and without the long forgiving stroke of a double-action revolver.

Also, officers under the stress of dealing with a dangerous perpetrator were forgetting to put their guns back on safe before re-holstering them, creating another issue that hadn't existed with revolvers. Compound these issues with the natural resistance to change, and the 1911 era was short-lived for many departments.

The next step was a progression to 9mm pistols and double-action operation. The 9mm Luger is a more powerful round than the traditional .38 Special, and yet it's remarkably easy to shoot. With the recoil issue solved, there was a big advantage to the double/single guns because they resolved the Condition One issue that had created problems with officers' fingers getting into the triggers during the draw. They can also be carried with the safety off, so officers didn't forget to disengage the safety under pressure. They had the extra capacity and fast reloading features of the 1911, and seemed a reasonable compromise. In fact, they were quite good and definitely better than the old service revolvers they replaced for law enforcement duty.

There were still some issues with officers re-holstering with cocked hammers, because a double/single action gun switches to single action after the first shot, requiring lowering the hammer manually or with a decocker/safety on the gun. Several makers designed double-action-only semi-autos to overcome this, but they didn't achieve a lot of success because double-action semi-autos never could get the trigger up to the standards of revolvers because of the linkage involved.

Eventually, the modern striker-fired pistol designed by Gaston Glock came on the market and took the law enforcement community by storm. Like a revolver, there was no external safety. The trigger pull was long like a revolver, but with a much shorter reset and a lighter pull to boot. Capacity of the original G17 with one in the chamber was three times that of a S&W Model 10, the most popular police service revolver, and another 17 rounds was only a couple seconds away for a well-trained officer. Guns could be fired and re-holstered without remembering to engage a safety, and the ultimate police pistol had arrived. The modern striker-fired pistol, in its many current forms, is an infinitely better gun for service than the swing-out cylinder six-shooter it replaced.

Armed with this knowledge of the evolution of the modern service gun, I still carry a revolver. While it's true that modern striker-fired guns are remarkably reliable, they still fail and an important part of any responsible law enforcement training problem is focused on managing the stoppages that will certainly occur with semi-auto pistols. With a semi-auto, it's not whether a malfunction will occur, it's when. There are simply too many complicated processes in the operation of a semi-auto and too many variables in ammunition and operators for 100% reliability to occur.

I can safely say that the majority of revolvers can be carried and used for 50 years without a malfunction that requires an action more complicated than another pull of the trigger. Compare this to the fact that the U.S. Army's "Mean Rounds Between Failure" (MRBF) requirement is 495 rounds per malfunction for 9mm pistols. It's certainly true that many semi-auto pistols can be fired hundreds and thousands of rounds without a malfunction, but any manufacturer of semi-auto handguns will tell you that an eventual malfunction is inevitable.

While law enforcement and military spend extensive time on the range learning to deal with malfunctions under stress, this isn't the case for civilians. While there are no studies on this, I suspect the average concealed carry civilian expends less than 50 rounds per year in practice, and this is far too few rounds to allow them to clear malfunctions properly and quickly under stress.

Further complicating this, while full-size semi-autos are remarkably reliable, smaller concealed carry guns lose some reliability because of their compact size. The complications in designing a reliable small semi-auto are considerable due to simple engineering. To get the proper action stroke of the slide, the spring must match the recoil of the round being fired against the weight and resistance of the slide, while also taking into account the amount of resistance there will be in the grip of the shooter. This isn't as hard with big, heavy guns because the weight of the gun and slide represent a higher percentage of the resistance. But with a smaller gun, the grip of the shooter becomes much more important.

If the gun is set up to function in the hand of a person with a strong and firm grip, a person who holds the gun loosely won't offer enough resistance for a full cycle of the slide. If the spring is lightened to work with the loose grip person, the slide will bang back on the slide stop with a firm-handed shooter and eventually damage the gun. Because the resistance of the slide changes as the mating surfaces wear in, many manufacturers caution that their guns require a 200-round break-in period before the owner can expect reliable operation. Many owners never fire 200 rounds through a gun during their period of ownership.

Am I saying that semi-autos aren't a viable choice for concealed carry? Absolutely not. What I'm saying is the choice of a semi-auto requires a much higher level of training than a revolver. There are certainly advantages to the capacity, slimness, and reload speed of the semi-auto, but those advantages come with a price. Ultimately, it's your choice, just make sure you consider all the factors so you'll choose wisely.

CHAPTER 8

TRAINING FOR MAXIMUM EFFECTIVENESS

While choosing and carrying an effective firearm is important, the time and effort you spend learning to properly operate that firearm will probably pay far higher dividends in effectiveness, should you ever have to use it. To be effective, you must be completely comfortable with every aspect of putting your concealed carry gun

Even low-pressure situations like competing in an organized competition degrades the performance of most people. That stress level will be ratcheted up ten-fold should your life be in danger. For the best performance, there's no substitute for confidence, and regular practice generates that level of confidence while developing the motor skills that allow performance under stress.

When you get in your car to drive to the grocery store, you know you have to step on the brake to allow the car to be shifted to drive. You don't think about this process, it just happens as a conditioned response to achieve the goal of making the car go forward. When you first learned how to drive, you had to consciously think about the process of stepping on the brake before it could be shifted into drive. Most likely, you tried to shift into drive without applying the brake and had to correct the sequence. After enough repetition, the act of stepping on the brake before shifting became a normal part of your routine that you weren't even aware you were doing.

Had you been sitting in an open Jeep during those first days of learning to drive and you were being charged by an angry grizzly, there's a strong chance you'd have tried to start the car and shift into drive without applying the brake. Early in your driving career, your mind related the brake to stopping, and with the charging bear, your objective would be to go. There's a possibility the bear might have eaten you when you didn't shift into drive because you simply forgot to press the brake. This illustrates why, as an armed citizen, you must practice until operating your gun comes as naturally as driving your car.

The best performance from humans always comes when we're using non-verbal, or operational thought. Verbal thought is when we work our way through a process using a mental checklist, such as mentally checking off the act of pressing the brake before putting a car into gear. New shooters must use a mental checklist in order to master the fundamentals. The

The stress level of a real life or death defensive situation dwarfs the pressure of competition, even at a national level, but competition does teach you to run your equipment under stress. Here I shoot the Celebrity Steel Challenge at the Bianchi Cup with the stands full of spectators. The pressure of this is nothing compared to a real-life threat.

sooner the new shooter shifts from a mental-checklist thinking to conditioned-response thinking, the sooner that shooter will progress.

While it's possible to shoot well using a mental checklist, it's not possible to shoot well while shooting fast because our brains simply don't run that quickly when processing a mental checklist. Operational thinking allows you to group sets of actions into one thought command and allow fast response. Instead of thinking grip, stance, breath, sight picture, trigger press, and follow through, in checklist thinking, operational thinking just processes the thought, "shoot." Eventually, by conditioning the shooter's response patterns, the process for firing a shot becomes "sweep jacket back, grip pistol, bring weak hand close to body, draw pistol and bring it to horizontal, bring the pistol to eye level and reinforce grip with weak hand, extend pistol, align sights on target, and fire if the threat continues."

Practice and developing your conditioned response allows grouping whole sets of actions into

"PROPER PRACTICE DOESN'T JUST INVOLVE THE ACT OF FIRING THE SHOT. YOU CAN BE A DEAD-ACCURATE SHOOTER AND STILL BE TOTALLY UNPREPARED FOR DEFENDING YOURSELF AGAINST A BAD GUY."

There is no substitute for a qualified instructor who knows how to teach as well as shoot. Here Chris Cerino demonstrates the value of trigger control to a student/instructor.

single responses, and this is why it's so important to learn to do things the correct way and do them that way all the time. As a younger man, almost everything I shot was reloaded, and I can certainly understand the practice. It's easier to pocket brass than to pick it up and when you dump it on the ground, it gets dirty.

Bill Jordan, former competitive shooter and Border Patrol agent, recalls other officers finding brass in their pockets after a gunfight with no recollection of how it got there. Certainly it's reasonable to assume that the conditioned response could be so strong as to commit such an error.

Proper practice doesn't just involve the act of firing the shot. You can be a dead-accurate shooter and still be totally unprepared for defending yourself against a bad guy, because being able to manipulate your gun up until the second you fire the shot is just as important as accuracy when you fire the shot. Gear manipulation is as important as shooting, and without it you're operating under a severe handicap. The acts of safe gun handling, drawing your gun, clearing a malfunction, and going through the loading process are just as important as marksmanship. All these tasks must be ingrained into your process to the point they

don't require conscious thought, and this should be done with your carry gun or with a gun that's operationally identical.

For this reason, practice for the concealed carry citizen should be done in the same way that person would fight back in the event of an attack. There's no doubt that simple shooting practice improves your shooting skills. Competition is even more likely to improve skills because it stresses accuracy, speed, or both, and because it adds a level of stress and performance anxiety to the equation. The action shooting games also teach the shooter how to deal with problems like malfunctions and handling complicated decisions while under the duress of time constraints. Having said this, you must perform a portion of your practice with the same gun, or a similar one, to the gun you carry for this to fully work.

An example of this is something my friend and former Federal Air Marshal, Chris Cerino, experienced during the History Channel TV show Top Shot. Chris was shooting a double-action revolver and a round failed to fire. Chris has extensive training with semi-auto pistols and most of his training work is training military, law enforcement, and civilians with semi-auto pistols. When the revolver failed to fire, Chris tried to tap-rack the gun. A tap-rack is the procedure of tapping the base of the magazine to make sure it's seated, and racking the slide to chamber a fresh round. Tap-racking a revolver does nothing since there's no magazine to seat in the butt of the grip and no slide to work.

When this happened, the show's host, Colby Donaldson, saw it and asked him, "Chris, did you just tap-rack a revolver?" Of course he had. Chris was so conditioned to tap-rack when a gun failed to fire that the conditioned response was to tap-rack the revolver, even though all he had to do with a revolver was pull the trigger again. On a TV show, this is a source of entertainment, but in a life or death situation it could be deadly. A lot of training with equipment other than what you carry can cause conditioned responses you don't want.

Choosing a quality instructor or training facility can be difficult because everyone in the business is certain he's ultimately qualified to share his vast knowledge. I once set up at a gun show with a group of young military-looking guys on the next aisle. Their booth was back-to-back with my booth and it featured videos of shooting scenarios with them moving around in tactical clothing. The production quality of the videos was very good and these guys looked like young Navy Seals or special forces operators. Conversation ensued, and I was shocked to find these guys were not law enforcement, past military, or even competitive shooters. They'd taken the NRA instructors classes for shotgun, rifle, and pistol and were setting up shooting classes with absolutely no practical experience at all.

There are shooting instructors across the country who apply SWAT or military tactics to concealed carry citizen situations and train citizens in these techniques. SWAT or military training simply doesn't apply to an armed citizen. Citizens have no right to attack the bad guys. In no state I know can civilians use deadly force to detain, much less attack, a criminal. Our odds of having a gunfight with multiple bad guys are similar than those of winning the Powerball lottery. Tactical training of this type might be fun, but don't fool yourself into thinking that shooting at multiple targets from a speeding vehicle is suitable

At Butler Tech Police Training Facility, Chris Cerino demonstrates proper stance and grip to police instructors.

training for the concealed carry citizen, and I'd advise a wide berth from someone who tries to tell you otherwise. If you want to do zombie training, that's fine, but it doesn't relate to concealed carry. In the zombie apocalypse, I plan to carry my three-gun rifle with a high-cap shotgun and a double-stack .45 for backup.

In recent times, it's become popular to start up a website and become a shooting instructor. For basic firearms training such as the NRA's First Steps programs, there's nothing wrong with a person who only has limited experience teaching safety, operation, and very basic shooting techniques to a new shooter. The problem comes when that instructor begins teaching more sophisticated aspects of shooting without having real-world experience. Conversely, some really good shooters simply can't pass along what it takes to shoot well because they're unable to analyze what they're doing and why they do it.

As an example, imagine learning to ride a bike: When you're learning, you have to turn the handlebars in the direction the bike is falling to keep it upright. As long as you have forward motion and you turn into the direction the bike is falling, you can keep the bike upright. At first, this process is done in verbal thought. The bike begins to lean, you remember to steer into the direction the bike is leaning and the bike straightens up. The process is jerky but you keep the bike upright. Later, the process smoothens out, and you can ride a bike. Based on what you've learned, you can also teach someone else to ride a bike.

Here Chris Cerino demonstrates proper trigger control with a Next Level Training SIRT Training Pistol.

Now, let's explain the difference between someone who can analyze situations and really teach, and someone who can only teach at a basic level. If asked which way you turn the bars of the bike to turn when it's traveling at speed, most people say you turn the bars in the direction you want the bike to go. Others say you don't turn the bike at all, but lean the bike and make it turn. Both statements are based on their honest beliefs. Both responses come from people who actually know how to ride a bike, but both are wrong.

The real analysis of what happens when you turn a bike is that the rider puts light pressure in the opposite direction he wishes to turn. This causes the bike to lean in the direction of the turn. The rider lightens the pressure that caused the bike to lean and then regulates the radius of the turn by manipulating the bars. Once the turn is made, the rider turns the bars into the direction of the completed turn, which lifts the bike back to the vertical position. If this doesn't make sense to you, get on a bike and try it. If I'm telling you wrong, I'll send you a check for the price of this book.

The point of this is to illustrate how easy it is to complete a task without understanding exactly what you're doing to get the desired result. In order to resolve problems that limit a shooter's performance, a good instructor breaks down what happens and can explain it to his student. A poor instructor tries to improve his student's performance by standing over him, repeating the same basic instructions, and encouraging him to run box after box of ammunition through his gun, while repeating the same mistakes.

EPISODIC VERSUS IMMERSIVE TRAINING

There are two types of firearms training: episodic training and immersion training. You can become a proficient shooter on your own with episodic training but only if you learn to shoot properly in the first place. This can be done through videos and text, provided you have the ability to critically analyze your own performance. Many people simply don't seem to have this ability and as a result, they aren't able to recognize their shortcomings and plateau at a point well below their potential. A better method is to train with a capable instructor who can critique your problems and help you correct them. Practicing on your own will accelerate your progress, provided you don't fall back on your shortcomings when you're not under the watchful eye of a good instructor.

Immersion training involves extended training over a full day or several days. This method will yield faster results, but unless you completely grasp the fundamentals and muscle memory involved, you'll likely regress later. The best way is to begin with a period of immersion training and follow up with regular practice sessions and occasional episodes of training. Remember than many aspects of learning to shoot don't require live fire. Almost all national level shooting competitors dry fire and learn gear manipulation skills that don't involve live rounds.

Concealed carry training should be done with the gun and holster or carry system you carry every day. It should be done wearing the same kind of clothing you wear and be practiced both with winter and summer clothes. While it's reasonable to say you can develop a high level of marksmanship and gun handling skills on your own, I find this very rarely happens.

You'll progress much faster by spending time with

At the Bianchi Cup, Springfield Armory's Rob Leatham gives me tips on proper grip just before my next stage. Proper grip is paramount in getting off accurate and quick follow-up shots.

a reputable trainer who shares a similar philosophy. If you're committed, after study and consideration to daily carry with a small revolver, you'll likely be frustrated with trying to learn with an instructor who advocates a full-size, high capacity semi-auto and who considers anything less as lunacy. He may convince you to change, but you certainly won't convince him your plan is solid.

While the average armed citizen is better equipped to survive a violent crime than an unarmed citizen, a properly trained armed citizen is much more likely to perform well. We can argue forever about what constitutes the best gun or caliber for concealed carry, but there is simply no argument about training: A trained concealed carry citizen is far better equipped to deal with an adversary than an untrained one.

CHAPTER 9

CONCEALED

Women often outperform men in shooting because it's a sport that doesn't favor strength and bulk. Julia Watson is shooting the Bianchi Cup. She's also a national champion rifle competitor.

My family has a close connection to the Cerino family, who run Cerino Consulting and Training Group. Recently, Michelle Cerino conducted an online survey of women relating to concealed carry. Taking into consideration the fact most women who took the survey take an active interest in issues of concealed carry, I believe a higher percentage of women who have concealed carry permits have the resolve for daily carry than men of similar circumstance. In the Cerino study, almost 54% of women who responded to the survey carry a gun every day, and while I have no similar survey of men, I suspect this is a higher percentage than men. I'm impressed with the dedication I see with the women who take my class, both in dedication to daily carry and the desire to train to a level of proficiency that improves their performance.

The situations that create the need for extra consideration for women involve three criteria: First,

many women spend more time in close proximity to children simply because they are mothers and mothers generally spend more time with the kids. Of course, there's no excuse for lack of vigilance in gun safety under any circumstances, but the presence of children ratchets up the level of responsibility even more. Guns should never be left unattended. Guns not under the direct control of the operator should never be loaded unless locked up in a lockbox. Children should be educated on firearms safety using the excellent educational materials that are available at no cost, like the NRA's Eddie Eagle program.

There's no reason that gun ownership and child interaction should create safety issues, but there are precautions that must be taken to insure this. The Cerino survey indicates that over 16% of responders use a purse as their only carry method and another 49% use a purse for carry at least some of the time. Purse carry

Just choosing a proper gun isn't enough. All concealed carry citizens should learn to properly handle their guns. Here, Cherie demonstrates how an improper grip makes a normally manageable .38 Special difficult to control in recoil.

makes sense because women's clothing styles often don't work well with on body carry, and purse carry is perfectly safe provided certain precautions are taken. Many concealed carry purses have locking zippers that prevent access, but those require constant vigilance in making sure they're locked when children could reach the purse and unlocked in situations where quick access is needed. Since quick access is always a good idea for defensive carry, a better idea is to never allow the purse to be in the reach of children, and use the zipper system as a redundant fail safe.

A better fail-safe could be accomplished in firearm choice. Both striker-fired and single-action semi-automatics have triggers light enough for small children to operate. Double-action firearms have trigger pulls heavy enough that small children simply can't activate them, even with both index fingers in a two-handed grip. I've tested this with my eight year old grandchildren, both active and athletic kids. Neither can activate a double-action trigger, because of the long stroke and energy required to overcome the hammer spring. Because of this, I recommend a double-action gun for situations where there's even a remote possibility of a small child acquiring control of a gun.

A second consideration that often affects female shooters is the strength to operate the action of the firearm. While double-action revolvers and semi-autos have this added level of safety, the heavy trigger pull can be problematic for those with low hand strength. In my classes, I have experienced students who simply don't have the hand strength

to operate a reasonable double-action trigger. This can be the result of age and physical issues such as arthritis and it can affect both men and women. In this situation, many semi-automatics are also problematic because they require a similar level of hand strength to cycle the slide. I have had clients who were only able to qualify by shooting a double-action revolver in single-action mode, having to cock the hammer for each shot. I've talked to instructors who said they wouldn't have qualified that person for concealed carry, but it's my conviction that anyone who's capable of responsible levels of accuracy and sound judgment should have the right to self-defense.

Certainly some double actions are easier to operate than others. The level of effort to pull the trigger on some guns is nearly double that of others, so purchasers should always spend some time making sure they can comfortably manage the trigger of a prospective purchase. The same is true when operating the slide of semi-autos. Often, the shape of the slide offers better purchase, and spring resistance can vary considerably. Many times smaller semi-autos are harder to operate with smaller hands, so a larger gun might be a better choice. Of course, technique plays a major part in this, and many shooters find that with practice, something that was very difficult becomes relatively easy. Regardless of age, strength, and gun choice, practice and training are invaluable.

The third consideration that might differ from a man's needs in concealed carry relates to carry methods. As already mentioned, women are more

Older women often have low hand strength and require special considerations when choosing a gun for defense. Sometimes the choice involves guns that allow low hand strength.

The carry method for women is often more complicated than men due to wider variations in clothing and accessories. Small and light guns like this Diamondback DB9 with a Sticky holster work well and can easily be switched from on the body to purse carry.

likely to vary their carry method based on what they're doing or wearing. This means their carry gun might require a higher level of concealability than a man's gun.

My daughter is a runner and her needs for a carry gun require a very lightweight gun that can be carried without jiggling around in a holster or bag. Her choice is a Diamondback DB9 in a Galco body band. While it tends to profile in her running clothes, it stays in place while running and isn't noticeable at a casual glance. In the Cerino study, the most popular method was some sort of waistband holster with a smattering of women using bra holsters, either exclusively or from time to time. Small guns always work better with close fitting clothes and women are more likely to dress this way than men. Certainly, under almost all conditions, light weight is desirable.

Purse carry also can involve some special considerations as well. While many women choose to use dedicated concealed carry purses, some choose to carry the gun in their regular purse. Certainly, I don't recommend loose carry of a loaded firearm, so there needs to be some kind of holster or dedicated

pocket for the gun. A smaller group use some form of fanny pack similar to Galco's Passport. It has a standard pocket for your stuff and a concealed carry holster behind the regular pocket next to the user's body. With a simple pull of a tab, the holster is revealed and the gun can be drawn. With this system, there's little need for a bobbed hammer, in many purse carry situations, an exposed hammer is a potential snag that could impede draw. For purse carry, the smoother the gun, the better.

All these issues potentially can affect men, but are of particular importance to women. Keep in mind that every guy behind a gun shop counter has his own ideas of what constitutes the perfect carry gun. Take the time to try different guns and see what you like. Many ranges allow you to test different rental guns and that's a great option. In my concealed carry certification courses, I lay out a variety of guns at the end of the class and allow clients to try what they think they might like. Once you decide to become a concealed carry citizen, your gun choice will be something you deal with every day, so put thought into the process and pick the right one first.

CHAPTER 10

SUB-COMPACT SEMI-AUTOS

One of the most popular, yet most controversial group of concealed carry firearms are the guns we'll call sub-compacts. These are guns that are small in size and generally small in power and capacity. The weight limit for this category is a svelte 14 ounces. These guns are all small enough for inside-the-pocket carry with little chance of being noticed. Everything in life involves a trade off, and what these guns gain in concealability costs them in other qualities.

They're controversial because many think they are simply too underpowered to be effective stoppers. As I've previously covered in this book, there are many opinions on just how much gun is required to effectively stop an aggressor, but we've also covered the importance of having a gun that will actually

> "THESE GUNS ARE ALL SMALL ENOUGH FOR INSIDE-THE-POCKET CARRY WITH LITTLE CHANCE OF BEING NOTICED. EVERYTHING IN LIFE INVOLVES A TRADEOFF, AND WHAT THESE GUNS GAIN IN CONCEALABILITY COSTS THEM IN OTHER QUALITIES."

action types. Most are internal-hammer semi-autos of blowback design. Using the operating spring to overcome pressure requires a spring of higher strength than systems that delay slide movement mechanically. Since these guns are already small, this makes them difficult for people with low hand strength to operate. A few of these have worked around this difficulty by offering a tip-up barrel that

BERETTA 21 A BOBCAT

It's a little-known fact that James Bond carried a Beretta .25 before he adapted to the more familiar Bond gun, the Walther PPK. The gun 007 sported was the M418, but were I making the choice, I'd much rather have the current Beretta 21A Bobcat. Chambered in both .25 ACP and .22 Long Rifle, the Bobcat is an exposed-hammer, double/single-action semi-auto. Double/single-action guns can fire the first shot in double action with a long pull of the trigger or the hammer can be cocked for a single-action shot. Like some of the earlier Beretta pocket guns, the Bobcat has a tip-up barrel that allows loading and unloading the chamber without cycling the slide. This is a popular feature with people who have low hand strength. The magazine holds seven rounds in both .22 and .25 with the release in a push button located in the grip near the bottom to the rear, an unusual placement to say the least, but it's a European gun and Europe doesn't seem to appreciate where Americans like our magazine release. Weight of both calibers is the same 11.8 ounces even with a steel frame and slide. Sights are small and unobtrusive, but might be tough to make out in low light, though most citizen/criminal confrontations occur at close range. Available in both black and stainless, the MSRP for both calibers is $410.00.

BERETTA PICO

Arguably, the most innovative pistol in this category is the Beretta Pico. The innovative part is that the Pico is a chassis design. The serial number is on the fire controls and the grip frame that holds the gun together is replaceable and interchangeable with other colors and styles, or future integral laser versions. The serial number in the fire control chassis is visible because of a notch in the grip/frame.

The Pico is an integral-hammer, double-action-only design. With a weight of 11.5 ounces, it's the slimmest of all the .380 pocket pistols, measuring just .728" thick. It's also a very snag-free design, despite a dovetailed three-dot sight system. There's a slide lock and no manual safety. Pocket security is covered by the double-action trigger system. The magazine capacity is 6 + 1 in .380. It comes with two magazines, one standard and one extended. The magazine release is a European paddle style. The Pico can convert to .32 ACP by switching barrels. Barrel length is 2.7" and overall length is just over five inches. MSRP is $398.00 with a soft case and two magazines.

COLT MUSTANG

Colt's Mustang is a scaled-down 1911 design with allowances made for tiny size and minimum weight. It's a locked-breech .380 single-action semi-auto. The front sight is fixed and the rear is dovetailed to allow for drift windage adjustment. The safety, slide release, and magazine release are in the familiar 1911 locations. In the interest of simplicity and weight, there's no grip safety, but the rear tang allows a generous (for its size) beavertail. Magazine capacity is the seemingly mandatory 6 + 1 for this category of pistols.

There's a Commander-style hammer, a solid aluminum trigger, the barrel length is 2 ¾" and Colt has lowered the ejection port for better reliability. Interestingly, the Mustang is offered with either an aluminum frame or a polymer frame. The polymer-frame version stays within the 12-ounce parameter of this category at 11.8 ounces, the aluminum version exceeds it by only a half an ounce. MSRP for the aluminum version is $698.00 and $672.00 for the polymer version. A Lasermax grip is available for the aluminum version.

DIAMONDBACK 380

Diamondback Firearms' first introduction was the DB380, a true striker-fired .380 with a strong resemblance to Glock pistols. Reports on early models were widely varied, with some purchasers ecstatic about how good the guns were and others reporting a myriad of quality problems. Apparently there were problems with consistency, but more recent reports I've heard are positive. Located in Cocoa, Florida, the company's firearms are now marketed and handled by Taurus USA.

If there's a smaller true striker-fired gun than the DB380, I'm not aware of it. With a weight of 8.8 ounces and a width of just ¾" it's a super subcompact .380. The comparison to Glock comes from the squared-off appearance of the slide, shape of the trigger guard, and the takedown method. Like the Glock and some other striker-fired guns, the DB380 requires a pull of the trigger for takedown. The trigger system is totally unlike the two-stage-style striker-fired trigger pull so popular today. It's a long, smooth stroke that resembles a double-action pull, but without restrike capability. Sights are a stacked two-dot arrangement that is a good compromise between concealability and effectiveness. The rear sight is in a dovetail and therefore drift adjustable. Capacity is 6 + 1 with the magazine release in the proper - in my opinion - 1911 position. Like the Glock pistols, the DB380 has a gripping surface on the front of the trigger guard. I don't use that surface on full-size guns, but it might have utility on such a small gun in allowing more grip purchase. The DB380 is available in a variety of color schemes and has an MSRP of $394.00.

DIAMONDBACK DB9

As a gun writer, I've used the term "Noisy Cricket" ever since I first fired a DB9. When I saw my first DB9 I was at Archdale Arms, the dealer who was handling the transfers on my test and evaluation guns. I was amazed that a 9mm could be so small. Intrigued, I bought it without even calling the company for a T&E gun. The Diamondback guns certainly have their detractors, but my first one, and the second one I purchased for my daughter, have both been absolutely flawless. There was no break-in period, they cycled with everything I ran through them, and the only malfunctions I ever experienced were when I intentionally held the gun so loose in my hand I could barely retain it, in an experiment to see just how loose I could hold it.

Apparently, there were issues with consistent quality control, but recent reports I've heard have been good and both my early guns must have been built on a good day. I talked to a local gunsmith who has a friend who claims to have shot well north of a thousand rounds through his, and he swears it's as good now as ever. As with everything else in life, individual experiences vary.

The DB9 is a true striker-fired pistol with a long-stroke trigger pull that feels like a double action, though there is no restrike capability. With a weight of just 11 ounces in 9mm, it was the inspiration of my use of the "Noisy Cricket" category for light and powerful guns that offer intimidating recoil. Simply put, many people won't shoot it twice. I find it reasonable for a gun I'm going to carry much more than I shoot. I strongly suspect that if a person had to use a DB9 to stop a bad guy, he wouldn't remember the recoil afterward. Besides recoil, the high power-to-weight ratio comes with another cost: There's no locking slide on the DB series and if you do experience a malfunction, it's tough to clear without the ability to lock the slide back. Capacity is 6 + 1 with the magazine release in the right place and the DB9 comes in a variety of colors with a base MSRP of $431.00.

GLOCK 42

Induced in 2014, the newest gun in this group is the Glock 42. The new .380 may be a single-stack .380, but it's Glock through and through. The 42 has the same Glock trigger, the standard easy-to-see Glock sights, and the same styling and controls of its bigger brothers. It's a little bigger than most .380 semi-autos, falling between the average .380 and the smaller 9s like the S&W Shield. While guns like the PPK are larger, I guess you could say the G42 is the largest of the sub-compact .380s. This makes it very easy to shoot, yet keeps it within the 14-ounce weight limit. Weight is 13.75 ounces and barrel length is 3.25". Like most other .380s in this group, magazine capacity is 6 + 1. MSRP is $449.00.

KAHR CW380

Kahr's CW 380 is the economy version of the P380. Many of the features are the same, but the CW comes with only one magazine and standard rifling in the barrel. The front sight is fixed rather than dovetailed and in general it has less bling. Otherwise it's operationally the same gun. I think perhaps it's a better buy with an MSRP of $419.00.

KAHR P380

Kahr's P380 is a striker-fired, locked-breech, double-action-only .380 pocket pistol. It has restrike capability and there's no magazine safety. It uses the now-traditional polymer frame and stainless slide with a drift-adjustable dovetailed two-dot sight system. With an overall length of less than five inches and weighing just under ten ounces, the P380 is certainly a pocketable pistol. Magazine capacity is 6 + 1 and the magazine release is in the proper 1911 position. Trigger pull is smooth and controllable. Many owners report disassembly for cleaning is more difficult than many guns in this class, with some saying at least three hands are required. There's no external safety since it's a true double-action-only gun and there is a slide lock provision.

The P380 uses polygonal rifling in their 2.5" Walther Lothar barrel for better accuracy. It comes with three magazines and as an all-black or bi-tone version for an MSRP of $667.00.

KEL-TEC P3AT

The Kel-Tec P3AT is a hammer-fired, locked-breech, polymer-framed .380. At 8.3 ounces, it's the lightest .380 in production. It has a barrel length of 2.7", a length of 5.2" and the magazine capacity is the usual 6 + 1. In order to keep weight down, the P3AT has no slide stop and no external safety. In the interest of concealability, the grip frame is extremely short with most shooters not able to get two full fingers on below the trigger guard.

Of course, concessions to small size always come with liabilities in shootability, and the P3AT was bound to garner some complaints from operators. The grip is small, the sights are rudimentary and tiny, and the gun is so small it's hard to manage the trigger. OK, so it's still the smallest and lightest, and there's always a trade-off. Available in bi-tone and all black, it has an MSRP of $318.00.

KIMBER MICRO CARRY

Kimber has been known for years as a primary producer of quality 1911 pistols. It's no surprise that their entry in the sub-compact carry gun market would bear at least some resemblance to the 1911, and in fact the Micro Carry looks very much like a scaled-down 1911, and borrows heavily from its design. The Micro Carry is a locked-breech, external-hammer, single-action, .380-caliber pistol.

At 13.4 ounces, the Micro Carry is the heaviest gun in this group. The reason for the weight is metal. Instead of the common polymer frame, the Kimber uses an aluminum frame and a steel slide. Magazine capacity is the normal 6 + 1 with the location of the magazine release being obvious when you look at the Micro Carry. All other controls are in the 1911 locations, but there's no grip safety. The sights are three-dot, fixed front and dovetailed rear.

As much as I love 1911s, the 1911 design might not be the best design for a pocket gun. Guns like this must be carried cocked and loaded for effectiveness and I've seen several situations where the safety on holstered 1911s have been accidently disengaged by seat belts or clothing. I'd suggest holster-only carry for any thumb safety single-action semi-auto for daily carry. It is extremely well made, and the Micro Carry has a base MSRP of $651.00. There are five models with the top of the line being the Micro CDP with ambidextrous safety, Tritium sights, Crimson Trace rosewood grips, and the highest MSRP of any gun listed at $1,406.00.

RUGER LCP

The LCP is the smallest of the subcompacts, and also one of the simplest. The Ruger design features a trigger that feels like a double action but doesn't have restrike capability. The trigger pull doesn't completely cock the hammer. Part of the energy to complete the cocking cycle comes from the complete operation of the slide and this means a dud round will require a cycle of the slide. Another distinguishing feature is the lack of a slide lock on the last round in the magazine. Although the slide doesn't lock to the rear on the last shot, you can lock the slide back manually for safety and cleaning with a small button on the left side of the gun. There's a real advantage to having a manual slide lock because clearing a malfunction on a tiny .380 can be a trying and potentially dangerous experience for a novice operator. It's difficult to remove the magazine when it's under pressure and without a slide lock, it's easy to get the gun pointed in the wrong direction.

Using an internal hammer system, the LCP has a long trigger pull that reminds one of a double-action trigger, but that's not quite the case. The spring resistance of the trigger doesn't completely cock the hammer and there is no restrike capability. In the event of a round that doesn't fire, the operator must manually clear the round and re-cock the hammer, a task that's not easy to complete under the mental pressure of a life-threatening situation.

On the plus side, the LCP is compact and lightweight at just 9.4 ounces and a barrel length of 2.75". It's really thin, just over .750 and has no external safety, relying on the long trigger pull for safe pocket carry. The magazine carries six rounds of .380 ACP with another round in the chamber. The magazine release is on the left side in the 1911 position. The glass-filled nylon frame offers a two-finger grip, which is the norm for pocket-sized pistols. For sighting, the Ruger has a small milled-in bump for a front sight and a milled groove in the rear. The new model has a more obvious photo luminescent front sight and a drift-adjustable rear. The smaller sights are more concealable and less prone to snag, but difficult to see in low-light conditions.

The LCP is offered in blued and bi-tone with a brushed stainless steel slide. The standard model has an MSRP of $389.00. There's also a Crimson Trace Laserguard model that sells for $575.00.

SMITH & WESSON BODYGUARD

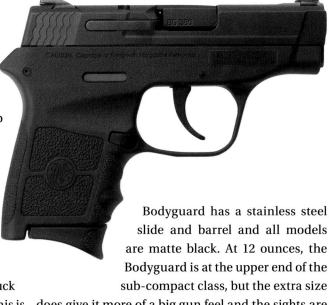

Smith & Wesson's Bodyguard uses a true double-action trigger system that completely cocks the hammer every time the trigger is pulled. It has other big gun features like a thumb safety and slide lock on the last shot. It operates as an internal-hammer, double-action-only pistol with a long stroke of the trigger required to fire each shot. The double-action trigger combined with a manual frame-mounted thumb safety makes the Bodyguard a very safe pocket pistol with an extra layer of security. The true double-action trigger system has real benefit in that a failed round can be struck again in the event of a misfire. Whether or not this is a good idea is argued by different trainers, but it's my belief that this ability has merit for inexperienced operators.

Like many other guns in this class, the light weight is achieved by use of a polymer frame. The Bodyguard has a stainless steel slide and barrel and all models are matte black. At 12 ounces, the Bodyguard is at the upper end of the sub-compact class, but the extra size does give it more of a big gun feel and the sights are large and easy to see. Magazine capacity is 6 + 1 and the magazine has a slight extension to allow a bit of purchase with a third finger. MSRP of the standard model is $379.00 and $449 for the Crimson Trace equipped version.

TAURUS 738 TCP

The Taurus TCP has been around for a while, and uses the familiar polymer frame and stainless slide. Like many others in the category, it has an internal hammer and a 6 + 1 magazine capacity with the magazine release in the familiar 1911 location. The sights are milled into the top of the slide and are small but usable and certainly compact enough for pocket use. The design has a spacy look that's very sculpted, making it a low drag pistol for slipping into small places. It has a width of about 7/8" so it rates high on concealability. Weight is 10.2 ounces and the TCP uses a 2.84" barrel.

The TCP uses a long hammer stroke as the safety feature and there is no external safety. The trigger pull is long, but it's quite smooth and manageable. A friend owns one of these and I remember a session on my range when Chris Cerino was staying with us. At 40 yards, Chris hit an 8" plate every shot for seven rounds and this is impressive for an inexpensive pocket pistol, and the TCP is certainly an inexpensive pistol, with an MSRP of just $254.02. It's available in blue, bi-tone, pink polymer and as a 3.3" version.

TAURUS PT25

As a young man, I heard a lot of jokes about grinding off the front sight of .25 caliber pistols or the installation of chocolate grips, but the fact is the diminutive .25 has carried its load in stopping bad guys. A friend who just happens to be the state's chief coroner once told me to never discount the effectiveness of the .25 ACP round, and I haven't since that day.

The Taurus Model 25 brings back memories of the tip-up-barreled Berettas of my youth and it's probably a better carry firearm than they were. It's an internal-hammer, double-action-only gun with re-strike capability. Because of its steel frame, it weighs 12.3 ounces. There's a polymer-frame version at just under 12 ounces, but it simply wouldn't fit in reasonably anywhere else.

Capacity in .25 is 9 + 1 with the magazine in the proper 1911 location. The grip is long enough to get three fingers on for most folks due to a magazine extension. It has a frame-mounted external safety and milled-in sights that are certainly unobtrusive. The tip-up barrel release is at the approximate location

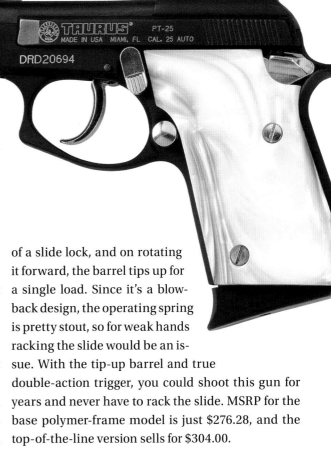

of a slide lock, and on rotating it forward, the barrel tips up for a single load. Since it's a blow-back design, the operating spring is pretty stout, so for weak hands racking the slide would be an issue. With the tip-up barrel and true double-action trigger, you could shoot this gun for years and never have to rack the slide. MSRP for the base polymer-frame model is just $276.28, and the top-of-the-line version sells for $304.00.

REMINGTON RM380

Remington was one of the earliest makers of a concealed carry pistol in the form of the Remington pattern derringer. The Remington derringer was produced between 1866 and 1935. Originally chambered for .41 Short, it was a true concealed carry gun with two single-action shots and a weight of less than 12 ounces.

The new Remington RM380 is an all-metal, modern concealed carry pistol chambered for .380 ACP. It has a smooth double-action-only trigger with re-strike capability. There's a locking slide on the last shot and an ambidextrous magazine release. Magazine capacity is 6 + 1 and barrel length is 2.9". The sights are fixed and low contour to prevent snagging. It has a dual-spring recoil system that's very easy to cycle. Weight is 12.2 ounces and MSRP is $417.00.

There's probably been more argument in recent years about what constitutes an adequate carry gun than almost any firearm-related topic. With record numbers of concealed carry citizens, and firearm sales at record levels, concealed carry is a hot topic. I teach the North Carolina Concealed Certification class, and the issue sometimes takes a life of its own in my classes. There's the "heavy caliber/high capacity" contingent and there's the "carry a small gun and be comfortable contingent".

I suppose I belong to the latter, because I carry an S&W 637 with a Crimson Trace laser grip and Remington Golden Saber ammunition. I know myself, and I know that if my choice was a heavy gun, I'd have the tendency to leave it at home or in the vehicle more, and if trouble comes to call, a .22 short in your pocket is more valuable than a .500 S&W on your dresser, unless you're standing next to your dresser.

One of the hottest classes of concealed carry guns for the small gun/comfortable group is the semi-auto .380s. They're very light, and very slim, and you can carry one anywhere without the slightest discomfort. There are a lot of models, and getting all of them together for a test was a daunting task. I don't like daunting tasks, so I chose the three I thought best represented the cream of the crop; the Glock 42, Ruger LCP and S&W Bodyguard.

The new gun on the block is the Glock 42. The new .380 may be a single stack .380, but it's Glock through and through. The 42 has the same Glock trigger, the standard easy-to-see Glock sights, and the same styling and controls of its bigger brothers.

It's a little bigger than most .380 semi-autos, falling between the average .380 and the smaller 9s like the S&W Shield. While guns like the PPK are larger, I guess you could say it's the largest of the subcompact .380s.

The second gun in the test is the iconic Ruger LCP. These little guns have probably been as close to being the cause of the shortage in .380 ammunition as any other model. The LCP is the smallest of the three, and also the simplest. The Ruger design is double action but doesn't have restrike capability. The trigger pull doesn't completely cock the hammer, meaning a dud round requires a cycle of the slide like the striker-fired Glock. Another distinguishing feature is the lack of slide lock on the last round in the maga-

With a larger grip, two-stage trigger, and full-size sights, the Glock was the easiest gun to shoot well. Seven shots in one hole at seven yards is respectable for a pocket gun.

Even the largest of the compact .380s is dwarfed by a five-shot compact revolver.

The subcompact semi-autos are incredibly slim, allowing them to hide almost anywhere.

zine. The slide won't lock to the rear on the last shot, but you can lock the slide back manually for safety and cleaning. Clearing a malfunction on a tiny .380 can be a trying and potentially dangerous experience without the slide locked back. For sighting, the Ruger has a small milled-in bump for a front sight and a milled groove in the rear.

The third gun is the S&W Bodyguard, a sub-compact with full double-action-only operation, a slide lock, and a built-in laser. The laser switch is activated with buttons on either side of the frame forward of the trigger guard. Slightly larger and heavier than the Ruger, the Bodyguard also has a thumb safety and uses a Baughman Quick Draw-style ramped front sight, and a ramped rear sight. Both front and rear sights are dovetailed into the slide.

All the guns use polymer frames and steel slides. All three also have 6 + 1 capacity, and all shoot the .380 or 9mm Kurtz round. All three guns represent what their manufacturers believe to be the best way to build a sub-compact .380. All have advantages. The Ruger is the smallest and lightest, at under ten ounces, but the slide doesn't lock back on the last round and it has tiny sights. The Glock is the easiest to shoot because of its size, has the best sights, and the benefit of the same trigger as larger Glock models. The Bodyguard has double-action restrike capability, a manual safety, and a laser as standard equipment. All three guns have valuable features that may appeal to some consumers.

The Glock 42 offers more gun to grip and handle. It's a scaled down version of the full-size gun, and has excellent sights.

The Ruger was tiny, and gave up some features to be small. The sights were very small, but allowed good accuracy in deliberate shooting.

The Bodyguard was a compromise between the tiny dimensions of the Ruger and the more full-size feel of the Glock. It had big gun functions and a drift-adjustable rear sight.

Shooting Impressions

The Ruger is certainly the smallest of the three guns. It's also the lightest, but has the fewest features. While an extended gunfight with a .380 seems unlikely, a slide that locks back on the last round is a valuable feature. At least there's a manual slide lock. Naturally the light weight and small size of the LCP resulted in the most recoil, and though it didn't feel out of control, I suspect follow-up shots were slower.

The LCP also had the longest trigger stroke and the shortest distance from the web of my hand to the trigger. I suspect this made the trigger feel less manageable, at least for me. A shooter with a smaller hand might not notice. The sights are tiny, but I shot a slightly smaller group with the LCP than with the Glock. There were no malfunctions, even when I held it very loosely in one hand, I couldn't make it fail to function.

I did notice one issue on the Ruger that might create problems for shooters with poor hand strength. In teaching concealed carry, I have a lot of new shooters, and many are older women. Most of those women have trouble cycling the slide on most semi-autos. I had a few women cycle the slide on all three of these pistols, and all agreed the Ruger was the most difficult. This is partially because of the small size, but it's also because of the way the Ruger unlocks. The initial movement of the slide on the LCP is similar to the other two pistols, but as the unlock sequence nears completion there's a secondary resistance that caused weaker hands to lose their grip of the slide. For older women with weak hand strength, cycling the slide might not be possible.

The Glock was certainly the easiest to shoot well, and it had the least recoil. It also had best trigger and hand position. In short, shooting it felt like I was shooting a real gun. Even though the grip is about the same length as the Bodyguard, it felt longer. I think this is because of the way the shape of the rear tang fits into the palm of my hand.

The Glock also clearly had the best sights, though it shot the largest group. If you look at the group, though, you'll notice that seven bullets went into a knot with an extreme spread of just .641. I suspect I bear the responsibility for the other three shots.

ALL THREE GUNS DELIVERED MORE THAN ADEQUATE ACCURACY FOR PERSONAL DEFENSE. THE BEST GROUP CAME FROM THE BODYGUARD, BUT ONLY BY A SMALL MARGIN.

With defensive ammunition, these guns have a reasonable amount of recoil, but they're manageable. Due to its size, the Glock was most manageable.

The Glock did experience one malfunction, a double feed on the second round from a full magazine. This happened when I was holding the gun normally. It cycled every time with the loose hold but in one session, the slide failed to lock back. As with the issue of hand strength, many weaker or inexperienced shooters fail to grip a pistol sufficiently for it to operate. I've noticed this a lot with the smaller 9mm pistols like the Shield, DB9 and XDs.

The most accurate of the three, by a tiny margin, was the Bodyguard. Like the Glock, it shot a cluster with three shots that were flyers. The total group was the smallest, but the seven-shot cluster measured only .462 center-to-center. At seven yards standing with a pocket pistol, this is remarkable accuracy. It also shot closest to point of aim, with the seven-shot cluster taking out the ¾" aiming point almost completely. The trigger has a long stroke, but it's very manageable, and sights are small but easy to see and line up. It was also the easiest to stroke the slide, stroking smoothly, and with a more comfortable gripping area. The safety is an added plus, and while it took a hard push to engage it, it was reasonably easy to disengage.

While many will disagree, the Bodyguard was, for me at least, the clear winner. Not as small as the Ruger, it has a slide that locks on the last round, a manual safety, good sights and trigger, and a laser to boot. It's mid-priced of the three guns, and cheaper than an LCR equipped with a laser. Add the fact that the Bodyguard is a true double action with restrike capability, and the features simply outweigh the other guns. The women who handled the guns, rating slide stroke and trigger pull, all gave it the best marks, and let's face it: many of the guns in this class wind up in purses. The restrike capability is invaluable for those who aren't the best at the tap/rack drill and I can assure you, few CCH permit holders practice their tap/rack drills.

Those who have preferences towards a more manageable gun will like the Glock better. Those most interested in small size will likely go for the Ruger, and of course brand loyalty can and will play a part in an individual's choice, but when I consider the whole package, the Bodyguard is the hands-down winner for me.

THE DIAMONDBACK DB9

In the movie *Men in Black*, Will Smith was taken to a cabinet full of exotic interstellar weapons. He wanted to choose one of the big, scary ones but Tommy Lee Jones insisted he take one that looked like a tiny water pistol. It was named the Noisy Cricket. Near the end of the movie, Smith had no choice but to fire the diminutive pistol and the recoil knocked him across the room while blowing out the whole front wall of the building.

As a concealed carry instructor and personal firearms trainer, I'm often asked about the best carry gun. I favor revolvers because they almost never malfunction and they're simple to use under pressure. They can also be quite small for the amount of power they can deliver. The balance of power, size, and accuracy is the whole deal in concealed carry guns. I live an active life and I carry every day so a big, heavy gun simply doesn't work for me. My carry gun is a small-frame .38 Special revolver because it offers the best compromise in power to weight and is almost as reliable as a rock.

Revolvers have a serious downfall in that they're thick through the middle and don't hide as well as a small semi-auto. I've looked at the .380s longingly because of their thin profile and light weight, but I simply don't consider the .380 to be enough of a man-stopper. Chambered for the 9mm Luger cartridge, the Diamondback DB9 is only slightly bigger and heavier than the numerous .380s on the market.

The DB9 is small enough to put in a shorts pocket and carry all day without being a burden. I carried the DB9 for two weeks and I liked it just as well at the end of that time as I did in the beginning. It represents an easier carry option than the five-shot snubbie revolvers and has a little more horsepower. Horsepower in a small package carries a penalty, though, and the penalty comes in the form of recoil. Recoil is always going to be a problem with carry guns that are light enough to carry comfortably and powerful enough to be effective. Personally, I don't find the DB9 uncomfortable, but others who've shot it instantly remarked that it has a bite. Well, it is a Diamondback.

Considering the recoil issues connected with small carry pistols and revolvers, you simply have to take into consideration that any gun light enough to carry and powerful enough to stop, is going to bite you a bit. Managing that recoil in a defensive situation isn't likely to be a huge problem because the defender is required by law to fear for his/her life. I teach my students to practice with lower-recoil ammunition or guns that operate like their carry guns. I don't know many folks who can afford to practice with quality defense ammunition, anyway. I run a cylinder load of defensive ammunition through my carry gun from time to time but most shooting is done with lighter loads. Work on sight picture and trigger management with rimfires and you'll be more confident and effective with you high-powered CCH gun.

Operationally, the DB9 gives up a few things to be a super small package and the lightest production 9mm. The DB9 slide doesn't lock back on the last shot, nor is there a manual slide lock. The trigger doesn't have the safety blade and there's no manual safety. I've heard the DB9 described as a baby Glock, though there's little similarity other than appearance. The DB9 disassembles like a Glock and does have a polymer frame. The six-shot single-stack magazines release is in the same place. Others have reported early reliability issues with these guns but mine has run flawlessly for me when I hold it normally. I say this because a friend, Ray Owens, has one and he remarked it stove-piped when he shot it in his weaker hand. Our test DB9 stove-piped once when my wife, Cherie, shot it; I told her to grip it tighter and she had no more problems. She also observed the recoil seemed less with a tighter hold,

something most folks don't consider. To replicate Ray's issue, I intentionally held the DB9 loosely and fired a magazine. On the last shot, I got a stove-pipe of an unfired round. Cherie's stove-pipe also came on the last round.

This is a common problem with lightweight, powerful pistols. The engineers balance the weight of the gun and the shooter's hand against the strength of the recoil spring. Hold the gun too loose and you have problems. If they make the spring too weak, the slide pounds the frame and beats the gun apart. While there's little to be done to correct it, any small

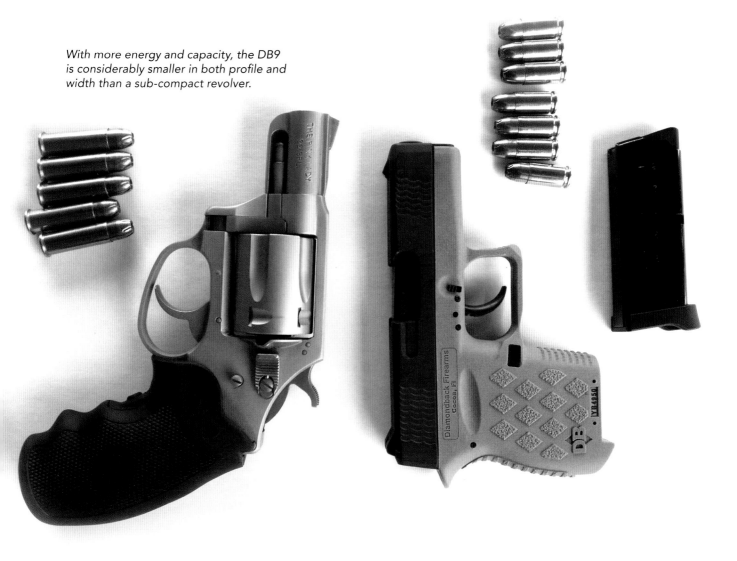

With more energy and capacity, the DB9 is considerably smaller in both profile and width than a sub-compact revolver.

semi-auto is prone to malfunction if not held tight. Take this into consideration and train yourself to really grip the pistol. A good grip will only help your shooting.

The DB9 isn't an easy gun to operate. The recoil spring is quite strong, due to the light weight of the slide. Since the slide is quite small, most women can't get a strong enough grip on it to rack the slide. Should a malfunction occur, it's difficult to clear because there's no slide lock. When I induced malfunctions by holding the DB9 lightly, malfunctions couldn't be cleared with the usual tap/rack.

I did find the DB9 to be accurate for a small gun. I shot a couple of groups, two-handed, at ten yards. I really focused on the small sights and came up with groups in the 2.5" range that were a couple of inches below the aiming point. This is really quite good for an 11-ounce 9mm pistol with tiny sights. At this

With a weight of under 12 ounces, the DB9 is a viable option for an active lifestyle and can be carried in high impact situations like this SmartCarry waistband holster.

At seven yards, two- handed, the DB9 makes a good accounting in the accuracy department. This target measured under 1.5" at the exact point of aim. The sights are quite small, though, and a laser would be a good choice in low light conditions.

point, Crimson Trace doesn't have a laser option for the DB9, though a laser would be a great option, as it is on any carry pistol or revolver.

In summary, the DB9 is a Noisy Cricket. It's deadly and powerful. It's accurate enough for a small carry pistol. My test gun was as reliable as one would expect out of a tiny but powerful carry , and it is hands-down the winner in a bulk versus power contest. It is, however, not a pistol for the inexperienced shooter in spite of the fact that you can buy it with a pink polymer frame. My experience spanning over 30 years of training new shooters has shown me

that inexperienced shooters need simple, easy to use guns. Having said this, my daughter has one. She's a runner and it's small, light, and slim enough to carry and not move around when she trains.

The DB9 is a great carry gun for the experienced shooter who needs the smallest, most powerful gun he can get. I like it and I own one, though it's not my everyday carry choice. I do carry it when the bulk of my snubbie revolver's cylinder is just too much. It is as close as you can come to an over-the-counter version of the Noisy Cricket and with good ammunition like the Remington Golden Sabre I carried in it, almost as deadly.

CHAPTER 11

SUB-COMPACT

The first of the small semi-auto movie guns I remember was James Bond's PPK, and even in the Ian Fleming-inspired movies, many of the other characters sported revolvers. In recent years, the move has been away from revolvers to semi-autos, both in the movies and TV and in real life. I suspect a fair amount of firearm choices are made based on visual media. Modern movies almost never depict revolvers, and when they do, the revolvers tend to be large and scary-looking.

Often in the discussion of revolvers and semi-autos, the issue of magazine capacity and fast reloads arises. It's true that the revolver is much slower to load and generally has a smaller capacity, but most civilian/criminal confrontations involve a very low number of shots, unlike the experiences of law enforcement and military. Even in law enforcement, it's rare for a confrontation to exceed five shots. Ultimately, it's the choice of the purchaser, and there are a lot of great choices both in revolvers and semi-autos available to the concealed carry citizen. You obviously make the choice for yourself. Nothing is ever written without bias on the part of the writer, so please excuse my unashamed preference for the small revolver.

For this category, I chose the upper weight limit at 16 ounces, a bit more than for the sub-compact semi-autos. There are only a few polymer guns in the group and all have steel or aluminum subframes because unlike semi-autos, the frame of a revolver actually contains the pressure of the round fired. Revolvers suffer in the area of thickness, an important issue for concealed carry, so for the ultimate in compactness and weight, they're eclipsed by semi-autos.

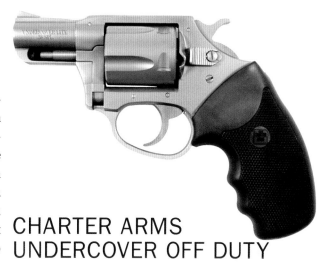

CHARTER ARMS UNDERCOVER OFF DUTY

My first sub-compact revolver was a blued steel Charter Arms Undercover. Though at the time we didn't have concealed carry in my state, I carried that gun for over 20 years. My normal carry method was in a kit bag that held my camera, binoculars flashlight, etc. I often slipped it in my belt when I felt I was in a dangerous situation. We went swimming twice by accident, it was only cleaned on rare occasions and it was just as reliable, though a bit less attractive, when I gave it to my son-in-law, many years later. Though he daily carries a S&W Shield, he still keeps that Charter Arms in his truck.

The base gun in the Charter Arms line is the five-shot .38 Undercover Blue Standard. It has a black finished stainless frame and cylinder, a 2" barrel, exposed hammer, and is chambered for .38 Special +P ammunition. Sights are a simple groove in the top strap and a milled-in ramp front. The cylinder release requires a forward push and the ejector rod is shrouded. With a steel frame, it weighs 16 ounces. It has an MSRP of $342.00. It's also available as the Aluminum Standard with an aluminum frame and matte grey finish at 12 ounces and an MSRP of $383.00. There are other options like double-action-only, shrouded hammers and Crimson Trace lasers.

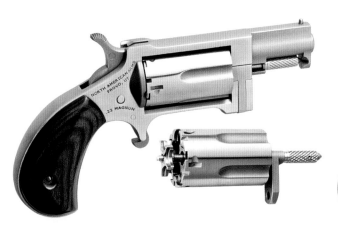

RUGER LCR

NORTH AMERICAN SIDEWINDER

Certainly the size and weight leader in the revolver category is the North American series of revolvers. The first rule of a gunfight is to have a gun, and no one could say a North American revolver is too big or heavy to carry. In .22 Magnum with a 1" barrel, it weighs just 6.7 ounces. While some might scoff at a diminutive gun this small, I can certainly see merit. The Sidewinder swings to the right rather than to the left and there's no side cylinder latch. Instead, the operator pulls the ejector rod forward, which disengages the locking mechanism and allows the cylinder to swing out. The ejector stroke is quite short, as can be imagined. The Sidewinder is a single action and from the cylinder back looks like a Remington-pattern derringer. The top-of-the-line Sidewinder has an MSRP of $349.00 in .22 Long Rifle or .22 Magnum and is available with a conversion cylinder for $419.00.

If the Sidewinder is too big for you, they also make the standard .22 Magnum with a weight of 6.2 ounces with a 1 5/8" barrel for $219.00 or with a .22 Long Rifle accessory cylinder for $254.00.

Ruger's LCR and the newer LCRx are traditional five-shot revolvers in function only. They're a radical departure from the look of the standard sub-compact revolver, using a polymer sub-frame mated to a steel structure that contains the pressure of the fired round. If it's possible in today's world for a revolver to have a modern look, the LCR is the top candidate. The frame is rounded with a swept look. The trigger guard and grip frame are polymer and the ejector rod is shrouded with a pushbutton cylinder latch. Some, especially people with arthritis or other dexterity issues, prefer the pushbutton instead of the forward-moving latch on most other revolvers because they find it easier to activate. Instead of the normal cylinder flutes, the LCR has an odd scalloped machining to reduce the weight of the cylinder. It looked strange to me at first, but now, I don't even notice. Grips are black rubber Hogue Tamer Monogrip and provide good purchase; sights are a grooved top strap and a pinned front ramp.

A real asset for the LCR is the smooth double-action trigger. If you plan to carry a small revolver, it's a good idea to learn how to manage a double-action trigger. The double-action trigger is both a safety feature and what makes the modern small revolver so simple. To shoot, you just pull the trigger until the gun fires. Once you learn how to manage the trigger, you can shoot as well double action as you can single action, not to mention much faster. Early LCRs were double-action-only, but in 2014 the company brought out the LCRx, an exposed-hammer model that allows single-action use. Weight is 13.5 ounces, Caliber is .38 Special +P, and barrel length is 1.875. Base MSRP is $545.00 with the Crimson Trace version at $825.00.

SMITH & WESSON 637, 638, AND 642

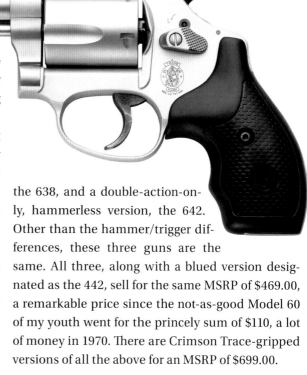

The basic modern equivalent of the Model 60 S&W from my teenage years is now the S&W 637 that resides in front of my appendix every day that I'm not in some location where me carrying it is against the law. Last year, I carried it 354 days. Four of those non-carry days were in Italy, the rest in New York. It's a basic working man's gun with few frills, just concessions to modern metallurgy and engineering that make it even better than my teenage dream carry gun. Chambered for .38 Special +P, it's a five-shot double-action revolver with an exposed hammer. The frame is aluminum; the majority of the rest of the parts are stainless steel. There's a machined-in serrated front sight and a machined-in groove rear. The barrel is 1.875" with a weight of 13.7 ounces. Finish is matte silver.

Although the 637 has an exposed hammer, Smith & Wesson also makes a shrouded hammer version, the 638, and a double-action-only, hammerless version, the 642. Other than the hammer/trigger differences, these three guns are the same. All three, along with a blued version designated as the 442, sell for the same MSRP of $469.00, a remarkable price since the not-as-good Model 60 of my youth went for the princely sum of $110, a lot of money in 1970. There are Crimson Trace-gripped versions of all the above for an MSRP of $699.00.

SMITH & WESSON M&P BODYGUARD

Smith & Wesson doesn't have an entry in the polymer revolver category. The M&P Bodyguard 38 is a modern departure design from the old J frame line of revolvers. The Bodyguard 38 is a foray into modern manufacturing and engineering methods introduced several years ago. It features an aluminum frame, a different top operating cylinder latch, and a Crimson Trace integrated laser. The sights are a milled-in front and groove in the top strap rear. Weight is 14.4 oz with a 1.9" stainless steel barrel. It comes with a matte black finish and is double-action-only. MSRP is $539.00.

SMITH & WESSON 340 AND 360 PD AND M&P

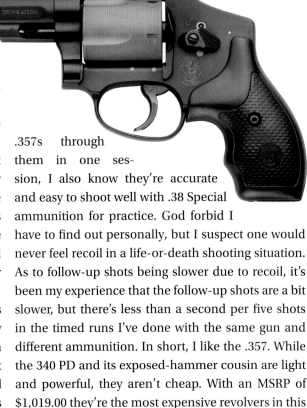

While most agree that the .38 Special +P round is sufficient as a concealed carry caliber, those who read this will be mostly Americans, and with Americans, more is always better. I suppose it was that spirit that caused engineers to design the ultimate concealed carry revolver, the Smith and Wesson 340 PD. I imagine a boardroom meeting with someone in sales talking to engineering with the purpose of cutting weight and increasing power. In automotive circles, this is referred to as the power-to-weight ratio, and the 340 and 360 PD revolvers are certainly contenders. At 11.4 ounces with a 1 7/8" barrel, the 340 PD is only surpassed by the Taurus Novue as the lightest five-shot centerfire revolver. Though the Novue weighs less, it's chambered for the standard .38 Special round and the 340 PD is chambered for the .357 Magnum round.

I am aware that a two-inch .357 doesn't generate as much velocity and power as a 6" .357, but I also know it generates more steam than any .38 Special load. I'm also aware that recoil is directly related to the weight of the gun and the energy of the load, so be informed that I'm aware an 11.2 ounce .357 has recoil that's as impressive as its power-to-weight ratio. Having said this, I've shot one of these guns quite a bit and while I know they're not pleasant when you run a box of hot .357s through them in one session, I also know they're accurate and easy to shoot well with .38 Special ammunition for practice. God forbid I have to find out personally, but I suspect one would never feel recoil in a life-or-death shooting situation. As to follow-up shots being slower due to recoil, it's been my experience that the follow-up shots are a bit slower, but there's less than a second per five shots in the timed runs I've done with the same gun and different ammunition. In short, I like the .357. While the 340 PD and its exposed-hammer cousin are light and powerful, they aren't cheap. With an MSRP of $1,019.00 they're the most expensive revolvers in this category. If you're willing to carry a bit more weight, you can opt for the M&P 340 with an MSRP of $869.00 and a weight of 13.3 ounces.

SMITH & WESSON 351 PD

The 351 PD is a bit outside the box in this category because almost all the guns here are chambered for the .38 Special round. The 351 PD is lighter than all but a couple of guns in the group and this is because it's an aluminum-cylinder, aluminum-framed .22 Rimfire Magnum. While many would argue the .22 Magnum is too light for personal defense, there are individuals who simply can't handle the recoil of light .38 Special guns. With a 1.875" barrel and a weight of just 10.8 ounces, the 351 is super light, reasonably powerful, and easy for a person with poor hand strength or pain issues like arthritis to shoot well. The cylinder holds seven rounds, there's the usual machined groove rear sight, but the 351 sports a hi-viz front. It has an exposed hammer in the event the shooter cannot pull a double-action pull and as one who teaches, I'm aware that many older people have this problem. With an MSRP of $759 with sculpted wood grips, this gun fills a niche.

TAURUS 85 ULTRALITE

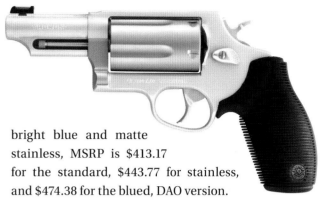

Taurus has been importing handguns into the U.S. since the mid-Sixties, The Model 85 is their iconic five-shot concealable revolver, with a barrel length of 2", chambered in .38 Special +P. At 17 ounces, it's a bit heavy for the sub-compact class but only in the weight department. The Ultralite series uses an aluminum frame with a steel cylinder and barrel, is available as a hammerless double-action-only, or with an exposed hammer and double/single action. The front sight is a fixed ramp; the rear is the familiar milled groove on the top strap. Offered in bright blue and matte stainless, MSRP is $413.17 for the standard, $443.77 for stainless, and $474.38 for the blued, DAO version.

TAURUS VUE/NOVUE

The smallest and lightest .38 Special revolver in history has been the Taurus Vue. At the time of this writing, it is listed on the Taurus website as discontinued, but during my recent trip to SHOT show, the Brazilian company was reintroducing it as the Novue. The Vue name came from the clear polymer side plate that allowed the user to see the action parts as they worked. Partially a novelty and part functional, since clear polymer weighs less than metal, the Vue had a 1.41" barrel and weighed just 9 ounces. It was a remarkable achievement in producing the ultimate lightweight five-shot revolver, besting the S&W 340 PD by over two ounces. Chambered in the same .38 Special chambering as the Vue, the Novue has an aluminum side plate and is otherwise the exact same gun. It seems the clear polymer plate cracked around the screw holes and simply didn't hold up as expected.

The two most remarkable functional features of the Novue are the tiny grip and the short ejection stroke. As one might imagine, a nine-ounce .38 Special has noticeable recoil and the tiny grip of the test Vue I reviewed required a firm grip. The double-action trigger pull was reasonable and quite smooth on my test gun and my wife really liked it, saying the recoil was a manageable compromise in return for the remarkably light weight. At the time of this writing, she was using the Vue as a daily carry gun. As to the short ejection stroke, it only lifts spend rounds out enough to pick them out individually. It would properly be called an extractor.

If this sounds like I'm not impressed favorably with the Taurus Vue/Novue, then I can assure you it's not the case. I think this gun has a place in the market and that the Novue, with an aluminum side plate will sell reasonably well. As I've stated before, you carry a defensive firearm more than you fire one and as long as you can perform with a gun, it isn't too small or light. I'd like to propose two more changes to the Vue/Novue.

First, offer a slightly larger grip as an accessory. The light weight is more important than the grip size, so give us the option for more purchase. Second, extend the extractor rod to the end of the barrel which would produce a reasonable extraction stroke and we might be able to call it an ejector. Along with the new aluminum side plate it would make the new gun a reasonable option. In fact, I even have a name for the new edition. I'd like to call it the Revue. MSRP on the Vue was $599.00. I suspect the Novue will sell at the same level.

THREE SUB-COMPACT REVOLVERS

The first rule for a gunfight is to have a gun. While this seems obvious, the fact is, we can never know when the gunfight will happen. Concealed carry, and the ability to intervene and save your life or the life of someone you love, should be an everyday commitment. The problem with intermittent carry is that the need can arise when you're not prepared. For everyday carry to happen, you either need a high level of discipline, or the gun and carry method must be non-intrusive enough to assure you won't get lazy and leave the gun at home.

Because of this, choice of the concealed carry firearm is always going to be a compromise between effectiveness and convenience. Personal preferences will always influence the choice, but, as stated elsewhere in the book, my choice for the last 30 or so years has been the five-shot, small-frame revolver. I choose this category of gun because I feel it offers the best compromise between power, size, and reliability.

I've used the term "Noisy Cricket" for very small, very powerful handguns. At the end of every class I teach, after my shooters have qualified, I get out some different handguns so they can try different guns and possibly refine their choices. Two guns that always come out are my wife's little Charter Arms Pink Lady and my Ruger .44 Magnum Super Blackhawk. Everyone assumes the Charter is a harmless little toy and the Redhawk will flip out of their hands, cut their face with the front sight, or break their wrist.

They're amazed when they realize the little pink .38 delivers more felt recoil and sting than the big, scary .44 Magnum. I've never had a student who didn't agree the Pink Lady kicks more with full-power loads than the huge .44 Magnum. Of course, effective defense ammunition doesn't have to be the +P kind, though more energy is always better. In fact, standard .38 Special with a quality bullet is a reasonably good stopper, and the light practice loads most

The Charter Arms Pink Lady is an Undercover Lite with a pink finish to make it more attractive to the feminine sex. Apparently it works, the gun sells as well as it performs as a low cost, light weight carry gun.

The LCRx is the most unconventional of the three. The unusual scalloping of the cylinder and polymer sub frame that comprises the grip and trigger guard sets it apart.

The Ruger's barrel is stainless and lines the gun's alloy frame.

people shoot recreationally are quite mild, even in a lightweight gun.

It's a fact that using a firearm for defense is all about stopping the threat. While there are no real numbers available, only a small percentage of the occasions when a firearm is used for self-defense involve the firing of a shot. In most situations, the presence of the defensive firearm ends the confrontation. In many situations, a single shot ends the confrontation, whether it incapacitates the assailant or not, and in some situations, the assailant only gives up when totally incapacitated.

The number of individual self-defense situations where a high number of shots are required is infinitesimally small. Consider how often you've read of a self-defense situation where the citizen reloaded his gun or ran out of ammunition. We see movies with extended gunfights and we get the high-volume mindset, but the reality is that while this makes great movies, it almost never happens in the real world for civilians, and rarely for sworn officers. While the potential is always there, and extra ammunition should be carried, the need for high capacity is a small percentage within a small percentage.

We all understand the stopping power of the firearm can have a profound effect on the number of rounds required to stop a determined assailant. Certainly, most would agree that a single well-placed, highly effective round would be more likely to stop a bad guy than one from a .22 rimfire. Because of this, I advocate carrying the most potent firearm you can handle. My choice of a five-shot compact revolver is the lightest and most powerful I can obtain.

Three such Noisy Crickets are the Ruger LCRx, the Charter Arms Undercover Lite, both chambered in .38 Special +P, and the Smith and Wesson 340 M&P chambered for the .357 Magnum round. I chose these guns for this comparison because they're both powerful and lightweight, and have excellent triggers that are light and manageable. I chose the .357 version in the S&W because it represents, as do the other guns, the highest power to weight ratio in their product line. Other companies make similar guns in .357, but those guns are heavier. The Charter Arms Mag Pug and the LCR both are available in .357, but both are based on heavier frames, the extra mass taking them up and into another weight class.

All three guns are similar in concept. The S&W is an updated, lightweight version of the time-honored Model 36 Chief's Special, using the small J frame and made of lightweight Scandium alloy with a stainless steel cylinder. The 340 M&P is the double-action-only, shrouded hammer version. At 13.3 ounces, it's a powerful lightweight with a good trigger pull and unobtrusive, but effective sights consisting of an integral U notch rear and a pinned, round, Tritium front sight.

The Charter Undercover Lite is a lightweight version of the standard Undercover I carried for about 20 years. It served hard duty, having the undesired experience of going swimming twice, not by choice. It traveled thousands of miles, endured minimal care, and never even thought of malfunctioning. It still serves my son-in-law faithfully. The Undercover Lite has a lighter trigger pull, though not as smooth as the other two guns. It has a machined-in ramp front and the same integral notch rear sight as the other guns.

The Ruger LCRx was chosen primarily because it's new in the Ruger line this year. While the S&W and Charter Arms designs have a long and storied history, the Ruger is a relative newcomer. The LCR product line was introduced in 2009. In spite of being a newcomer, the LCR series has received a warm reception in the world of personal protection revolvers. My sample version weighed the exact same on my scales as the S&W at 13.3 ounces, both guns being a half-ounce heavier than the Undercover.

The Ruger uses less conventional materials to achieve its light weight. The functioning part of the LCR frame is aluminum, but the grip frame and trigger guard are of polymer. A conventional pinned ramp front sight mates up with an integral notch rear sight providing adequate sights for a short-range carry gun. The Ruger has a less traditional look with the cylinder sculpted for weight reduction rather than the more conventional fluting on the Smith.

With .38 Special +P and .357 Magnum chamberings, and weighing less than 14 ounces, these guns generate levels of recoil that aren't for the faint of heart. They're not the kind of gun you want to burn a lot of defense level ammunition through. Recoil, though stout, is manageable. I'm a mid to back-of-the-pack guy at an action shooting event and I could manage five shots into the A zone of an IDPA target at seven yards within four seconds with both .38s using Remington Golden

Five shots, double-action-only at seven yards with Remington Golden Sabre 125-grain .357 loads. The 340 was spot-on point-of-aim and under an inch.

Sabre defense ammunition, and lost an additional second with the .357 S&W.

While there's room for argument that follow-up shots would take more time with such a powerful combination, the most important shot is the first, and a well-placed shot from a +P .38 or .357, even one with a short barrel, should discourage even the most determined attacker. And while we're on the subject, yes, I do know a two-inch .357 isn't as powerful as one with a six-inch barrel, but it's considerably more powerful than a .38 Special with a two-inch barrel.

Of course, there are guns with more weight that are easier to handle than these super light thumpers, but the primary issue with civilian everyday carry is comfort, and the plain fact is that you'll carry the gun far more than you'll shoot it. For a civilian to use deadly force, there must be a real threat of loss of life, serious bodily harm, or sexual assault. Under those conditions, the defender won't be likely to remember feeling any recoil at all.

In teaching the North Carolina Certification, our curriculum requires a discussion of the seven-yard standard of the Tueller drill, involving an assailant without a firearm. Though civilians using firearms for defense are almost never criminally charged, most

Recoil with the .357 M&P 340 is stout, but manageable. The extra level of power assures the 340 has penetration and stopping power.

My personal daily carry S&W 637 is capable of shooting flies at seven yards. If you notice the paster aiming point is missing, it disappeared after the third shot. Little guns can be very accurate, even in double action.

defense-with-a-firearm situations eventually involve a lawsuit, and shooting an assailant without a gun at ranges of less than seven yards will put the defender in a bad position in a civil suit. Having said all this, all three guns tested delivered quarter-sized groups at seven yards, more than enough accuracy for 99 percent of all civilian/aggressor confrontations.

Accuracy levels of guns like this are more dependent on your ability to achieve good sight alignment and manage the trigger than on the actual accuracy capability of the gun and ammunition. Recently, I did a video with Chris Cerino, of Top Shot fame, and Chris hit a 12" by 16" target on the third shot, double action, at 100 yards with a two-inch S&W .38. A couple of years back, I shot a 25-yard, five-shot group with the S&W 637 I was carrying at the time. I shot the group in low light, using a Crimson Trace grip laser rather than the sights on the gun. Off a sandbag, the two-inch-barreled belly gun produced a three-inch group, centered in the target.

The average distance in defensive shootings is generally agreed to be less than three yards; anything beyond seven is rare indeed. Adding a laser contributes both to low light capability and accuracy, though the laser should be set to be below the shooter's line of sight for practice purposes. Lasers are great and the reliability levels are spectacular, but depending solely on a battery in a life or death situation might not be the best

practice. Of course, grip laser systems are available for all three guns tested.

It still makes sense to carry ammunition for a possible reload, and reloading should be a part of your training exercises and drills. Speed loaders and speed strips are an asset in fast loading and they make the extra ammunition less fumble proof, an important factor when your life is in danger. Since the extractor rod is shorter on the two-inch guns, making sure ejected rounds clear the gun is important. The ejector stroke on the Ruger is .656, compared to .618 on the Smith, and .616 on the Undercover, but all three guns require a strong ejection stroke with the muzzle pointed skyward to assure that all brass clears the chambers, even then there's a possibility of a case or two needing removal.

Between these three guns, there's no bad choice. Your wise choice depends more on your product preference than on quality of features. I carry the S&W because I like the .357 round. I admit it's hairy to shoot, but I manage it just fine. I carried a Charter Undercover for years and it never let me down. The Ruger is as good as either, just a little different. Yes, a five-shot revolver gives up magazine capacity and speed of reloading, but they're as reliable as a hammer and offer a lot of power in a small package. In spite of the clichéd name, the snub-nosed .38 is still a viable choice.

My first reaction to the Taurus Vue was that it was more novelty than serious defensive firearm. After spending time with one, and my wife proclaiming it to be her daily carry gun, I've changed my mind. At a bit over nine ounces, the Taurus Vue, and now the Novue, is the lightest .38 Special revolver in history. It isn't perfect, but it certainly is small and light, and in concealed carry, small and light are very important because the first rule of a gunfight is to bring a gun.

I have friends who swear the only gun they'll carry for defense is a full-size .45 or a high-capacity 9mm or .40. The problem I've observed with their logic is they rarely have the big gun on them at the time they're swearing by its superiority. There's a current commercial based on the premise that you don't get a warning of when your heart attack will occur. The same logic applies to the need for personal defense. We don't know when we'll meet an aggressor, so we have to be prepared all the time. Being prepared all the time means carrying a gun all the time and if you like carrying a big heavy and difficult-to-conceal gun every day and everywhere you go, you're an unusual soul. My life simply doesn't allow me carrying a full-size, double-stack, .45 and even if it did, I wouldn't be able to conceal it without completely changing the way I dress to a style that's completely unacceptable to me.

My wife carries her carry gun in a purse with a Velcroed-in holster. She was carrying a 12-ounce gun until I brought the Taurus home and she instantly claimed it as her carry gun. I advised her it was a kicker due to the light weight so we went out in the yard to the plate machine and she demonstrated

The Vue/Novue is about the same size and weight as a Ruger LCP, one of the smallest and lightest of the .380 semi-autos. It is a bit thicker.

Recoil from a .38 Special in a nine-ounce gun is more than noticeable. If the grip was larger, it would be reasonable, but the tiny grip makes keeping the muzzle down tough.

she could not only shoot it, but she didn't mind the recoil, and at under ten ounces in .38 Special, the recoil is certainly substantial. In fact, to me, the Vue is more uncomfortable to shoot than a .460 S&W, and that's saying a lot. When I asked if the recoil bothered her, Cherie's logic was unassailable because she was quoting me. Her reply was, "I'll carry it a lot more than I shoot it and I can control it and hit a target." I was satisfied with that answer and sent Taurus the check.

For those unfamiliar with the Taurus Vue, and now the Novue, it's an abbreviated version of their popular line of alloy-framed, five-shot revolvers. It has a 1.5" barrel, a groove on the top strap for a rear sight and a ramp front. The most noticeable features are the tiny grip and the see-through side plate. The see-through side plate concept has been scrapped, presumably because it develops little cracks around the screw holes, but the Novue with an alloy side-plate only weighs an ounce or two more. I suspect

Cherie's gun will be going back to Taurus for a new side plate, but for now, her gun is OK.

Shooting the Vue/Novue, you instantly notice two things: First - and foremost - is recoil. There are guns that have more recoil than the Novue, but they don't hurt as much to shoot because they offer a more secure purchase. In order to get the gun as small and light as it is, Taurus fashioned a tiny, butter knife-sized handle for the gun that's not only small, but also curved. The idea is to allow keep the butt of the gun close to the shooter's body, but the effect is it's harder to fashion a set of respectable-sized replacement grips.

Shooting the Vue/Novue isn't comfortable, but the tiny little gun groups remarkably well in spite of the tiny barrel. Shooting at seven yards I was able to put three of five shots in the same hole with the other two an inch or two out while shooting two-handed and double action, which is the only option, since the tiny little gold hammer is bobbed. The trig-

The ejector is proportioned with the barrel length and should extend to the end of the barrel. The ejector stroke is so short it's better described as extraction.

ger is pleasantly smooth and reasonably light and manageable. The gun's sights are no worse or better than other five-shot belly guns, but it does print a couple inches high. This can't be corrected by filing the front sight, so for best accuracy the user will need to hold low. There's a possibility one might find a load that shoots lower, but I suspect it's a flaw to be corrected later. I've asked Crimson Trace if they plan a laser grip option for the Vue/Novue because it would cure two of the more noticeable shortcomings, the tiny grip and the gun shooting high. As of now, they have no plans for one.

Loading and unloading the Vue/Novue is pretty standard, and Smith J frame speed loaders work fine. Unloading does often require pulling cases out of the chambers because the stroke of the ejector rod is remarkably short. It would better be described as an extractor rather than an ejector, but the cases of the Winchester Train and Defend ammunition I used for the test fell out easily.

Having read the shortcomings, one might think I wasn't too pleased with the Vue/Novue, but this would be an incorrect assumption. In fact, I liked the little gun and I'd carry one myself, if I needed something even smaller than the 637 I currently pack. When I first tested the Vue a while back, I decided it needed three things to be a really great pocket carry revolver. Taurus has already taken care of the see-through side plate, which I saw as an unnecessary gimmick. They need to extend the extractor rod out to the end of the barrel, which will add negligible weight and bulk ,but make the gun much more usable and easier to reload, and they need an optional set of grips that are still small but substantially bigger than the standard ones that come on the gun. Making the front sight a bit taller would help,

In spite of tiny grips and rudimentary sights, the Vue was remarkably accurate for such a small gun. At seven yards, double-action-only, my group is pretty good, though a little high. Next time I see Lew Danielson at Crimson Trace, I'm going to beg him to add a laser grip for the Novue into their line.

but as a concealed carry instructor, I'm aware that armed citizens rarely take shots beyond seven yards and the existing sights are adequate for that, especially since most of my students shoot low anyway. If Crimson Trace comes up with a set of laser grips, that would be even better.

It's true that there are .380s that equal the light weight of the Vue/Novue. With modern ammunition they also come very close in power and energy, with the added bonus of slightly more capacity and much faster reloading, but capacity and fast reloading are rarely an asset in citizen defensive firearms. The little revolver offers something no small semi-auto can offer and this is the almost infallible reliability of a

revolver and an instant second shot in the admittedly unlikely event of a dud round. While small semi-autos tend to be sensitive to different loads and how the user grips the gun, the revolver remains 99.99% reliable. I suspect the Vue/Novue wouldn't hold up to thousands of rounds, but it's certainly reliable as tested and few concealed carry guns are called upon for regular practice, even though it's a good idea.

Overall, the Vue/Novue is a groundbreaking little gun that's a great example of how less is more. Ounce for ounce, it delivers a remarkable and almost unprecedented level of power, reliability, compactness, and light weight. It's not without flaws, but it's a remarkable little gun and I like it.

CHAPTER 12

COMPACT SEMI-AUTOS

Ultimately, everyone gets to choose his or her own carry gun. There are so many quality guns today that it makes the choice more difficult, but the blessing is that almost any set of qualities one might wish for in a gun are available to us. The compact category of semi-autos is probably where most concealed carriers will choose their weapon. These guns offer easy concealment and powerful calibers, some offer slim profiles, others offer high capacities in small packages.

While the .380 has become a much more effective caliber through the development of better defensive loadings, many still wish for the power of the 9mm Luger. Several of the guns in this category are chambered for .40 S&W and two are chambered for .45 ACP. From economy guns to top-of-the-line bling-laden carry pistols, there are a lot of great choices in this category.

BERETTA NANO

Like the Pico, Beretta's 9mm Nano is another chassis-based gun with a serialized fire control system, though the Nano is a striker-fired gun. It features a polymer frame to encase the fire controls and connect the magazine, slide, and barrel into one unit. The whole gun is snag-free with few protuberances to tangle with clothing. The standard three-dot sights are low profile, and the top corners of the slide appear to have been shaved off for easy holster carry. Total width is less than one inch, allowing for ease of concealability. Like the Pico, other frames in different colors are available to complement or allow for some appearance changes, based on your mood or for functional changes like a laser.

Not a super lightweight at almost 20 ounces, but slim and certainly concealable. Magazine capacity is 6 + 1 and overall length is a bit over five inches. MSRP is $475.00.

BERSA THUNDER

Founded in the mid-1950s, Bersa is an Argentinian firearms manufacturer. In 1994 they introduced the Bersa Thunder, a double/single-action, blowback operated semi-auto that bears a strong resemblance to the Walther PPK. The barrel is fixed, the sights are small, but useable in good light. Trigger pull is a fairly smooth double action on the first shot, reverting to single action on subsequent shots. The safety de-cocks the gun and I'd have to be pretty nervous about an accidental discharge to worry about carrying the Thunder with the safety off due to the trigger pull. With a 3.54" barrel the Thunder weighs 20 ounces. Because of the all metal construction, it's a bit heavy for a .380, but this certainly makes it easy to shoot and light on recoil. Magazine capacity is 8 + 1 and MSRP is $569.00.

GLOCK 36

Glock was the leader in bringing the striker-fired pistol into widespread use. The Glock 17 wasn't the first polymer-framed, striker-fired pistol, but it certainly was the first commercial success. Glock's 36 is a concealed carry-specific pistol chambered for the popular .45 ACP cartridge. Unlike almost all other Glocks in the US, it's a single stack gun with compact dimensions and a thin profile. Length is a tad under seven inches and it's just 1.1" wide. It features all the standard Glock operational features, from the striker-fired "safety action" to the familiar white outline U rear sight and dot front. Like other Glocks, there's a bladed trigger with a two-stage trigger pull.

The magazine and slide release are in the familiar locations. The single stack magazine holds 6 rounds and weight is 22.4 ounces. Barrel length is 3.77". MSRP is $637.00.

GLOCK G26, G27, G33, G29, AND G30

Glock has a whole series of double-stack carry guns in almost every popular concealed carry caliber. All feature the familiar Glock polymer frame, trigger, sights, and controls. The Glock G26 is a 9mm, the 27 is a .40 S&W, and the 33 is chambered for .357 SIG. All are the same width at 1.18" with a weight of 21.8 ounces. All have the same barrel length of 3.42". Magazine capacities are 10 for 9mm, 9 for .357 SIG and .40 S&W.

The Glock 29 is chambered for 10mm, and the Glock 30 is a .45 ACP. Both these guns weigh 26.3 ounces with a width of 1.27" and a barrel length of 3.77". The Glock 29 is chambered for .45 GAP, and weighs 24.1 ounces with a width of 1.18" and a barrel length of 3.42". The Glock 30s is a later, narrow-slide version of the standard Glock 30. Magazine capacity is 10 + 1. Weight is 22.95 ounces with a 3.77" octagonal rifled barrel and width is 1.27". MSRPs for these compact double-stack models range between $599.00 and $637.00 in standard and $649.00 and $687.00 in Generation 4 models.

KAHR CM9, CM40

The Kahr CM9 and CM40 pistols are true striker-fired pistol with a polymer frame and a stainless steel slide. It's chambered for both 9mm and S&W .40 and has a magazine capacity of 6 + 1 in 9mm and 5 + 1 in .40 and has a 3" standard rifling barrel. The magazine release is in the proper 1911 position and the gun has slide lock on the last round. Trigger pull is a long, smooth pull, feeling like a double-action revolver and like a revolver, there's a long reset. Fortunately, the trigger system also has double strike capability. The dovetailed rear sight has a vertical bar aligning with a pinned-in dot at the front. At just .90" wide in 9mm and .94" in .40, it's certainly slim enough for most folks, and with a magazine, the CM weighs less than 16 ounces empty. With such light weight, recoil is going to be stiff in .40 and not for sissies in 9mm. MSRP is $460.00.

There's also a more expensive PM version of this design featuring polygonal rifling, two magazines instead of one, and a milled slide release instead of a cast one. The PM series sells for $810.00.

KEL-TEC P-11

Chambered in 9mm Luger, the Kel-Tec CNC Industries P-11 is a locked-breech semi-auto with an aluminum frame and a stainless steel slide and 3.1" barrel. While the frame is aluminum, the grip is high-impact polymer and comprises both the trigger guard and magazine well. Capacity with a double-stack magazine is 10 + 1, quite remarkable in a pistol that weighs just 14 ounces empty. The trigger is a true double action with a long reset, but allowing restrike capability. MSRP is $333.00.

KEL-TEC PF9

The Kel-Tec PF9 was introduced in 2006 as a smaller, slimmer, and lighter version of the P11. In spite of the fact that it weighs only 12.7 ounces and is only .88 inches thick, it has usable sights, an accessory rail and a slide stop. There's a stainless steel slide and an aluminum and polymer frame, with a stainless 3.1" barrel. The slide comes with a Parkerized, blued, or chrome finish and the frame comes in different colors. It does have a locking slide and the magazine release is in the 1911 location. The trigger is a restrike-capable double action with a long reset, not a target trigger but a reasonable trigger for a carry gun. The single-stack magazine allows for 7 + 1 capacity and MSRP is $333.00.

KIMBER SOLO

While Kimber is known for its 1911-style pistols, the Kimber Solo is a complete departure from that design. Chambered for 9mm Luger and with a 2.7" barrel, it sports an aluminum frame and stainless steel slide. It's a striker-fired gun with a typical striker-fired trigger that's a long-pull first stage with a perceptible second stage. At 17.2 ounces, it's a mid-weight in its class. Magazine capacity is 6 + 1 with the safety and magazine release in the standard 1911 location, and the magazine release and thumb safety on the right side as well, to allow ambidextrous operation. Sights are drift-adjustable three-dot with rounded edges to make them non-snagging. In fact, the whole gun is smooth and rounded for easy pocket and holster carry. Early reports found the Solo to be a picky feeder, and Kimber recommends only using premium ammunition, but more recent reports reflect solid performance.

Selling for an MSRP of $765.00 with one magazine, the Solo isn't cheap, but Kimber has a reputation for making high-quality guns and quality workmanship is apparent in handling the Solo.

MAGNUM RESEARCH MICRO DESERT EAGLE

The Micro Desert Eagle is a bit heavy for the sub-compact class and a bit small for compact. Chambered for .380 ACP and with a 2.2″ barrel, the Micro is an enclosed-hammer action with twin recoil springs instead of a single spring in the center under the barrel. It's small for a compact, but due to all-metal construction, it comes in at about 14 ounces, a bit heavy for sub-compact. It uses a double-action-only trigger which should provide second-strike capability and a gas-assisted blowback action. Sights are fixed and machined into the slide, the magazine capacity is 6 + 1, and the magazine release is in the conventional location, but there's no slide lock. The magazine well is radiused for easy magazine changes, but the magazines protrude oddly from the well. MSRP is $467.00.

NORTH AMERICAN ARMS GUARDIAN

Known for its tiny single-action revolvers, North American also makes the Guardian. A traditionally-made, concealed-hammer .380 ACP semi-automatic, the Guardian is a double-action-only gun with a traditional look. The frame and slide are stainless steel with black polymer grips. As an all-steel gun, the Guardian is a bit heavy for a .380 with a 2 ½″ barrel at 18.72 ounces, but the extra weight will allow comfortable recoil. There's no slide lock or magazine safety and the magazine release is in the normal location. Capacity is 6 + 1 rounds. There's also no manual safety because the Guardian relies solely on the double-action trigger pull to prevent unwanted discharges. This does allow second-strike capability. Sights are minimalist with a tiny front blade and machined rear notch, but there is an optional Crimson Trace grip-activated laser. MSRP is $449.00.

RUGER LC9S

Ruger has been a power player in almost every aspect of firearms manufacture, and their LC9 garnered its share of laurels when first introduced. The original LC9 was a hammer-fired semi-auto 9mm with a polymer frame and alloy steel slide. There were complaints concerning the trigger and since we now live in a striker-fired world, the LC9s was introduced in 2014 to address the trigger issues. With a weight of 17.2 ounces and a width of .90", the SR9s is not a super lightweight, but certainly slim and light enough for easy concealment. With a barrel length of 3.12", overall length is 6". Sights are three-dot drift-adjustable and the trigger is the bladed type without second-strike capability. There's a left-side thumb safety and a visual chamber indicator port. Magazine capacity is 7+1 rounds and the gun comes with a finger grip extension for the magazine floor plate for more comfort. The standard model comes with a magazine disconnect, but as of 2015, there's a Pro model that has neither the thumb safety nor magazine safety, no doubt a concession to those of us who dislike a magazine safety. With one magazine and a soft case, both models have an MSRP of $449.00.

RUGER LC380

Many consumers have trouble handling small, lightweight 9mm semi-autos. With lightweight guns, the recoil of +P 9mm ammunition can be intimidating, and the added power requires a stronger operating spring, which makes stroking the slide more difficult than would be the case with a lighter round. To answer the call of this niche, Ruger makes the LC380, an almost identical gun to the LC9 but chambered for the milder .380 ACP round. The LC380 has the same MSRP as the LC9 but is also available with the Crimson Trace Laserguard system with a grip activated laser for an MSRP of $629.00.

RUGER SR9C AND SR40C

The SR9C and SR40c are compact striker-fired versions of the SR series service pistol from Ruger. They feature a polymer grip frame and a stainless steel slide and 3.4" barrel. Weighing in at 23.4 ounces, magazine capacity is 17 + 1 in 9mm and 15 + 1 in .40 with the extended magazine, and 10 +1 in 9mm and 9 + 1 in .40-caliber with the standard magazine. The extended magazine has a sleeve that extends the grip to allow more purchase. Most users will likely carry the gun with the smaller mag for concealment, and the larger for backup. The SR series of guns also feature a magazine safety. There's an ambidextrous magazine release and thumb safety.

Sights are the drift-adjustable three-dot system. The SRc series also has a reversible back strap to allow better fit for shooters with smaller hands. Sights are the three-dot system with adjustment for both windage and elevation. There's a rail on the bottom of the frame for lights and/or lasers. Trigger pull is the standard striker-fired pull with a bladed trigger. MSRP in both calibers is $529.00 and the guns are available with black nitride or brushed stainless slides.

SCCY CPX

Located near the Daytona Speedway in Florida, SCCY produces the CPX series of concealed carry 9mm pistols. The CPS pistols are internal hammer, double-action-only polymer-framed pistols with an internal aluminum receiver and stainless steel slide. The barrel is 3.1", the gun is 1" wide in spite of using double-stack magazines, and the SCCY CPX weighs 15 ounces. Sights are the familiar three-dot system with a drift-adjustable rear.

MSRP is $319.00 with two magazines, a trigger lock, and two plain baseplates for the magazines. It's available in several different color combinations and with or without a thumb safety.

SIG P238

SIG has a reputation for high-quality pistols and in handling the 238, there's no doubt in one's mind that it's a quality gun. Chambered in .380 ACP, it's a single-action, locked-breech semi-auto with many 1911 characteristics. The magazine release, safety, and slide release are in familiar 1911 locations; the hammer resembles the roweled Commander version, and it's obvious the trigger is going to have a 1911 feel just looking at it. There's an alloy beavertail frame with a stainless steel slide and at last count, there were 22 color/grip/option combinations. Standard sights are drift-adjustable three-dot.

Early reports included feeding issues, though current reports indicate those issues have disappeared. There certainly are advantages to single-action pistols, the first and foremost being a precise trigger pull. The trigger on the 238 is exactly what one would expect on a service-grade 1911, a clean break, with a bit of overtravel. Not so light to be dangerous, but precise enough for accurate shooting. This type of trigger is great on a service pistol that's holstered with a protection over the safety or hammer. For a concealed carry gun, it might not be such a great system. The only way to quickly respond with a single-action gun is to carry in Condition One, cocked and locked. Most of the 238 owners I know are simply too nervous to carry in this mode because of the possibility of inadvertently disengaging the safety in an inside waistband or pocket holster. With a 2.7" barrel and a weight of just 15.2 ounces, the 238 is a little jewel of a gun, but consider your carry method before plunking down the cash. MSRP for the standard Nitron model is $679.00.

SIG P938

For those who'd like a bit more horsepower than the .380 ACP, Sig has the P938. The P938 is a single-action semi-auto that, like the 238, shares looks and basic design with the 1911. Still a lightweight at 16 ounces, it's less than an ounce heavier than the .380 P238 and less than a half-inch longer. Other features are the same, with 16 color, grip and sighting options. The Nitron base model sells for about $750.00.

S&W SHIELD

My first experience shooting the Smith & Wesson M&P Shield was when my son-in-law brought one by the farm for his first shots. I decided right away that it's a remarkable gun: thin, light, powerful enough to be considered a serious stopper, and no frills affordable. The Shield has certainly been a commercial success for the company and it's a top-tier choice for practical everyday carry.

There's nothing unconventional about the Shield; in fact it's as standard as modern striker-fired concealed carry guns can be. There's a polymer frame and a steel slide and barrel. The trigger is hinged instead of bladed, but the effect is the same. The trigger pull is the standard two-stage with the first stage for safety and a reasonable, but not remarkable break at the second stage. Barrel length is 3.1", and weight is 19 ounces. It's one inch thick in profile and just over 6" long. It has three-dot sights that are drift-adjustable for windage. The controls are all in the normal locations. Magazine capacity is 7 + 1 in 9mm and 6 + 1 in .40. It's available with or without a thumb safety and of course there's a Crimson Trace laser option. There are - as of 2015 - a couple of choices for the look of the polymer frame, but there aren't a dozen color options. In short, the M&P Shield is a no-nonsense, practical gun that works. Though I don't carry one, I am a fan. MSRP is $449.00 for the standard gun with a standard and extended magazine, and $589.00 for the Crimson Trace model with the grip switch laser.

SMITH & WESSON M&P COMPACT

The S&W M&P has been successful as a service, recreational, and competition pistol. It's also available as a concealed carry pistol with reasonable concealability and weight. With a barrel of 3.5" and a weight of just 21.9 ounces, it's a double-stack, polymer-framed, striker-fired compact. It uses the S&W style of hinged triggers for safety; the trigger is a two stage. There's a bottom rail on the frame, the slide release is ambidextrous, and the magazine release is convertible for lefties. It's available in both 9mm and .40 S&W with a magazine capacity of 12 and 10 rounds, respectively. Sights are the familiar three-dot system and both front and rear are dovetailed. It comes with three interchangeable palm grip inserts. MSRP is $569.00 and $829.00 for the Crimson Trace version equipped with a rear grip activation button.

SPRINGFIELD ARMORY XDS

Springfield Armory is a relatively new company when you consider the impact they have in the industry, but the name is one of the oldest names in firearms. The original Springfield Armory was created in 1777 as a U.S. Government arsenal. Manufacture of guns began in 1794 and the armory was closed in 1968. In 1974, the Springfield Armory name was resurrected as the manufacturer of the M1A rifle and in 2007 they introduced the successful line of XD pistols made in Croatia.

In 2012, they introduced the XDs, a slim, single-stack striker-fired pistol with XD characteristics for concealed carry. First introduced in 9mm and then shortly later in .45 ACP, it drew instant attention as a small and light powerhouse in the extremely popular .45 caliber. Like the M&P Shield, the XDs is a no-nonsense pistol, polymer-framed, with a bladed trigger and standard striker-fired trigger pull. There's no thumb safety option but there is a standard grip safety, a feature I feel is a viable addition to a concealed carry semi-auto.

The XDs weighs in at 23 ounces, making it a bit heavier than other contenders in this class, but the extra weight makes it manageable enough for regular practice with little discomfort. Magazine capacity is 7 + 1 in 9mm and 5 + 1 in .45 with the flush magazine, and 8 + 1 in 9mm and 6 + 1 in .45 with the extended magazine. In addition to the standard 3.3 model, the XDs is also available in a 4.0 4" version. MSRP is $599.00 with two magazines, a holster and magazine pouch, and a hard case.

SPRINGFIELD ARMORY XD COMPACT

Springfield's XD Compacts are double-stack 3" barreled versions of the popular XD line. They feature the same polymer frame and stainless slides of other guns in the XD line but with shortened grip frames to match the 3" barrels and concealed carry purpose. Sights are three-dot dovetailed front and rear. They have a bladed, two-stage, striker-fired style trigger and a grip safety. The magazine release is ambidextrous. Weight is 26 ounces. Available in 9mm with a capacity of 13 + 1 and .40 S&W with a capacity of 9 + 1. They come with an extra extended magazine, a holster, magazine pouch, and loader in a hard case. Available in both all black and bi-tone, MSRP is $599.00.

TAURUS MILLENNIUM G2

The Taurus Millennium G2 fits the current mold of polymer-framed, striker-fired pistols. Chambered in 9mm, it has a double-stack 12 + 1 capacity. Barrel length is 3.2" and weight is 22 ounces. Sights are three white dots, with the rear being adjustable and the front fixed. There's an accessory rail on the bottom of the frame and a loaded chamber indicator. The trigger is a bladed two-stage system similar to many current striker-fired pistols, but it has second-strike capability. There is an external thumb safety in addition to the thumb safety and long, two-stage pull. The magazine has a finger hook and the grips have stippled panels for better purchase. MSRP is $434.59.

TAURUS 709 SLIM

The Taurus 709 SLIM is a 9mm single-stack, striker-fired, polymer-framed pistol with a magazine capacity of 7 + 1. It uses a bladed two-stage trigger that, unlike most striker-fired pistols, features second-strike capability. Some argue that second-strike capability is of limited virtue, but it's been my experience that most rounds that don't fire on the first strike often fire on the second. It costs no time to pull the trigger again as the hand is moving around to tap the magazine for the tap/rack sequence, so I see an advantage. Sights are the three-dot variety with the rear sight being adjustable for windage and elevation. Weight is 19 ounces and barrel length is 3". The grip area offers a grooved front and rear area and there's an external thumb safety and adequate gripping surfaces on the slide. It's available in all black and bi-tone with an MSRP of $503.73.

WALTHER PPK

Walther's PPK is probably the longest-running production pistol in this category. Released in 1931, the PPK is best known as the gun 007 carried in the early James Bond movies. It also has the dubious distinction of taking the life of one of history's most notorious villains, Adolf Hitler. While the design is an older one, the PPK has a very solid feel many still like today. It's a steel-framed, double/single action, exposed-hammer, semi-automatic, using the simple blowback operating system. While this system is simple, it requires a stronger operating spring than some other systems, making the slide a bit difficult to cycle because of the strength of the spring. The double-action trigger system has merits in that the gun can be carried hammer-down, and a simple pull of the trigger will fire the shot. After the first shot, the trigger becomes a single-action trigger. This system also allows the operator to manually cock the hammer for a single-action pull on the first shot if more precise trigger management is required. The slide locks back on the last shot, but there's no external slide release.

While it might be considered underpowered with the .380 ACP chambering, modern defensive .380 ammunition outperforms the roundnose .38 Special ammunition popularly used for law enforcement for a half century. With a barrel length of 3.3" and a weight of 20 ounces, it's much larger than many .380s but the weight and size make it extremely pleasant to shoot. Sights are small and fixed. The magazine release is conveniently located and the safety de-cocks the hammer. Magazine capacity is 6 + 1 and it's available in both blued and stainless as well as a PPKs version with a longer grip and an extra round of magazine capacity.

WALTHER PK380

If you'd like a more modern Walther, the PK380 is a new Walther pistol that performs the same purpose. Everything about the PK380 is modern and up-to-date except the exposed hammer and double/single-action trigger system. It's a locked-breech, exposed-hammer, polymer-frame pistol with a modern under rail for lights and/or lasers. It uses modern three-dot sights, a loaded chamber view port, a side takedown lever, and an ergonomic polymer grip frame. The magazine release is the European paddle style. It's in a convenient location, but the transition under pressure might be difficult for those used to a release button. With a 3.66" barrel it weighs 18 ounc-

es and has 8 + 1 magazine capacity. At 1.2 inches wide, it isn't super slim, nor is it small for a .380, but it's very comfortable and easy to shoot. The safety de-cocks and blocks the hammer and it's available in black and bi-tone or with a laser set. MSRP is $399.00.

WALTHER PPS

The PPS is a striker-fired, polymer-framed, locked-breech pistol chambered in both 9mm and .40 S&W. It uses a typical striker-fired, bladed trigger. It has a lower rail for lights and lasers and three-dot sights with the rear being drift adjustable for windage. There's a loaded chamber view port, a cocking indicator and a no-snag slide release. The magazine release is the paddle type and is ambidextrous. Both compact and slim, the PPS weighs 19 ounces with a 3.2" barrel and a width of just .9". Magazine capacity is up to 8 rounds in 9mm and up to 7 in .40. MSRP is $599.00.

REMINGTON R51

The original Remington Model 51 was designed by John Pedersen in 1915. It was a personal favorite of General George Patton and he carried one often during the World War II era. The modern version released in 2014 got off to a rocky start. At the time of this writing, the upgraded versions have not yet been released, but it seemed prudent to include it in this category anyway.

The R51 is a hammer-fired semi-auto firing from a locked breech. The original offering was in 9mm Luger, with a .40 S&W version promised. It uses a stainless barrel, has a drift-adjustable two-dot rear sight and fixed-dot front. It has an ambidextrous magazine release and uses a grip safety. Weight is 22 ounces with a 3.4" barrel and a double-stack magazine. Future release plans and MSRP are to be announced.

About the same profile as my 637, but slimmer, the XDs carries more rounds and has considerably more power.

The XDs comes with two five-round magazines and there's an available seven-round extended version.

There's a whole generation of new pistols for concealed carry and I'm impressed with the thought and engineering that's gone into some of them. Recently, I assisted in a test of four .45 ACP single-stack concealed carry semi-autos. I was impressed with the XDs then, and when I got a chance to test one myself, I jumped on it. Springfield Armory's line of XD pistols has been a smashing success. The features of these striker-fired guns make them unique in that they are ambidextrous and they feature a grip safety, a valuable asset in a striker-fired gun that allows a lighter, shorter stroke trigger with a similar or greater level of safety.

I used a Springfield XDm 5.25 in last year's Bianchi Cup. My choice was based on the XD's reputation for accuracy and reliability, so when my editor suggested shooting production class, the 5.25 was an easy choice. Made in Croatia and parented by the

The only striker-fired guns with a grip safety, the Springfield XD series adds an extra level of safety for concealed carry guns.

first Croatian pistol manufactured, the PHP, the XD series of pistols have become viable contenders for the civilian as well as police and military markets. My XDm has yet to malfunction through thousands of rounds.

Like other XD-series guns, the XDs is well finished for a utility gun. The controls are similarly placed with the takedown lever and slide release on the left side and an ambidextrous magazine release. The sights are really good with a drift-adjustable two-dot rear and a hi-vis front. The trigger is undistinguishable in pull from the larger XD pistols, which is to say it's very good. There's a fairly short initial travel and a distinct second stage that breaks consistently and cleanly.

The standard magazine holds five rounds and there's an available extended seven-round magazine. While the seven-round magazine is handy for range use, it increases the profile of the gun considerably. With one in the chamber, six rounds is reasonable in a concealed carry handgun. If you can't do it with six, you should practice more. Striker-fired, with no manual safety, the XDs relies on a blade in the trigger and a grip safety to prevent accidental

discharge. Carrying a round in the chamber is, in my opinion, a prerequisite for using a semi-auto for concealed carry and with a holster that protects the trigger, I'd feel perfectly safe carrying this gun with a round chambered.

At 21.5 ounces, the XDs is not a lightweight. With a loaded magazine, it approaches the empty weight of some service-level pistols. While it occupies about the same profile as a J frame S&W, it weighs more empty and considerably more loaded. What this pistol has going for it is that it's a .45. It's thinner in profile than a small revolver and it carries a lot more punch. That punch also translates into recoil. In a recent range session where I fired 300 rounds with the XDs and a couple of other compact .45s, I managed to escape without having a sore hand the next day, but this isn't a gun for the faint-hearted.

Operation of the XDs is both simple and convenient. The magazine is fairly easy to load, the slide operates well and may be easier to manipulate than some of the larger XD series guns with slides that taper towards the top. The controls are where they should be, making the gun easy to adapt to. With a good trigger and good sights, I expected it to per-

Shooting the XDs involves recoil levels beyond that of larger guns. It is manageable, but it is not for the faint of heart.

form well and I wasn't disappointed. I don't bench test carry guns because the short sight radius makes it difficult. My test is to determine reasonable accuracy for the purpose of the gun's intended use. At ten yards, two-handed, with a magazine change, I managed a 2.5-inch, ten-shot group that was centered in the target. Recoil recovery is slower than larger or less powerful guns, but it was reasonable and the good sights and trigger aided greatly. I fired this with the five-shot magazines because I see the seven-shot magazine as too large for everyday concealment.

Overall, this is a very good concealment gun for those who feel the need for serious power, and it has little other utility. It's larger and considerably heavier than the gun I carry every day but every aspect of concealed carry firearms choice is a tradeoff between effectiveness and concealability. This gun is as powerful as any concealed carry gun needs to be. It's reliable, accurate, and safe to carry in normal carry situations. It's not a gun for those who have problems dealing with recoil. Once loaded, it's heavier than I'd want to carry every day but you simply can't argue with a gun this small with this kind of power and accuracy.

Accuracy is good, but inexperienced shooters might have issues with recoil anticipation. I shot this group at ten yards and was impressed that the XDs shot exactly where the sights were pointed.

GLOCK G26 AND G30 COMPACTS

There is an ongoing debate in gun circles on whether the Glock pistol was the most influential handgun design of the second half of the 20th Century. While the Glock wasn't the first striker-fired, double-stack polymer pistol, it was the first one that found commercial success, and that success spawned a whole generation of similar designs, some so close as to merit lawsuits. Now, we have a whole generation of striker-fired double and single-stack polymer-frame pistols, and they're almost all excellent guns.

While it would be interesting to do a comparison between the major players, it's been my experience that most of these guns are excellent and that preferences as to which is better is more personal preference and brand loyalty than practical differences. To not have included a test of the compact Glocks would have been an unforgivable oversight, and I obtained two representative Glock compacts for a hands-on test. The guns I chose were the G26 in 9mm and the G30 in .45 ACP.

The Glock 30 is a .45 ACP with a weight of 26.3 ounces, a width of

In profile and bulk, there's a considerable difference between the G26 and G30. As a carry gun, the G30 is bulky, but it's a powerful package in .45 ACP with ten rounds.

1.27" and a barrel length of 3.77". Weight for the G30 I tested was 28.5 ounces. There's a smaller version; the Glock 30S, a narrow-slide version of the standard Glock 30 I tested, and that version weighs just under 23 ounces. Both guns have the standard Glock features with the same standard Glock sights and Safe Action two-stage, striker-fired trigger. The 26 has a frame that's substantially smaller and allows only two fingers on the grip using the smaller and more concealable magazine. Shooting the G26 is fairly comfortable in spite of the short grip and light weight. At ten yards, shooting two-handed unsupported, I managed nine of ten shots in just under an inch, with the flyer opening the group up to just over 1.5".

The sights were easy to see and the trigger is a good one for a concealed carry gun; manageable, but not too light. Recoil lifted the gun, but fast follow-up shots were easy and I didn't notice having to rotate the gun forward as I do with larger Glocks. My issue with having to rotate the gun forward comes from years of shooting guns with the more abrupt grip angle of most

At ten yards deliberate fire, I managed an impressive group with the G26. Seven shots were in one hole. The G26 was so on in point-of-aim that an early shot took out the paster aiming point and I finished by using the group as an aiming point.

The G30 is a handful in the recoil department and the fat grip forced me to readjust my grip every few shots.

The G30 was also spot-on for point of aim. Both guns had good triggers for a defensive gun, certainly not light on the break, but consistent.

The standard Glock sights were more than adequate and work well for precise shooting as well as allowing quick acquisition.

other semi-autos. The Glock grip angle is more like the grip angle of my old High Standard space gun target pistol. My only complaint was that the G26 tossed the spent cases straight back with most of them hitting my hat, and the occasional one actually hitting me in the face. Probably something a gunsmith could fix, but I once had a G19 that suffered from the same malady.

Shooting the .45 G30 was less pleasant than the 9mm G26. While the larger frame affords getting three fingers on the grip and magazine base plate, the large diameter of the G30 made it hard for me to maintain my normal grip through more than three or four shots. I know this is partially from the recoil of the .45 round, but I don't have this problem with a Springfield XDs, which weighs several ounces less. I suspect the problem is the large diameter of the grip, necessitated by the fat double-stack .45 magazine.

At the same ten yards, I managed nine shots in just over an inch with one flyer at about 1.5 inches. I suppose the term Glock Perfection doesn't apply to the guy holding the gun, because I'm sure the error was

mine. With both guns, this is more than adequate accuracy for a carry gun, and both guns have a respectable capacity as well. I experienced no malfunctions with either gun, though the test involved less than a hundred rounds with each gun.

As to concealability, both guns were fairly bulky, about as bulky as a medium-frame short-barreled revolver. They are both concealable, but the G26 had a considerable advantage. I suspect the G30s with its narrower slide would be considerably better than the standard G30, but with six ounces less weight, I suspect it would be a handful in the recoil department.

There's no doubt these are both viable choices for concealed carry when the thickness is offset by the extra magazine capacity. Certainly, no one will argue that Glock pistols are less than capable performers. Their history in law enforcement is a testament to just how reliable and durable these guns are.

SMITH & WESSON M&P 9MM SHIELD

The dilemma in choosing a concealed carry gun is a tough one. A concealed carry gun must be effective and comfortable to carry and yet the two are directly contradictory to each other. Most experts agree that the minimum reliable stopper is 9mm or .38 Special. The sub-compact .380 guns are wonderful to carry, yet most agree they're underpowered. Having said this, I'd rather have a .25 ACP in my pocket than a can of pepper spray or a stun gun.

In spite of what's currently available in semi-au- tos, I'm old school and I carry a .38 snubbie every day. I know a lot of highly experienced law enforce- ment officers who do the same thing, even those who swear by their striker-fired duty guns. With the revolver, there are never worries about reliabil- ity and that compensates for the bulky cylinder and small capacity.

I admit, the thin frames and magazine capacities of the tiny nines beckon me, and every time I see one I think could be a winner, I get excited. So far,

I've stayed with my S&W 637 but a couple of recent pistols have tempted me sorely. When the Shield was introduced at SHOT Show, Bill Booth of Blue Heron Communications pulled me aside to show me the new Shield. Frankly, I'd seen the ads and I wasn't really excited.

I'd already done the test on the Diamondback DB9 (see sub-compact auto chapter) and, for a small auto-loader, it was impressive. The Diamondback weighs in at barely over 11 ounces and is just slightly bigger than the .380 compacts. I acquired a test gun and found it to be both accurate and brutal. The super light weight and tiny grip assure a noticeable reaction when you fire 9mm ammunition. It's simply the laws of physics at work. I dubbed the DB9 the Noisy Cricket, after the tiny little gun Will Smith used in the first Men in Black movie. I carried it a while and loved the size but I kept thinking about how difficult the DB9 would be if it malfunctioned since it has no slide lock. I went back to my 637.

When Bill put the Shield in my hand, my first reaction was admiration for the sights. They're the same good sights as those on an M&P duty pistol, easy to see and substantial. The second positive reaction I got was when I dry fired the gun to try the trigger. I'm very sensitive about triggers. I come from a competition rifle background, and triggers are very important in that kind of shooting. It took me a while to adjust to striker-fired pistol triggers, but the large M&P pistols have good triggers and the S&W Shield has a trigger that feels just like the big M&P guns.

I can adjust to the long first stage of modern, striker-fired pistols, provided I get a second stage that breaks with some repeatability, and the Shield trigger is just that - repeatable with a reasonable second stage for a carry or duty gun. The Shield also had a slide release that locks the slide back on the last shot and facilitates easier clearing of malfunctions. That second feature may be even more important on a carry gun than the added speed in reloading. The average confrontation involves an average of 2.3 rounds to resolve so I don't worry so much about capacity of a small carry gun.

I keep referring to malfunctions and I realize that

While the Shield has about the same profile as a five shot revolver, it has a much slimmer thickness and carries two more rounds of more powerful ammunition.

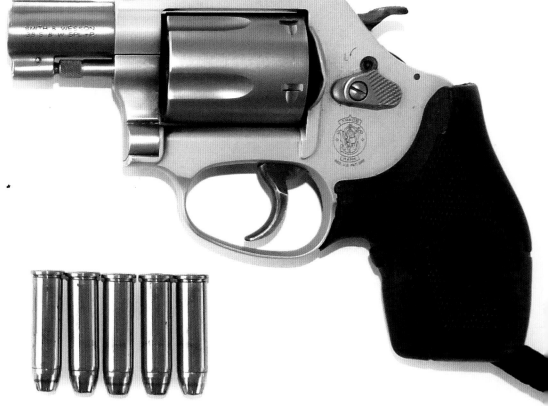

The sights on the Shield are small enough for easy concealment, but large enough to be seen in low-light conditions.

modern semi-autos are very reliable, but there are special considerations for concealed carry pistols. Much of the reliability of modern semi-autos comes from the shooter using a firm, consistent grip. Years ago, I learned that new shooters experience many more malfunctions than those of us who shoot a lot. Eventually, I figured out that many of these malfunctions came from improper grip. Teaching proper grip in a classroom or range setting is simple, but when you add fear induced adrenalin and awkward shooting positions to the equation, proper grip is much less likely to occur, so ease of clearing malfunctions in small concealed carry pistols is important.

When I shot the Shield the first time, I wasn't disappointed. I found the quality sights and repeatable trigger to be enough of an asset to allow me a very good test group. I accuracy-test concealed carry guns at ten yards, a very long distance for exercising deadly force if you're a civilian. I shoot a fairly fast cadence, not race gun speed, but much faster than the most deliberate fire. My first group with the

Powerful small guns produce recoil, and the Shield is no exception. Recoil is brisk, but manageable with Black Hills +P 9mm defensive ammunition.

Shield generated a seven-shot group that was about one inch left of center and measured less than two inches, impressive for a tiny concealed carry gun.

The Shield becomes even more impressive when you consider that it's available in .40 S&W. In .40 this is a very compact and powerful gun and probably about the best combination of power, size, capacity, and accuracy to be found. While the 9mm Shield is fairly manageable, especially with the longer gripped, larger magazine, the .40 definitely gets into the Noisy Cricket category.

This is a very good gun. It's reliable, accurate, and powerful. It's a little heavier than some pistols, but it has a very slim profile. In 9mm it's a powerful compact package with excellent magazine capacity; in .40 S&W it's probably the most potent for its size carry gun available. Is it so good that this writer is leaving his little wheelgun in the drawer? Not yet.

The Shield provides excellent accuracy by virtue of a great trigger and sights. Seven shots at seven yards produced this standing under two-inch group.

CHAPTER 13

COMPACT REVOLVERS

The compact revolvers in this category are an excellent choice for concealed carry. They offer better accuracy and hence are easier to shoot well than the sub-compact guns, and many offer superior energy and stopping power. Calibers range from .38 Special to .45 Colt/.410 shotshell. Weights range from over 15 ounces to about 24 ounces, and barrel lengths range from under two inches to three inches. They're small enough to conceal, but beyond reasonable pocket carry.

CHIAPPA RHINO DS 2" ALLOY

There's little doubt that the Chiappa Rhino is the least-conventional-looking gun in this book. In appearance, it looks like something dreamed up for an action adventure movie. It's a fact that the design is based on sound theory and engineering and the strange looking design has real function. What makes the Rhino look so strange is a design that allows it to fire from the bottom chamber of the cylinder, rather than the top, as do all other revolvers in existence. The reason for this is to put the axis of recoil more directly in line with the shooter's wrist, eliminating - or certainly reducing - muzzle rise. While this is described as theory, I've fired a Rhino and it does work. Surprisingly, the Rhino isn't named for its unusual shape; the name comes from its designer, Rino Chiappa.

The Rhino 2" is an exposed-hammer, double/single-action revolver with a capacity of 6 rounds. It has the usual swing-out cylinder with the cylinder latch located beside the hammer. In fact, the hammer I mentioned really isn't a hammer at all, but more of a visual cocking indicator that allows de-cocking as one would a conventional revolver. The cylinder is hex-shaped rather than round, and fluted to allow a slimmer, flatter profile. Chambered in .357 Magnum, .40 S&W, and 9mm Luger, all three guns come supplied with moon clips for faster loading and unloading. Weight is 22 ounces and the Rhino comes in both black and chrome finishes with rather unusual looking stippled wood grips.

CHARTER ARMS BULLDOG

I carried a Charter Arms Undercover for about 25 years. During that time, it traveled countless miles and required only cursory attention. That same gun is still in my family and probably will be when I've turned to ashes and dust. Charter Arms has the reputation of building reliable and affordable revolvers and they continue to do so. They're basic in design and functional in operation. When they came out with the larger Bulldog series in .44 Special, there was a lot of talk about brutal recoil, but I find the recoil quite reasonable for a lightweight and compact revolver with serious horsepower. In recent years, they've expanded the line of larger-framed guns to include the .357 Mag Pug, the .40 S&W Pitbull and by the time this reaches print, the Pitbull in .45 ACP will be in production.

The Charter "dogs" are a larger frame than the original five-shot .38 Special guns and feature 2.5" barrels with the usual milled groove rear sight and milled-in ramp front. There's a forward-moving cylinder release and they have a shrouded ejector rod. The 9mm and .40 S&W versions use Charter's unique rimless ejector system that allows ejection of rimless cases without use of moon clips, as will the .45 ACP version. Available with an exposed hammer, a shrouded hammer, and as a double-action-only, hammerless version, they weigh around 21 ounces have a five-shot capacity and a base MSRP of $405.00 for the Blue Standard with the Stainless Crimson Trace Mag Pug selling for $603.00.

RUGER LCR .357

The .357 version of Ruger's sub-compact LCR (see sub-compact revolver chapter for info) weighs 17.2 ounces, putting it above the sub-compact revolver class, but it's still quite small and light. Capacity is still five rounds and MSRP is $619.00 for the standard or $899.00 for the Crimson Trace laser grip model.

RUGER LCR 9MM

While the .38 Special +P LCRs come in the sub-compact category, the 9mm Luger versions pick up enough weight to put them in as compacts. They feature the same 1.875" barrel length and five-shot capacity, but carry extra weight in the form of a steel frame to handle a more potent round. In energy, the 9mm round is between .38 Special and .357 and offers considerably cheaper options for practice ammunition than .38 Special, and milder recoil than the .357. It also makes a great companion/backup gun for officers who carry a 9mm duty gun. The 9mm version comes with three moon clips to allow rimless ejection, while all other LCR features remain the same. Weighing in at 17.2 ounces, MSRP is $619.00.

RUGER LCRX 3"

In 2014, Ruger brought out an exposed hammer double/single-action version of the popular LCR. In 2015, they upped the ante and released the 3" version with good adjustable sights. Adding adjustable sights and another inch of barrel made the new LCR a totally different proposition. The new gun focuses on accuracy and overall utility over just concealability, but for many, it may prove an excellent compromise. The 3" barrel is fully shrouded to the muzzle and the adjustable rear sight is matched with a higher ramp front, adding considerable capability for accuracy. When you consider the features that provide superior accuracy, it makes the LCRx 3" a great choice as a utility kit gun for general outdoor use as well as an excellent choice for concealed carry. Construction is the same steel, aluminum and polymer and the trigger is the same super-smooth double action as the other LCRs. With a weight of 15.7 ounces and an MSRP of $545.00, it's available in black only.

RUGER SP101

Ruger's SP101 is a traditional stainless steel five-shot double/single-action revolver. It has a machined-in rear and ramped front sight and a shrouded ejector rod. The grip is black rubber in standard models with engraved wood panels in the four-inch model. Rugers are known for reliability and for their push button cylinder release. The 2" SP101 weighs in at 25 ounces and the base model has an MSRP of $679.00 and the fiber optic, adjustable sighted, model's MSRP is $719.00.

RUGER GP100 3"

With a weight of 36 ounces, the Ruger 3" GP100 certainly isn't a lightweight, but it is a compact revolver. It's a six-shot double/single-action revolver with a fixed groove rear sight and a pinned ramp front. Finish is satin stainless and it uses the popular Hogue Monogrips and is all stainless steel. MSRP is $749.00.

SMITH & WESSON MODEL 60

The Smith & Wesson Model 60 has been an iconic concealed carry gun since its release in 1965. When first released, Model 60s were so popular they often brought upwards of twice the retail price. They were considered by many to be the ultimate snubbie revolver, and as a young man, I fell to the allure of the almost indestructible little gun. I still have a healthy respect. The 60 is a basic exposed-hammer double/single-action five-shot on the small J series frame. While the original guns were dimensionally identical to the popular Chief's Special, the current Model 60 comes with a ¼" longer 2 1/8" barrel and is now chambered for the more potent .357 magnum round. Finish is satin stainless and empty weight is 22.6 ounces. While not a lightweight, the new 60 is both rugged and powerful. MSRP is $729.00.

SMITH & WESSON MODEL 36

One of the most popular carry guns in history has been the S&W model 36. Introduced in 1950 on the then-new five-shot .38 Special J frame, the model 36 has been the star of countless black and white TV shows, along with its commercial nemesis, the now defunct Colt Detective Special. Offered with a 1 7/8" or 3" barrel, it was available as both a round or square butt and in nickel or blue. The only current version is now the 1 7/8" round butt version. It has an un-shrouded ejector rod for light weight and an exposed hammer. It weighs 19.5 ounces and has an MSRP of $749.00.

SMITH & WESSON MODEL 60 3"

While both guns are designated as model 60s, the 3" model is so different it's really a different gun. It's the same frame, but with the excellent S&W revolver sights on the top strap instead of the standard milled-in groove rear sight. It also has a Baughman Quick Draw front sight, a fully shrouded 3" barrel, and oversized checkered wood target grips. Chambered in the powerful .357 Magnum caliber, it's a serious contender as both a concealed carry gun and an accurate camp gun. I recently tested one and managed to ring a man-sized gong target five times with five shots at 100 yards. Weighing 23.2 ounces and still quite small, it's a tough and versatile camp/carry gun with punch and accuracy. MSRP is $799.00.

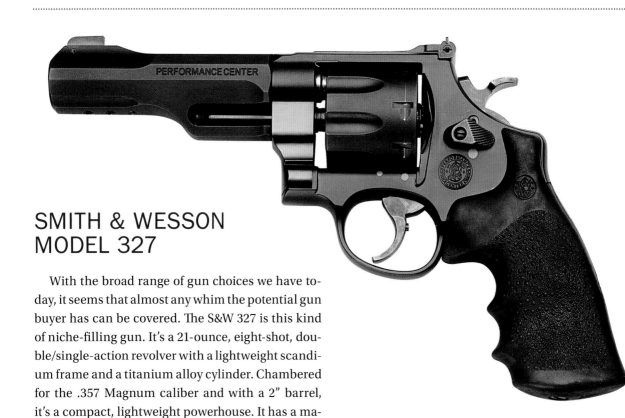

SMITH & WESSON MODEL 327

With the broad range of gun choices we have today, it seems that almost any whim the potential gun buyer has can be covered. The S&W 327 is this kind of niche-filling gun. It's a 21-ounce, eight-shot, double/single-action revolver with a lightweight scandium frame and a titanium alloy cylinder. Chambered for the .357 Magnum caliber and with a 2" barrel, it's a compact, lightweight powerhouse. It has a machined groove rear sight and dovetailed red ramp front. Finish is matte black and there are round butt wood grips with finger grooves. MSRP is $1,309.00.

SMITH & WESSON MODEL 627

As a younger man, I was told guns with short barrels could not be accurate. As a life-long shooter, I've learned that's not always the case. This fall, I was at a writer's conference on shooting day when a S&W rep invited me to shoot a couple of their guns. I chose the 2.625-inch barrel 627 because the shooter who shot it before me said the sights were off. I shot one sight-in shot at ten yards and hit the bullet hole I was using as an aiming point. I then shot 16 rounds at an 8" plate at 50 yards, hitting it every time. The second cylinder load was fired double action. Well-made short-barreled guns are capable of remarkable accuracy.

At 37.6 ounces, the S&W 627 is no lightweight, but it's fairly compact, though a bit thick in the middle.

It has an un-fluted eight-shot N frame cylinder, a full-length shrouded barrel, an adjustable trigger stop and the excellent S&W adjustable rear and dovetailed red ramp front. The double-action pull is smooth and predictable; the finger-grooved wood grips provide good purchase, and it has enough weight for accurate shooting. With 8 rounds of .357 Magnum power, it's a capable performer. The stainless steel frame, cylinder and barrel are finished in a pleasant matte. MSRP is $1,079.00.

SMITH & WESSON 686 PLUS

The 686 Plus is on the S&W seven-shot L frame. It's satin finished, stainless steel, double/single action, and has an adjustable white outline rear and red ramp pinned front sight. The fully shrouded barrel's length is 2.5" and it weighs 34.1 ounces. Chambered for .357 Magnum, it has enough weight for comfortable practice. The grip is black synthetic. MSRP is $849.00

ROSSI 38 SPECIAL AND .357 MAGNUM

Rossi's line of .38 Specials are no-frills guns with basic features. They use a five-shot double/single-action design, are made of steel or stainless steel and have machined-in front and rear fixed sights. Grips are hard rubber, barrel length is 2" and weight is 24 ounces. The blued version has an MSRP of $390.78 and stainless is $454.89. Built on a larger six-shot platform, the Rossi .357 line has a weight of 26 ounces. The ejector shroud is full-length and MSRPs are the same as the .38-caliber guns.

TAURUS 85 AND 605 PLY

The use of polymer in firearms construction is here to stay, and a recent entry from Taurus is the 85PLY revolver. It's a five-shot, .38 Special, double/single-action revolver that uses a polymer grip frame over an internal metal chassis to reduce weight. The polymer frame covers most of the gun, including the trigger guard and barrel shroud. Sights are fixed rear and a high-vis front over a ventilated rib and the grips are ribbed rubber. Barrel length is 2.5" and weight is 18.5 ounces. Finish is bi-tone, black with a bright cylinder. MSRP is $428.47.

The 605 PLY is the big brother to the 85 and chambered for .357 Magnum. It's also a five-shot, double/single action with similar features and a 2" barrel. Weight is 19.75 ounces and MSRP is $471.32.

TAURUS JUDGE 4510 POLYMER

The Taurus Judge line of shotgun caliber pistols had been controversial from the beginning. They're revered by some and reviled by others. I find them to be interesting and I see they fill a niche for certain circumstances. I've spent quite a bit of time shooting them and I find them accurate with pistol ammunition and intimidating with shotgun loads. They're somewhat bulky, with a width of 1.5", but not everyone needs a super-slim handgun. Recoil is considerable, but manageable. The real potential for these guns is in situations where it's a good idea to limit the range and penetration of the gun for safety considerations. A 9mm, or .40 simply doesn't make sense for an apartment dweller because of penetration issues. In a recent test of the Public Defender PLY, I tested it at close ranges and found it to be devastating at close range with certain shotshell loads and yet incapable of penetrating wall board beyond about seven yards with that same load. Loaded with .45 Colt, it's both accurate and powerful and not hard to shoot well. MSRP is $653.32 and weight is 23 ounces.

TAURUS JUDGE PUBLIC DEFENDER

The Public Defender is a five-shot, 2.5" barrel .45 Colt double/single-action revolver with a stainless steel frame. Trigger pull is reasonable in both double and single action for a defensive gun. Weight is 28 ounces with a barrel length of 2.5". The frame is matte black and the cylinder is matte stainless. Like the polymer version, it's a five-shot double/single action but with a fixed rear sight instead of the windage-adjustable rear on the PLY model. The front sight is a high-vis ramp. The grip is the same soft ribbed rubber that helps make the considerable recoil more comfortable. The additional weight of the all-steel gun makes recoil a bit less unpleasant. MSRP is $653.32.

IN-DEPTH

My first experience with a combination shotgun/handgun was in the late 60s with the Thompson Center Contender. It was an interchangeable-barrel, single-shot break-action pistol, and the shotgun version was chambered for .410 and .45 Colt. In order to get better patterns with the rifled barrel, there was a screw-on choke that had longitudinal grooves to negate the spin of the shot charge generated by the rifled barrel. The National Firearms Act of 1938 does not allow for shotguns with barrels of less than 18" without a short-barreled firearm tax stamp. Thompson Center got around that by chambering the Contender barrel in .45 Colt but extending the chamber to also allow using .410 shotshells. Of course,

TAURUS JUDGE PUBLIC DEFENDER

The Taurus Judge Defender uses a polymer trigger guard and grip frame to reduce weight.

The rear sight on the Defender is windage adjustable and the gun is accurate enough that this is a valuable option.

the Contender was hardly a contender as a personal defense firearm with a substantial size and weight and a single-shot configuration.

The Contender was preceded by a shotgun/pistol that was intended for personal use. Manufactured between 1921 and 1934, the Ithaca Auto and Burglar was a double-barreled 20-gauge shotgun pistol with 10" and later 12" barrels. It wasn't a concealed carry firearm by any means, but it was certainly formidable as a defense weapon. Production ended when the National Firearms Act required the $200 tax stamp.

When Taurus introduced a .45/410 revolver, they found instant popularity and sales. The series was dubbed "the Judge" when the company discovered the .410 revolvers were popular as a defensive sidearm for judges, since a .410 shot load would have excellent short-range stopping power and less chance of collateral damage to bystanders at even medium

The choice of ammunition that can be run through the Judge is diverse. The Judge will digest anything from snake loads to serious defensive ammunition. Least effective were the .410 slugs; they were less accurate and powerful than .45 Colt, and more expensive.

ranges. The Judge has a solid following and remains one of the more popular handguns in the Taurus line. In my experience, there are two kinds of people: those who love the Judge and those who hate it. It seems a lot of gun writers view it with a certain level of disdain, but the Judge, especially the Public Defender, has a lot of redeeming virtues.

In the standard all-metal configurations, the Judge is a bit heavy and bulky for daily carry, though no more than the full-size service pistols some carry. My test gun came in at 23 ounces, so a fully-loaded Defender would come in with a loaded weight a bit less than a compact double-stack .40. Due to the fact it's a revolver, it would be a bit thicker, but would have a slightly shorter profile.

What makes the Defender attractive is the level of versatility it offers. With bird shot, it would be a spectacular snake killer and a devastating defense firearm at very short ranges. For an apartment dweller, the potential for a stray round could be disastrous and by judicial choice (no pun intended) of shot size, unwanted penetration could be negated. Most

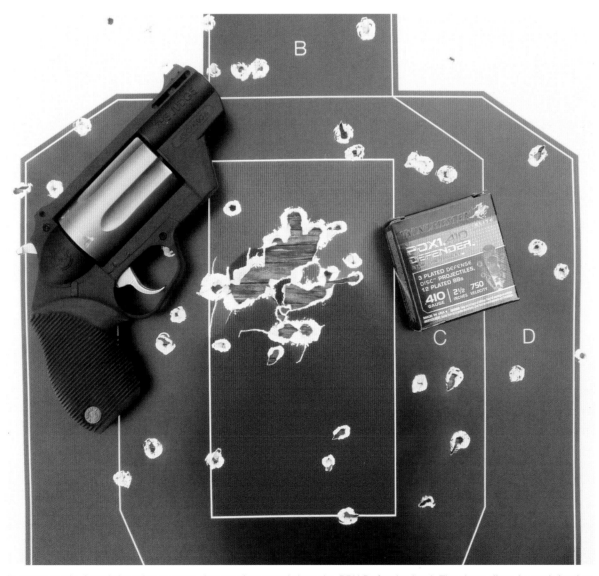

At seven yards, I can't imagine a more devastating round than the PDX Defender load. The three discs in each load go into the center of the group and the BBs scatter around the target for effect. Scary.

defensive situations occur under three yards, and backup .45 Colt loads could certainly be loaded for subsequent shots. Of course, not all handguns are purchased for urban defense; many are used as protection from both two and four-legged aggressors. In the event you need a broad-based revolver capable of handling many different situations, the Judge has real merit.

All the talk over gunshop counters proves nothing except that opinions are like a certain body orifice in one's nether regions; everybody has one. I decided to form an opinion based on actual testing and I came away a bit surprised. Since a Public Defender will handle everything from serious .45 Colt defensive

rounds to skeet loads suited for dispatching snakes, I decided to test the whole gamut. I called Winchester Ammunition and requested #9 shot AA skeet loads, #4 hunting loads, rifled slugs and the popular PDX1 .410 Defense Disc loads. I also tested .45 Colt loads: the 750 fps, 250-grain Cowboy Action load and the Super X 255-grain, 860 fps load that delivers a whopping 410 foot/pounds of energy. No one will argue that the .45 ACP isn't a capable stopper and the Super X 255 load exceeds the energy levels of the Winchester Defender .45 ACP load at 392 foot/pounds. True, the Public Defender only has five rounds in a cylinder, but most compact .45s with similar weight and dimensions only hold six or seven.

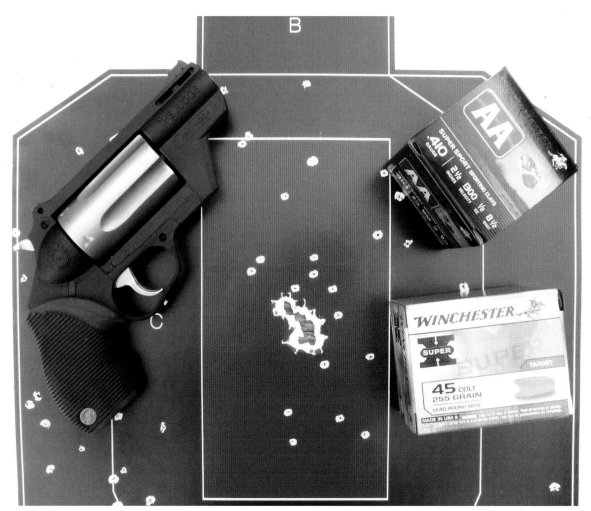

Even at short range, #9 shot loads are only viable for snakes and small pests. Accuracy with the .45 Colt 255-grain bullets was remarkably good. The five-shot group and shotgun pattern were shot at seven yards.

Shooting the Public Defender is fun, provided you don't mind recoil and muzzle blast. I actually enjoyed my morning of testing, though I admit the Defender is a hard kicker. I began with AA skeet loads. At about five yards, they provide a dense enough pattern to allow only a very skinny and lucky snake to avoid destruction. For defense, they'll certainly deter, but even at a distance of five feet, they failed to penetrate ½" oriented strand board (OSB) as used for construction. For the apartment dweller, I'd recommend the #4 load. For shooting snakes, the pattern would be pretty spotty at five yards, but at five feet, they penetrated the hard OSB and blew out sections of it. Certainly they would penetrate a rib cage and cause massive hemorrhaging, which is the only reliable stopping factor with handgun calibers. While I didn't build wall sections for testing, I seriously doubt the #4 shot load would penetrate two thicknesses of drywall gypsum.

The most impressive looking effect came from the PDX1 Defender load with three plated discs and 12 plated BB shot. The PDX1 simply beats the center out of a target. At normal defense distances of under seven yards, it would be both painful and devastating, the discs would likely penetrate the rib cage and the BBs would pepper the attacker all over the targeted area. I also tried shooting rifled slugs, but they're less accurate and more expensive than .45 Colt loads and therefore not recommended.

Shooting the .45 Colt loads, I was impressed by the accuracy potential of the Public Defender. To center the X in a USPSA Dirty Bird target, I needed to hold about two inches low at ten yards, but based on my experience as an instructor, most novice shooters tend to shoot low because of recoil anticipation, and probably would benefit from a gun that shoots a bit high. While the rifling of the Judge series is more shallow than normal because of the .410 chambering, accuracy was certainly acceptable for a defensive gun. My ten-yard, five-shot groups were always ragged holes unless I called a shot a bad one. As mentioned earlier, recoil with both shot and ball was stiff, but manageable.

The real argument for the merit of the Polymer Judge is versatility. In the same cylinder, the user

With #4 shot loads, the Judge penetrated through a half-inch of oriented strand board at point-blank range, making it the practical minimum for defensive use. It might make good sense in urban areas or for an apartment dweller because of limited penetration at distance.

can carry two #9 shot snake loads and three hard-hitting 250-grain .45-caliber bullets. For the backpacker, this means real utility. The time it takes to swing out the cylinder and switch from a bear or pig stopper to a snake-dispatching load is less than two seconds; I tried it as part of my test.

For quite some time, I carried a Charter Arms Bulldog .44 Special revolver as my daily carry gun. I eventually began leaving it in the safe in favor of a lighter, but similarly powerful 340 S&W .357. No one will argue the viability of the Bulldog, yet the Public Defender is only a few ounces heavier and a bit thicker through the waist. The Bulldog is a defensive carry gun only. The Public Defender is much more versatile and the .44 Special and .45 Colt have almost identical ballistics. Everyone is certainly entitled to their own opinions, but as for me, I can certainly see a lot of merit to the Public Defender, and it would be my first choice as a kit gun for an extended outing in rough country.

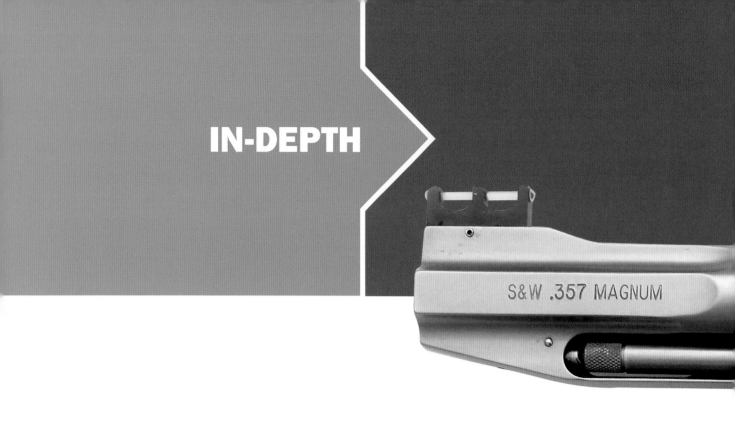

IN-DEPTH

S&W .357 MAGNUM

The theme of compromise has been constantly mentioned throughout this book. Carry guns are all about compromise, so the term multipurpose is now being used for the first time. Few guns work well as multipurpose firearms, and yet when I think about the Smith & Wesson Model 60 with the 3" barrel, the best description I can think of is multipurpose. The word, by definition, almost always means something that doesn't do anything well, but will suffice for multiple needs. Somehow, in my mind, the Model 60 3" seems it could do anything well, even if I know this isn't true. For some reason, I've fallen in love with the little gun, and worse yet, it isn't mine.

A few months ago, a friend showed me his Model 60 3" and allowed me to shoot 50 or so rounds through it. Since then, I've been afflicted to get one, and I plan to add one to my gun safe at first opportunity. It's a long way from the original Model 60 in .38 Special I coveted as a young man. With a three-inch barrel, adjustable sights, .357 Magnum chambering, and a full-sized synthetic grip, it's a lot more gun than that original stainless belly gun, but it only weighs a few ounces more.

The three-inch Model 60 is a perfectly proportioned little gun that is as fun to shoot as it is good looking.

SMITH & WESSON MODEL 60 3"

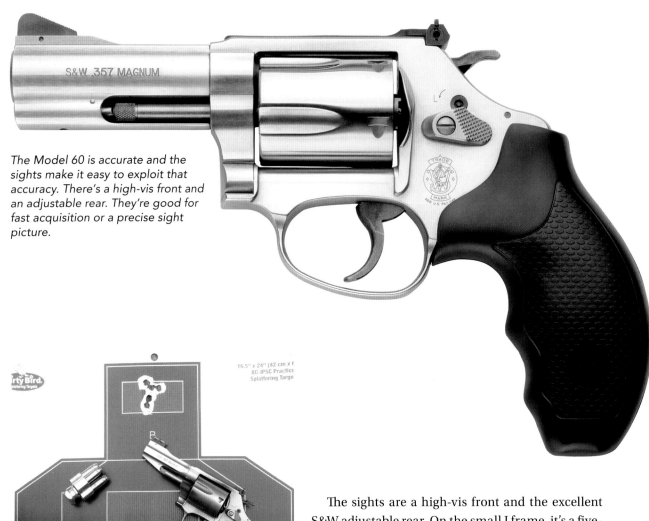

The Model 60 is accurate and the sights make it easy to exploit that accuracy. There's a high-vis front and an adjustable rear. They're good for fast acquisition or a precise sight picture.

With defensive Black Hills .357 125-grain loads, my ten-shot group, shot at defensive speed, was well centered and just over two inches for ten shots. Deliberate fire in double action rendered ragged one-hole groups when I did my part.

The sights are a high-vis front and the excellent S&W adjustable rear. On the small J frame, it's a five-shooter. The barrel is sculpted with a top rib and flat sides. It weighs 24 ounces, but feels much lighter. The Hogue Monogrip grips fill the hand and allow great control even with hot defensive .357 loads. On Mike's gun, the trigger is smooth from the factory, but with a slight bit of stacking at the very end of travel. This makes it as easy to shoot in double action as in single action, and there's enough accuracy to exploit the manageable trigger. At ten yards, it shoots one ragged hole and when shot quickly, as one would with a defensive gun, it's controllable and easy to shoot well. The sights allow fast acquisition, and yet they're precise enough for accurate deliberate shots.

I've coined a new phrase, one that probably won't catch on, but why not try? My new phrase is the SUG, or Sport Utility Gun. I shot the little Model 60

The 3" Model 60 begs for adventure and makes a low maintenance, reliable, powerful, and accurate outdoor companion.

just prior to SHOT Show and when I got to the Ruger booth, there was the new three-inch LCRx. Both guns hold attraction for me, but the little S&W is a .357 Magnum and I've been a fan of that round since I bought my very first handgun, a Ruger Blackhawk.

Guns like this are perfect for everyday outdoor use. The Model 60 is durable stainless and the grips are almost indestructible, providing a good grip wet or dry. It's light enough you won't notice it in your kit bag and if you decide you need to conceal it, that won't be a problem either because it's slim and compact. In .357 Magnum, there's plenty of power for almost anything, and while it might not be considered a bear stopper, I'm willing to bet it's more effective than a can of spray.

There's enough accuracy to bag a squirrel or rabbit for the pot if you run out of jerky and it would be dandy for dispatching a snake. I have to admit, I'm not a guy who's normally impressed by styling, but the Model 60 3" appeals to me on the visual level as well, very nice looking, but capable of conducting serious business when called upon. With an MSRP of $759.00 and all this going for it, I imagine it's the kind of gun that becomes a family heirloom because it begs to be brought along for outdoor adventures that make lasting memories.

CHAPTER 14

MID-SIZED SEMI-AUTOS

This is perhaps the most popular category of concealed carry semi-autos. While they are bulky and heavy to carry every day and conceal in warm weather, they find favor because of their magazine capacity and the fact they're easier to shoot well than smaller guns. Guns in this category range from 9mm to .45 ACP, with one gun chambered in .22 Magnum, but with a magazine capacity of 30 rounds. Most provide both energy and penetration in a more compact package than the duty-sized guns they're often based on. They range in weight from under 20 ounces to 33 ounces.

BERETTA PX4 STORM COMPACT

The Beretta PX4 Storm Compact is a polymer-framed double/single-action semi-auto with an exposed hammer, and one of the newest editions from this oldest of established gunmakers. It uses a double-stack magazine for a capacity of 15 + 1 in 9mm Luger and .38 Super, and 12 + 1 in .40 S&W. Sights are the three-dot variety with the rear being drift adjustable for windage. It fires from a locked breech and uses a rotating barrel unlocking system. The magazine is in the standard location and is reversible for southpaws. The slide release is ambidextrous and there's a bottom rail for mounting

lights and lasers. The safety is located on the slide, sweeps down and is also ambidextrous. There are three different grip inserts to accommodate shooters with larger or smaller hands. MSRP is $575.00.

BERETTA 92 COMPACT

Developed in 1972, the Beretta 92 series has been a monumental success for the company. It was adopted by the U.S. military to replace the 1911 .45 in 1985, and has proven itself as a worthy performer since that time. The 92 Compact is a reduced-size version with an abbreviated barrel and grip frame, making it 2.3 ounces lighter than the standard model. It's a double/single-action semi-auto with an open-topped slide using a falling block to unlock the action. The ambidextrous safety is mounted on the slide and sweeps down, serving as a de-cocker. The magazine release is in the standard position and reversible for left-handed operation. There's a bottom rail for mounting lights and lasers and the front and back straps are checkered for grip. The 92 Compact is chambered in 9mm Luger and has a magazine capacity of 13 + 1. Barrel length is 4.25 inches and unloaded weight is 31.6 ounces. Sights are three-dot, drift adjustable at the rear. The standard model uses a black Brunton finish and comes in a hard case with two magazines and a lock with an MSRP of $745.00. The stainless or Inox version has an MSRP of $775.00.

BERSA BP9CC

Bersa has a reputation for producing quality guns for a very affordable price. They have a strong following and the BP9CC is no exception in the area of value. It's a striker-fired, polymer-framed compact with a single-stack magazine. Barrel length is 3.3" and weight is 21.5 ounces. The BP9 is thin at .94" so it certainly is a reasonable choice for concealed carry. The sights are the three-dot system, both dovetailed in with the rear being polymer and the other appearing to be cast steel. There's no external safety as is the case with many striker-fired guns and the trigger relies on a long sweep of the trigger for the first shot with a shorter reset for subsequent shots. It has a tactile or visual loaded chamber indicator on top

of the slide. The magazine release is in the 1911 position and ambidextrous and there's an external slide release. MSRP is $429.00.

COLT NEW AGENT

Colt is the iconic company when one thinks of the 1911, and for good reason. For years, the only source of a quality 1911 was a new Colt or a rebuilt GI gun. Now everyone is in the 1911 game, but Colt is still Colt and they're very much in the 1911 business. Their dedicated concealed carry gun is the New Agent. Everything about it is centered around making a powerful and reliable gun than can be carried with a minimum of difficulty in concealment or comfort. Since most defensive situations involving concealed carry occur at close range and protruding sights snag clothing, the New Agent uses a machined barrel channel as a sighting system. Grooved top straps have been used as rear sights for revolvers for years and the groove down the top of the slide on the New Agent looks like it would work remarkably well out to at least 15 yards or so.

The New Agent features a bushingless, 3" bull barrel, and combined with an alloy frame, this keeps the weight down to a respectable 22.5 ounces. Most features are standard 1911 with a standard magazine release, the normal 1911 grip safety and a 1918-style safety. The grip safety has an extended top to keep the web of the hand safe, the trigger is drilled for weight, and the ejection port is flared and lowered for reliability. Magazine capacity is seven with the standard magazine and of course, caliber is .45 ACP. MSRP is $1,078.00.

45 cal

COLT DEFENDER

The Defender is designed for concealed carry, but with a bit more emphasis on tactical options. It uses a bushingless, 3" bull barrel and is available in .45 ACP and 9mm Luger. It features Novak Low Mount Carry sights, and has an extended beavertail grip safety with a bump for better engagement with the palm. The ejection port is lowered and flared, the aluminum trigger is lightened, there's a Commander-style hammer and a rail for lights and lasers. Weight is 24 ounces and available in stainless and bright alloy, black or bi-tone, MSRP is $973.00.

CZ PO1

CZs P01 is a double/ single-action semi-auto with a steel frame. The slide is mounted on rails inside the frame to keep slide weight down and make the top of the gun more compact. The safety/decocker is frame-mounted and conveniently located, as is the reversible magazine release. There's a lower rail for lights and lasers and sights are three dots, with a drift adjustable rear. Barrel length is 3.8" and weight is 28 ounces. The double-stack magazine gives a capacity of 14 + 1. CZ pistols have a reputation for reliability and CZ touts a test where the PO1 had only seven stoppages out of 15,000 rounds. Finish is basic blade and MSRP is $627.00.

CZ P07

The P07 is a compact version of CZs P09 duty pistol. It's a polymer-framed, double/single-action with an exposed hammer. The safety is located on the frame and the de-cocker/safety is interchangeable for left or right-hand operation. The magazine release is ambidextrous and sights are three-dot with drift adjustability. The 3.8" barrel is hammer-forged and magazine capacity is 15 rounds. MSRP is $510.00.

CZ COMPACT SDP

CZ's Compact SDP is a CZ custom shop gun specifically designed and crafted as a defensive concealed carry pistol. Built by the same guys who do work on the competition guns, it's a P01 that's been hopped up and tuned for maximum performance as a personal defense gun. Chambered for 9mm Luger and using the standard double-stack P-01 magazine, it has a capacity of 14 + 1. It uses a T6 aluminum frame and thin aluminum grips for reduced weight. The sights are Tritium Slant Pro at the rear and a dovetailed dot post at the front. The trigger is tuned to break at 3.5 to 4 pounds in single action and smoothed and lightened for about 8 pounds in double action. Inside, there are custom parts like a solid firing pin stop and trigger pin, extended firing pin and a stainless steel guide rod, to make it even more reliable. Weight is 28 ounces and caliber is 9mm Luger. MSRP is $1,420.00.

GUNCRAFTERS CCO

I have no idea just how many companies are currently building 1911 pistols. I can tell you who is building some of the very best ones and that answer would be Guncrafters. I tested the Guncrafters CCO a couple of years back and was thoroughly impressed with the attention to detail. While many newer 1911s feature trick spring arrangements, extended guide rods and barrel bushing to barrel engineering tricks, the Guncrafters CCO is basic 1911 design through and through. Even as a downsized Officer-sized gun, it is as accurate as any 1911 I've ever shot, based on my ability. The trigger is like a fine match gun, but heavy enough to use as a defensive gun. The slide works like a fine bullseye competition pistol and it with both light match, hardball and defensive ammunition, I have yet to experience a malfunction.

Guncrafters achieves what most 1911 builders aspire to and they do it without tricks, but with quality craftsmanship. Every part in the inside looks as good as any part on the outside and everything fits perfectly. One might argue that with an MSRP of over $2,800.00 one should expect perfection, and I agree, but I've seen guns that cost substantially more that didn't perform any better than a $500 service gun.

The CCO has a 4.25" barrel over an Officer-sized frame. Chambered for .45 ACP, it uses a seven-shot magazine and comes with two that are fitted to the gun. The grip safety is a high sweep beavertail with a palm bump. The front and rear straps are checkered for grip, and the safety is right side only. Sights are tritium and designed for the ability to allow stroking the slide against a solid object. The magazine well is beveled, and the top of the slide is flat-topped and grooved from rear to front sights. Inside, everything is finished as well as it is on the outside. True, the Guncrafters CCO isn't affordable to some, but to the discriminating buyer who wants an ultimate carry .45, it's a bargain. Available in stainless, bi-tone, reverse bi-tone, or black Melonite, the CCO weighs 33 ounces in steel and 27 with the aluminum frame. MSRP starts at $2,899.00.

FNH FNX9

FN's FNX9 is a compact stainless steel slide and polymer-framed double/single-action semi-auto. It uses an external extractor and has a loaded chamber indicator. The 4" barrel is hammer-forged stainless and magazine capacity is 17 + 1. The sights are three-dot with a drift adjustable rear. There are two interchangeable grip inserts for better fit and the de-cocker safety, slide release, and magazine release are ambidextrous. There's a bottom rail for lights and lasers, front and rear grip surfaces on the slide, and magazines come with a polymer base pad. Frame rails are replaceable for long life. Weight is 21 ounces. Available in black or bi-tone, MSRP is $799.00.

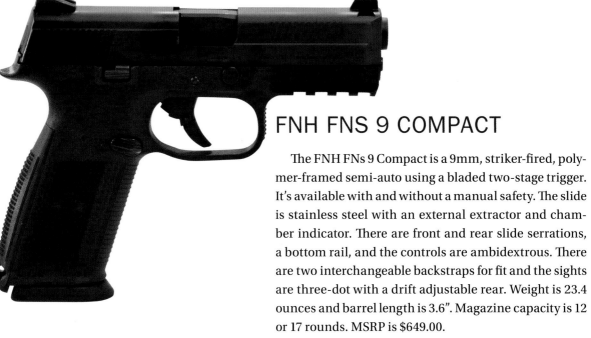

FNH FNS 9 COMPACT

The FNH FNs 9 Compact is a 9mm, striker-fired, polymer-framed semi-auto using a bladed two-stage trigger. It's available with and without a manual safety. The slide is stainless steel with an external extractor and chamber indicator. There are front and rear slide serrations, a bottom rail, and the controls are ambidextrous. There are two interchangeable backstraps for fit and the sights are three-dot with a drift adjustable rear. Weight is 23.4 ounces and barrel length is 3.6". Magazine capacity is 12 or 17 rounds. MSRP is $649.00.

GLOCK G19, G23, G32, G38

The Glock 19 is the compact version of the gun that one might argue began the polymer-frame, striker-fired trend that has swept the firearms world. It's reliable, simple to operate, and accurate. There are guns that are more esthetically pleasing, have better triggers, are more accurate, and a dozen other qualities, but no one can argue with the fact that Glock builds an effective and usable gun. The G19 has a barrel length of 4" and with the shortened for compactness grip frame, capacity is 15 + 1. It's a polymer-framed gun with a steel slide using the bladed trigger system that many other companies now use. The trigger system makes accidental discharge less likely by requiring full engagement to fire the weapon. Normal trigger pull is about 5.5 pounds. Sights are the now familiar Glock U white outline and a dot front. Magazine release placement is in the standard 1911

location and there are three different backstrap units to assure better hand fit. Glocks use hexagonal rifling that requires use of jacketed bullets and precludes use of lead bullets. The 19 weighs 23.6 ounces comes in matte black only and has an MSRP of $599.00. Glock models 23, 38, and 32 are similarly-sized models chambered in 40 S&W, .45 GAP, and .357 SIG respectively.

H&K P30

The H&K P30 is a polymer-framed semi-auto for personal defense and duty use. On the trigger guard it has a paddle style magazine release. It comes with both interchangeable backstraps and grip panels for a better fit. There's a bottom rail for lights and lasers and is available in multiple trigger operation modes. The standard double/single action has a frame-mounted de-cocker/safety. The LEM or Law Enforcement Modification allows use as single action on the first shot with the safety working as a single-action system would. This system also allows second-strike capability in double-action mode in the event of a misfire. P30 models have an ambidextrous safety on the frame. The extractor serves double duty as extractor and a visual and tactile loaded chamber indicator. There are fixed three-dot sights with the rear in a dovetail allowing drift-adjustable windage. Barrel length is 3.86", magazine capacity is 15 + 1 and weight is 23 ounces. MSRP is $1023.00 and finish is matte black.

KAHR T9

KEL-TEC PMR 30

My instant impression of the Kahr T9 is reminiscent of the Model 39 Smith & Wesson I once owned. It's a stainless steel double-action-only single-stack semi-auto with handsome checkered grips. A traditional-looking pistol, it uses a three-dot sight system with a drift-adjustable rear. The magazine and slide releases are in the standard location. There's no magazine safety but there is a passive striker block for safety. The 3.865" barrel uses polygonal rifling and weight is 26 ounces. Magazine capacity is 8 + 1 and it comes with three magazines and an MSRP of $857.00.

KIMBER

Kimber's line of Commander and Officer-sized 1911s begins with the Pro Carry II, an aluminum framed Commander sized pistol with a flat mainspring housing and skeletonized hammer and trigger. It has a matte black finish, a 4" barrel and weighs 28 ounces. Sights are low profile fixed and grips are double diamond, black synthetic. MSRP is $919.00. The compact Kimber line features dozens of models in different configurations of sights, grips, materials, finishes, up to the Onyx ultra with an ambidextrous safety, beavertail grip safety, Tactical Wedge night sights and PVD Cut scroll engraving for an MSRP of $1,652.00.

The Kel-Tec PMR 30 is as unconventional as the Kahr T9 is conventional. It's a striker-fired pistol that uses more polymer than any pistol in this group. It's also the only rimfire in this group, but I couldn't quite figure out where else to put it. Construction resembles a Super Soaker more than a conventional semi-auto pistol, but the PMR is a remarkable, if unusual, gun. Chambered for the .22 Winchester Rimfire Magnum, it has a magazine capacity of 30 + 1. That remarkable capacity is matched by the fact that it only weighs 13.6 ounces. The most striking attribute of the PMR 30 is that with two loaded magazines, it weighs less than a single loaded AR15 magazine. As a utility gun it's remarkable, but I see potential as a personal defense/concealed carry pistol.

I teach shooting, and I often have students who abhor recoil. I also have students who don't have the hand strength to operate the slide on many guns. The PMR 30 has mild recoil, is easy to cycle even for weaker individuals, and more than accurate enough for personal defense. The sights are as unconventional as the rest of the gun with a hi-vis red front and two hi-vis green dots at the rear. Trigger pull is a two-stage striker-fired pull that's adequate for self defense, and there's a rail for lasers or lights. Barrel length is 4.3" and it's available in multiple different colors. MSRP is $415.00.

PARA EXECUTIVE CARRY

Para's Executive Carry is a 3" bull-barreled 1911 with a full-length grip frame. It offers Tritium sights, and an aluminum frame with an Ed Brown mainspring housing that's rounded at the rear for better concealability and less chance of snagging clothing. Since the grip is full length, the Executive Carry has full 8 + 1 capacity in .45 ACP. The trigger is skeletonized and match grade with a crisp break. The grip safety has an extended beavertail and a healthy bump for guys with thin palms. The stainless barrel is ramped and doesn't use a bushing. Grips are VZ machined G10 and it has an anodized finish. It comes with two magazines with an MSRP of $1,399.00.

REMINGTON R1 COMMANDER

Remington's 1911 R1 Commander is a downsized version of their successful full-sized R1. It uses a carbon steel frame and slide with satin black oxide finish. The barrel is stainless as is the barrel bushing. There's a three-dot sight system with an adjustable rear sight. Chambered in .45ACP, it has a 4.25" barrel and weighs 38.5 ounces. Grips are checkered walnut and it uses the flat mainspring housing. It comes in black only and MSRP is $729.00.

RUGER SR SERIES

The Ruger SR series pistols are striker-fired, polymer-framed and use the bladed trigger popular with modern striker-fired pistols. They have a barrel length of 4.14" in 9mm and .40 S&W, and 4.5" in .45 ACP. Sights are the three-dot system with the rear being drift adjustable. There's a bottom rail and the frame-mounted safety is ambidextrous as is the magazine release. In 9mm, weight is 26.5 ounces and capacity is 17 + 1. In .40, magazine capacity is 15 + 1 and weight is 27.25 ounces. In .45 ACP capacity is 10 + 1 and weight is 30.15 ounces. MSRP on all three calibers is $529 in a hard case with two magazines in black on black or bi-tone. The Ruger 9E is a basic model of the SR series with a base MSRP of $429.00.

SIG P220 COMPACT

The SIG P220 Compact is a steel-framed double/single-action semi-auto. It's chambered in .45 ACP and uses a single-stack magazine with a capacity of 6 + 1 rounds. Barrel length is 3.9". The grips are polymer, sights are three-dot Siglite night sights. Being an all-steel gun, it's no lightweight at 29.6 ounces. MSRP is $1,166.00.

SMITH & WESSON 1911 SW1911 SUB-COMPACT

The SW1911 sub-compact is a downsized 1911 using a Scandium alloy frame and stainless steel slide. Sporting a 3" bushingless bull barrel, it uses the Officer-size frame to create a compact .45 ACP carry gun. As are all 1911s, it's single action semi-auto with a single-stage trigger. For better reliability it uses an oversized external extractor. It uses the three-dot sight system with both dovetailed in so windage adjustments are possible by drifting the sight in the dovetail. Grips are synthetic and the weight is 26.5 ounces. There's an oversized beavertail grip safety with a palm bump and lightened hammer and trigger with a trigger over travel adjustment. Magazine capacity is 7 + 1, it comes in black only and MSRP is $1,229.00.

SPRINGFIELD ARMORY RO COMPACT

Springfield Armory made a name for itself in the rifle world with the M1A and they continued in the pistol world with their basic 1911s. When they released the Range Officer series, buyers were impressed with the value of a gun with so many features at a reasonable price. The RO Compact continues that tradition of winning over the gun world and with good reason. The RO Compact features a ramped, match-grade, stainless, 4" bull barrel. The frame is forged aluminum alloy and the slide is forged carbon steel. Sights are drift adjustable, Novak style, with two dots at the rear and hi-vis front. There's a dual-spring full-length guide rod. Finish is black nitride and grips are checkered and engraved cocobolo. Magazine capacity is 6 + 1 and the RO Compact comes in a hard case with holster, loader, magazine pouch and two magazines for an MSRP of $899.00.

SPRINGFIELD ARMORY XD 4"

Springfield's XD 4" is a compact 9mm, chambered in .40 S&W, .45 ACP and .357 SIG. The 4" barrel is mated to a shortened frame for concealability. Other features like drift-adjustable three-dot sights, the accessory rail, bladed trigger and grip safety remain the same. Magazine capacity is 16 in 9mm, 13 in .40 and .45., and 12 rounds in .357 SIG. Weight is between 28 and 30 ounces for the different calibers. The XD 4" is also available with a manual thumb safety in .45 ACP. Available in black or bi-tone, MSRP is $599.00.

TAURUS 840

The Taurus 840 is a .40 S&W double/single-action semi-auto with a polymer frame and steel slide. The safety and slide release are located on the left side of the frame and the magazine release is ambidextrous. There's a rail for lights and lasers and the front of the trigger guard is hooked as a gripping surface. Magazine capacity is 17 + 1, barrel length is 3.625, and sights are three-dot with a drift adjustable rear. MSRP is $486.93.

SPRINGFIELD ARMORY RO COMPACT

Inside, the Range Officer Compact's bull barrel design makes disassembly a bit different. Springfield supplies a tool for compressing the recoil spring that makes the field-strip process pretty easy.

Elsewhere in the book I review Springfield Armory's Range Officer in 9mm, but Springfield also makes a compact version of the excellent Range Officer.

The Range Officer Compact has a four-inch barrel and an aluminum alloy frame, and an Officer-length grip. The front strap is smooth and the flat back strap is checkered in a high grip fine checkering pattern.

There's an extended beavertail grip safety with a generous bump at the bottom to allow shooters with thin hands to engage the grip safety. My hands are slender enough that I can't rest my thumb on the thumb safety of guns without the bump and still be sure I'll keep the grip safety engaged. The thumb safety is oversized and on the right side only. I think this is a good idea on a carry 1911.

While I haven't carried a 1911 as a daily CCH gun, I've had friends in law enforcement advise me that an ambidextrous safety might not be a good idea on a carry 1911, because it can be disengaged by seat belts and other objects the shooter comes in contact with. If you need a left-hand safety, it's an easy and economical addition.

The trigger is a long, lightweight, speed trigger. On my test gun the trigger broke with a slight amount of creep at just over five pounds, reasonable for a concealed carry defense gun. There are generous angled cocking serrations on the rear area of the slide. The hammer is a skeletonized, Commander-style. Sights are a combat-style two-dot rear and a high-vis front with both green and red replacement material provided. Finish is a flat Parkerized on the slide, and the aluminum frame is black Hardcoat anodized and matches well. The grips are thin cocobolo with double diamonds at the attachment screws and the familiar crossed cannons Springfield Armory logo.

While the standard Range Officer is straight-laced all the way, the design of the Range Officer Compact is drastically different from the conventional build of older 1911s. The Compact is a bull-barreled gun without a barrel bushing. The stainless steel match-grade barrel features a fully supported ramp. There's a full-length recoil spring guide rod and dual recoil

With a Novak two dot rear and a hi-vis front, the Compact Range Officer offers excellent sights. Ergonomic features like the beavertail grip safety with a palm bump and a skeletonized hammer and trigger round out the package.

The bull barrel design puts a little more weight up front to speed recovery.

springs.

Shooting the Range Officer Compact is similar to shooting an old-style Commander except with better sights and more ergonomic controls. Recoil with 230-grain hardball and +P defense loads is snappy, but manageable. It's my theory that you carry a gun more than you shoot it and if you use the gun to defend yourself, you'll never feel the recoil. Obviously, second shot recovery is always an issue with hard-kicking guns, but no one will argue the potential of the .45 ACP round, and heavy guns often get left at home.

Accuracy was more than adequate, though it seemed to take 50 or so rounds for it to settle down, but of course, this might have been me. After a couple hundred rounds, I managed a pretty respectable ten-shot group at ten yards, slow fire and rapid fire was both manageable and plenty accurate. It wasn't a problem running the plate machine at ten yards and staying on the standard six-second time limit. Most of my shooting was done with Winchester 230-grain Target and Win 1911 230-grain Target. I also ran a couple of boxes of 185-grain Silvertips and there wasn't a single malfunction.

Like the standard Range Officer, The Range Officer Compact is a lot of gun for the money. If I were to voice a suggestion, it would be to include at least one slightly longer magazine for pocket carry or perhaps to extend the magazine just a bit to allow for seven rounds. Of course, longer magazines for 1911s are hardly hard to find. Extra magazine capacity is always a good thing. The RO Compact functions flawlessly and is more than accurate enough for

The Range Officer Compact was easy to shoot and produced an almost one-hole group at ten yards standing with deliberate aim. Speeding up the string still produced a pretty nice group in the head of the target, but with my typical low left grouping that comes from my bad habit of managing recoil before it happens.

the purpose intended. It comes with the usual-for-Springfield Armory accessories, but generous for others in the industry. There's a hard plastic case with a holster, magazine pouch, two six-round magazines, tools ,and extra sight insert material. As is the usual case for Springfield Armory, it's a lot of gun and an excellent value.

Keltec's PMR 30 is unusual, but might serve as a viable defense/utility pistol. With a magazine capacity of 30 rounds of .22 Magnum ammunition, it's both light and powerful. With two loaded magazines of 61 rounds, it weighs less than a loaded AR15 magazine.

It's the most non-traditional pistol I have ever reviewed, and maybe ever shot. I once handled a GyroJet pistol from the 60s. Though it's truly non-traditional, it is highly sought after. I recently saw one sell on an auction site for $900, over twice the retail price.

I suppose the concept of the kit pistol was first approached by Smith & Wesson. I had a square butt Model 34 Kit Gun once, and it was truly an interesting little gun with a specific purpose. Designated as a broad-based utility gun to be kept handy by an outdoorsman, the Kit Gun was a J Frame, the smallest of the S&W revolver frames, in .22 Long Rifle or .22 Winchester Magnum. It was a six-shot gun with adjustable sights and a four or two-inch barrel. Lightweight and accurate, it could be relied on to dispatch snakes, take small game, or serve as a survival gun. It was an unusual concept gun based on a time-tested traditional design. Though the idea behind the PMR 30 is the same, the design of the gun is far from traditional.

With both magazines loaded and one in the chamber, a total of 61 rounds, a Kel-Tec PMR 30 weighs less than a loaded AR15 magazine.

The PMR 30 is a .22 Magnum, 30-shot, semi-automatic pistol that weighs just 13 ounces empty, considerably less than that two-inch Kit Gun. I can think of no other pistol that has a similar capacity even at twice the weight. While the .22 Magnum round isn't in the same league as the 9mm, it produces 137 foot pounds of energy with a 40-grain bullet. The PMR 30 is reasonably accurate, though hardly a match gun. The frame construction is of two polymer halves that fit around the slide assembly and bolt together with hollow head screws and nuts that are contained in hex recesses in the polymer frame.

The slide and barrel are steel but the top gripping area and rear sight housing are polymer and screwed to the frame with hollow-head screws. The 4 ½" barrel measures just .375" in the chamber area and .332 nearer the muzzle. There are twin extractors to extract the case and a thin ejector to toss it clear of the slide. Other than the slide release, it's completely ambidextrous, the safety is located in a similar fashion to a 1911, and the magazine release is at the bottom rear of the grip. The trigger is also polymer and is decent enough; not competition grade, but better than some popular striker-fired pistols. The sights are a fixed fiber optic rear and a dovetailed green fiber optic front.

Having fired and tested a PMR 30, I can certainly understand why they would sell at their suggested retail price of $415.00. I suppose the most revealing thing I can say about this gun is that it works for what I think it was originally intended for. The intended use is as a utility gun. For a fishing guide, a coastal commercial fisherman, a surveyor, or anyone else who spends lots of time outdoors, needs a defensive/utility firearm, and doesn't want to carry a lot of weight, it's a perfect gun. I have a friend who's a rancher and he wants one to carry as hog medicine. Maybe you can't drive staples with the handle, but it would serve a cowboy or rancher much better than the iconic 1873 Colt that made its name as the cowboy's perfect sidearm.

There is no doubt the most successful pistol design system in history has been the 1911 pistol. It's now 102 years since its acceptance as the U.S. service pistol, and it's still going strong. When the 1911 was replaced, there were many naysayers about the wisdom of leaving such a successful system, but things must be kept in perspective: As much as many of us love the 1911, we have to accept its limitations.

First, 1911s in .45 ACP are not easy pistols to learn to shoot well. The recoil is quite heavy and the single-action system is somewhat complicated for a novice to master and use effectively under stress. This problem came to light with police departments that went with the 1911. There were problems with carrying the gun in Condition One, which means cocked and locked on a loaded chamber. There were issues about the operation of the safety. There were also issues with the officers failing to get the pistol back into safe condition before re-holstering, since many were used to using revolvers with no safety.

Of course, another issue was the seven-plus-one capacity of the 1911. With most modern pistols having a capacity of at least twice that amount, this was seen as a serious shortcoming and made the 1911 seem archaic. As my friend and former Federal Air Marshal Chris Cerino has said, a fully-loaded 1911 is already half empty.

There were some teething problems with the Model 92 that were soon resolved, and the clamor eventually died down. I've talked to a lot of servicemen since that time and they've been happy with the Beretta, and it's performed well in combat and service pistol matches.

The double/single operating system of the Beretta is hardly an unproven system, and recent developments with striker-fired guns have made the double/single system guns seem even more archaic than the ancient 1911 system. Still, these are good guns, proven on battlefields, city streets, recreational ranges, and competitive events.

The 92 Compact is a cut-down version of the standard 92 that's designed to be a little friendlier for concealed carry and defense use. Other than the shorter barrel and grip, and with a lower magazine capacity, it's the same gun. With a capacity of 13 + 1, it's still a high-capacity pistol and there are many departments now considering going back to the 9mm in light of recent improvements in ammunition.

The tricky issue with double/single-action guns is the different trigger pull between the first and second shot. It's often cited as a major problem, so I decided to see just how much it affected my ability to get off two quick shots. I set up a ten-yard target and, firing from the low ready position, I fired a series of five, two-shot drills, firing the first shot double action and the second single action. I was surprised when I realized my first shots were better centered and formed a tighter group than the second, single-action rounds. Based on my experience, I believe the double/single worry to be a non-issue and I certainly can see the security in carrying a double-action trigger over a lighter-triggered striker-fired gun.

I'm certainly not saying the Beretta is superior to the current generation of striker-fired guns, but it's certainly far from obsolete, and a great choice if you're nervous about stuffing a light-triggered gun with no external safety in your pants. In this regard, I see it as vastly superior to the 1911.

CHAPTER 15

FULL-SIZE REVOLVERS

While most concealed carry citizens won't wind up carrying a full-size revolver, they do have real attributes for defensive use, and even daily carry under certain circumstances. I've a friend who shoots three-gun and action pistol events. He's always steered clear of revolvers since they only work for competition when placed within their own class. They reload slowly, and they lack the precision trigger of modern 1911 and striker-fired competition pistols. I brought a Smith & Wesson M&P R8 over to his range and he shot it out of curiosity. He was amazed at how much he liked shooting it and later bought one of the large-frame 9mm Performance Center Smith & Wessons. Now he's amazed that he can shoot that revolver more accurately in double action than his tricked-out competition 1911. He's also noted that with thousands of rounds, it happily digests everything he runs through it, even ammunition his semi- autos balk at.

Full-size revolvers are the most accurate and reliable handguns available, and they require very little tweaking and maintenance to stay that way. Most are a pleasure to shoot, once you learn to manage a good double-action trigger, and you don't have to scrounge around on your knees looking for scattered brass. It's true they're considered passé, but spend some time shooting a good one and you may find yourself to be an admirer of the ancient wheel gun.

CHIAPPA RHINO

The unconventional Chiappa Rhino has a space gun look, but the unusual look comes from a totally novel approach to revolver design. While almost all designs evolve over time, most continue to position components based on the original design. In the beginning, when revolvers were first conceived, there was a need for the ability to charge the chambers from the front, because the first revolvers were cap-and-ball guns. In addition to loading the powder and ball, the ball needed to compress the powder for uniform burning. The early Colt and Remington revolvers used a loading lever and plunger to seat the ball and compress the charge. It made sense for the barrel to be on top since it held the front sight and the rear sight was a simple slot in the hammer. As a result, all subsequent revolvers fired from the top of the cylinder because that's where the barrel was.

The only problem with this is that due to the way the gun is constructed, the recoil comes from an axis above the shooter's hand, causing the gun to rotate upward in recoil. On heavy, low-powered single-action guns, this wasn't a problem, and the grips were even designed to let the gun roll upward in the shooter's hand during recoil to allow easier access to the hammer for cocking.

Today's revolvers are much lighter, and much more powerful. They also are now double action, making them faster to shoot and precluding the need for thumb cocking after each shot. When Rino Chiappa designed the Rhino revolver, he pretended the revolver as we know it had never existed and began with a clean sheet of paper. He placed the barrel in line with the bottom of the cylinder, so it was in a direct line with the shooter's wrist, almost eliminating muzzle rise in recoil. He did want the ability to shoot the gun in single action, so he positioned a cocking lever in a location similar to the hammer spur on traditional revolvers. He designed the lock work so the gun could be fired double action, or cocked and decocked using this lever. He put a raised rib above the barrel in order to align the front sight with the top strap for sighting purposes and the result of all this is the very unconventional but functionally reasonable Chiappa Rhino revolver.

All versions of the Rhino use the same frame and internal parts. The cylinder is no longer fluted as has been the tradition as a way to reduce weight. Instead, it's hexagonal with flats to slim the profile. The grip is only present where it contacts the hand, creating an unusual shape that feels fine, but looks really strange. Available in 2", 4", 5", and 6" barrel lengths and in 9mm, .357 Magnum, .40 S&W, and .38 Super. Weights range from 22 ounces for the 2" to just a bit over 32 ounces for the 6" guns with steel frames. There's also a Polylite version with a 2" barrel that gets by at just under 20 ounces. The two inch guns have fixed sights and the rest are feature adjustable rear sights. Available in Black or Chrome.

SMITH & WESSON M&P R8

In my early years of shooting, I mostly shot revolvers. I shot my first handgun match with a Smith & Wesson Model 19, and I still own one. In fact, I don't think a gun safe is complete without a Model 19 because in my mind it's probably one of the top ten guns ever made. It was small enough to carry comfortably, and heavy enough to be comfortable to shoot with real .357 Magnum loads,. It had a great trigger and was accurate enough that I won my first Hunter's Pistol Metallic Silhouette match with one, and I hit several 100-yard ram targets in the process. The Model 19 is no longer in the S&W catalog, though the stainless version Model 66 is still there.

As much as I love my Model 19, I like the M&P R8 even more. Built on the large N frame, the .357 Magnum R8 holds eight rounds. It has the same butter-smooth trigger in both single and double action and offers an inch more sight radius because of a 5" barrel. Surprisingly, it weighs less than my old classic 19 by virtue of a lightweight Scandium frame. It also uses moon clips for fast loading and positive extraction. The R8 also comes with a bottom rail for lights and lasers and a removable top rail for optics. It does everything you can expect from a full-size revolver, and it operates flawlessly every time. Weight is 36.3 ounces and MSRP is $1,329.00 in matte black only.

SMITH & WESSON MODEL 69

The S&W Model 69 is a medium-frame .44 Magnum built on the S&W L frame. Cylinder capacity has been reduced to five shots, which would have completely changed the plot of the iconic Dirty Harry movie that made the Model 29 almost impossible to buy for several years. Only a bit larger than the Model 66, it features the excellent Smith & Wesson adjustable rear sight and a red inserted Baughman Quick Draw front sight. Double action and stainless with black synthetic grips, it has a weight of 39 ounces and a barrel length of 4.25". MSRP is $849.00.

SMITH & WESSON 686

The 686 Smith & Wesson was the Springfield, Massachusetts version of Colt's king of revolvers, the Python. Built on the medium L frame and with a seven-shot .357 cylinder, it's arguably a better gun than the much-revered Python, though I probably just made a lot of enemies by saying so. It has a full-length barrel shroud, a black synthetic grip, and adjustable rear and red ramp front sights. It's available with a four or six -barrel and has a satin stainless finish. Weight in 4" is just under 40 ounces and MSRP is $829.00.

SMITH & WESSON 686 SRS

The SSR is an upgraded 686 with checkered wood grips and a tapered barrel shroud. It also has an adjustable trigger stop to allow the elimination of trigger backlash and enhance accuracy. Available in 4" and with a weight of 38.3 ounces, it's a little lighter and faster than the standard 686. Finish is satin stainless and MSRP is $999.00.

SMITH & WESSON 625

Jerry Miculek's revolver world record is probably one of the most-watched shooting videos on YouTube. In the video, Jerry fires 12 shots from a modified Smith & Wesson Model 625, hitting a target in less than three seconds, including the reload. The 625 JM is a Champion and Pro series gun that commemorates that event. It's a .45 ACP revolver that uses moon clips for extraction. Sights are the S&W rear and a gold bead Patridge front. It has an over-sized hammer and a full-length barrel shroud. The round butt grip frame has Jerry's custom shape walnut grips and the JM logo on the butt. In a satin finish stainless, the MSRP is $979.00.

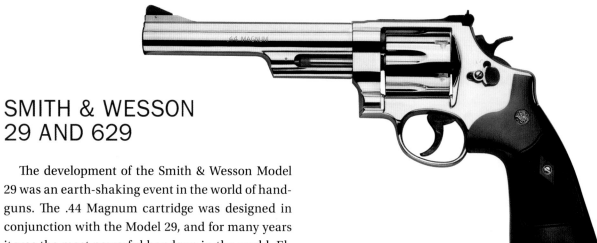

SMITH & WESSON 29 AND 629

The development of the Smith & Wesson Model 29 was an earth-shaking event in the world of handguns. The .44 Magnum cartridge was designed in conjunction with the Model 29, and for many years it was the most powerful handgun in the world. Elmer Keith generated both fans and detractors by claiming to have shot a whitetail deer with one at a reported 600 yards. Whether this really happened or not, the Model 29 was potentially capable of the task. The 629 is the stainless steel version of that iconic revolver. The 629 has a heavy ribbed barrel and oversized synthetic black or wood grips, depending on the version. Models are available with a partial or full-length ejector shroud and in barrel lengths of 4", 5" 6.5" and 7.5". MSRP is $949.00 on the basic model and up to $1,619.00 for the tricked-out Stealth Hunter. The Model 29 is a S&W Classic and is available in blue with walnut oversized grips with 4" or 6.5" barrels. MSRP is $999.00.

SMITH & WESSON 27 AND 627

Smith & Wesson's 27 is the gun that introduced the magnum pistol to the world. In the form of the original .357 Registered Magnum, the .357 was the most powerful pistol in the world when introduced in 1934. The original factory round developed by Winchester featured a 158-grain bullet with a muzzle velocity of 1,515 fps and 812 foot-pounds of energy. The round operated at pressures unheard-of in handgun calibers and spawned a whole generation of new handguns and calibers. The Classic version is currently available with a six-shot cylinder in bright blue with oversized walnut grips. MSRP is $1,059 with a 4" or 6.5" barrel.

The 627 is a modern version using the current eight-shot cylinder. It uses a round-butt frame, has a shrouded ejector rod and a black synthetic grip. MSRP is $999.00.

SMITH & WESSON 627 AND 629 V COMP

The Smith & Wesson V Comp guns are designed with a compensated barrel for reduced muzzle rise. They're competition-tuned guns with competition features like adjustable front sights to complement the adjustable rear sight, oversized hammer, black synthetic grips, and an adjustable trigger stop to eliminate backlash. The 629 is a six-shot .44 Magnum in all-matte stainless and a 4" barrel. The 627 is an eight-shot .357 Magnum with a 5" barrel and bi-tone black and stainless finish. MSRP on both guns is $1,559.00.

SMITH & WESSON 929 AND 986

In 2014 Smith & Wesson introduced two revolvers in 9mm Luger. The 929 is an eight-shot N frame with a 6.5" compensated barrel. The 986 is a seven-shot L frame with a five-inch flat-sided barrel with a tapered ejector shroud. Both guns have competition features like adjustable rear and Patridge front sights and oversized synthetic grips. Frames are stainless steel with titanium alloy cylinders. Since the 9mm is a rimless cartridge, both guns use moon clips to allow extraction. Weight of the 929 is 44.1 ounces with an MSRP of $1,189.00. MSRP on the 986 is $1,149 with a weight of 34.9 ounces.

SMITH & WESSON GOVERNOR

The Governor is the Smith & Wesson answer to the Taurus Judge. With a Scandium frame and stainless cylinder, the Governor has a six-shot capacity. Chambered for 2.5" .410 shotgun, .45 Colt, and .45 ACP with moon clips, the Governor has a 2.75" barrel with a shrouded ejector rod. Sights are a grooved top strap and ramp front and the grips are black synthetic. Weight is 29.6 ounces and it's available in matte bright or black. MSRP is $829.00 for the standard version and $1,119.00 for the Crimson Trace-equipped version.

RUGER REDHAWK

Ruger's Redhawk is a six-shot, double/single-action revolver with adjustable sights and a ramp front sight. It's chambered for .44 Magnum and .45 Colt. There's a shrouded ejector rod and finish is satin stainless. Available with 4", 5.5", and 7.5" barrels, there are two grip options; smooth wood and Hogue Monogrip. Weight of the 4" is 47 ounces and 54 for the 7.5". The .45 Colt version is only available in 4". The Hunter model comes machined for scope mounting on the barrel rib. MSRP is $1,029.00 for standard and $1,089.00 for the Hunter version.

RUGER GP100

Ruger's GP100 series are .357 Magnum, six-shot double/single-action revolvers. They have full-length shrouded ejector rods and come in 3", 4.2", and 6" versions. The 3" version has fixed sights, the others have a ramp front and adjustable rear. Grips are black synthetic Hogue Monogrip. Weights range from 36 ounces for the 3" to 45 ounces for the 6" version. With MSRPs ranging from $725.00 to $779.00, they're available in blued or satin stainless.

RUGER SUPER REDHAWK

The Ruger Super Redhawk sports a heavier frame and is chambered for .44 Magnum, .454 Casull, and .480 Ruger. The scope mount for the Super Redhawk is standard and on the top strap rather than the barrel. Sights are red ramp front and adjustable rear. Grip is the Hogue Monogrip and finish is satin stainless. The .44 Magnum chambering is available in 7.5" or 9.5" barrel length. .454 and .480 are 7.5" only. Weight is 53 ounces for the 7.5" and 58 ounces for the 9.5" version, MSRP for the .44 is $1,079.00 and $1,119.00 for the .454 and .480.

TAURUS MODELS 65 AND 66

The Taurus line of medium-frame revolvers features both six and seven-shot-capacity guns with almost identical features otherwise. The 65 series are the traditional six-shot version and the 66 series has an extra chamber ,upping the capacity to seven rounds. Both lines feature adjustable rear sights and ramped front sights. Both lines offer both four and six-inch versions in both stainless and blued. Grips are black synthetic, the hammers are oversized target style and the barrels feature a full-length shroud for the ejector rod. Weights for the 4" are 38 ounces and 43 for the 6". MSRP begins at $488.46 for the Model 65 in blue and tops out at $590.74 for the stainless Model 66.

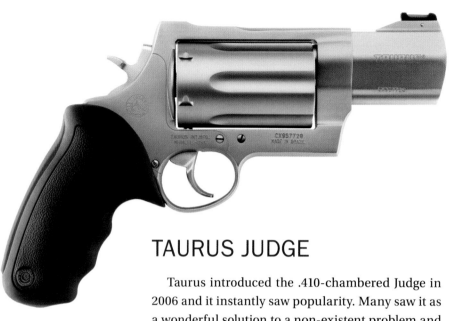

TAURUS JUDGE

Taurus introduced the .410-chambered Judge in 2006 and it instantly saw popularity. Many saw it as a wonderful solution to a non-existent problem and many saw it as the greatest thing since sliced bread. While controversial around gun shop counters, it's certainly seen success. The basic models are chambered for the .45 Colt and 2.5" .410 shotshell. The Judge comes in barrel lengths from 2.5" to 6.5" and with a variety of finishes and options. The base model five-shot with a 2.5" barrel weighs 28.2 ounces and has an MSRP of $607.53. The top-of-the-line Raging Judge is a six-shot .454 Casull/3".410 that weighs a hefty 73 ounces and has an MSRP of $1,012.00.

TAURUS MODEL 44

The Taurus Model 44 is a stainless steel, large-frame, six-shot, .44 Magnum with an adjustable rear sight and a ramped front. There's a full-length ejector rod shroud and the longer-barreled versions have a ventilated top rib. All come in matte stainless finish with black soft rubber grips and the muzzle is ported. The 4" version has a weight of 45 ounces and an MSRP of $726.59. The 8.375" barreled version weighs 57 ounces and has an MSRP of $741.86.

TAURUS 608

The Model 608 is a large-frame, stainless, .357 Magnum with an eight-shot capacity. The rear sight is adjustable and the front is a pinned ramp. The ejector rod shroud is full length, grips are soft rubber and the muzzle is ported. The 608 is available with a 4" or 6" barrel and the 6" version has a ventilated rib. The 4" version weighs 44 ounces and has an MSRP of $688.43. The 6" version weighs 52 ounces with an MSRP of $741.36.

Shooting is a sport that evokes passion, and lifelong friend Mike Byrd, of B&B Precision Machining, has such a passion for shooting that he's converted his front yard into a recreational pistol/rifle/shotgun range. His front yard contains multiple plate racks, dueling trees, a Texas star, multiple gong targets in various sizes, and stands for four by tens, a popular target for shotguns and pistols in three-gun competition. Targets range from ten to 100 yards and sometimes we've been known to use a 100-yard silhouette as a stop plate for pistols. There's a door with keys in a functioning door frame, a stairstep barricade (as used in three-gun matches), loading tables, and seating for when you just get too tired to shoot.

Mike holds weekly sessions, and invites his friends over for impromptu challenges. We take turns dreaming up scenarios and everyone shoots his way through, then we dream up another plan and continue. Most of the firearms used relate to three-gun competition, but I recently brought a wheelgun to the party. It wasn't an ordinary wheelgun like my 637 carry gun, it was as tactical as a revolver can get. I brought my S&W M&P R8, an eight-shot, N frame wheelgun that my wife, Cherie, used in the Bianchi Cup.

I shot my very first match with a S&W revolver, and I won the civilian class with it. It was a four-inch Model 19 and I still have it. I've been fond of Smith & Wesson revolvers ever since. Another favorite revolver of mine is a six-inch Highway Patrolman Model 28 that I used to win multiple metallic silhouette matches and earn an AAA classification.

Before you shrug and think I'm pulling your leg about a revolver staying in the hunt with double-stack semi-autos or striker-fired guns, take a few things into consideration: First and foremost is absolute certain reliability. Our recent session at Mike's range occurred on a pretty cold day. Some powders are temperature sensitive and all metals are affected by extreme cold. All the semi-autos were serious competition guns, while the R8 was almost totally stock. All three semi-autos had some form of malfunction that needed to be cleared. The revolver was 100% reliable.

I love semi-auto pistols as much as anyone, and I'm really happy that double-stack 1911s can be purchased for less than the price of a family car. The modern striker-fired guns are super-reliable, accurate, and have great triggers, but there's one issue that no autoloader can ever get around: All semi-autos use the energy of the previous shot to prepare them to fire the next round. If there's a bad round, the operator has to perform the task of cycling the gun to get it in condition to shoot again. This is not the case with the revolver.

With a revolver, the operator supplies the energy to bring the next round into position and preloads the spring that drives the hammer. This makes is-

Loading isn't as precise or fast as with an autoloader, but the use of moon clips or loaders helps. For competition like plate matches, these Five Star loaders and loading block are just the ticket.

While the trigger pull is a long-travel double action, the travel is smooth and controlled, and there's an adjustable trigger stop to eliminate backlash.

sues with bad magazines, different ammunition types, and changes in the way the gun is gripped a non-issue. Eventually, all semi-autos malfunction. Most revolvers go through decades of use and never malfunction during their entire lifetime.

It's true that no double action revolver can have both fast operation and the crisp, short travel of a 1911 trigger, or that a revolver will ever have the capacity of a double-stack, striker-fired pistol, but that reliability factor will always be an important issue. There's no need to learn a fast tap/rack sequence, no need for another hand, or a reposition of the grip because, if a round fails to fire, you simply pull the trigger again. As long as this is the case, the revolver will continue to thrive as a viable firearm in the minds of thinking people who need absolute reliability.

Revolvers can have quite functional triggers if properly set up. The M&P R8 came with a fairly smooth and decently light double-action trigger. There was little backlash and it was easy to prep the trigger and have only a slight movement when the pull fell through and dropped the hammer. The process of properly prepping the trigger is the secret to successful double action shooting. As an instructor who adheres to the teaching of former Federal Air Marshal Instructor Chris Cerino, of Chris Cerino

Testing the R8 off the Ransom Rest, I got 25-yard groups under two inches with several brands of ammunition.

The M&P R8 was made for shooting falling plates. The excellent sights and trigger made knocking the plates down a breeze, and the mild recoil made lining up the next shot easy.

The R8 cylinder is machined for moon clips, but we used Five Star speed loaders in our testing.

Training Group, I see trigger management as the most important aspect of pistol shooting. The R8 has a nice trigger out of the box, but I had a little more cleaning up and lightening done. I also installed a small foam pad inside the trigger guard to cushion the small amount of backlash there is. This is an old trick from the days of Police PPC matches.

Chambered for the old reliable .357/.38 Special, the R8 sports a 5" two-piece barrel. There's an under-the-barrel rail for lights or lasers, and the top of the barrel sleeve is drilled and tapped for an included upper scope mount base. The big N frame now sports eight chambers as opposed to my old Model 28's six, the cylinder is machined to allow use of full moon clips.

The front sight is interchangeable; the rear is a standard version of the excellent S&W adjustable rear sight. The grip is a synthetic rubber grip with finger grooves. I think I might prefer the old standard S&W Target grips, but I've had pretty good success with the standard grip, and Cherie liked it

The rail mount that comes with the R8 allows easy mounting of optics for hunting or competition. There's also a bottom rail for lights and lasers.

better than the big wooden grips. (I want to try the Hogue Big Butt grip when I get a chance.) The finish is matte black and the frame is Scandium alloy with a black stainless cylinder. Empty weight is just over 36 ounces, light enough to carry well but heavy enough to handle the recoil with little disturbance of sight picture.

The M&P R8 isn't a glamorous revolver. It's a workhorse designed to serve the purpose the purchaser plans for it. It would make an admirable service revolver with eight-shot capacity and weighing only an ounce or so more than the old S&W Model 19, which was the Cadillac of service revolvers when every police department depended on wheel guns. It's a viable choice as a home defense gun, with a rail for laser and flashlight. It would be an admirable hunting sidearm, coming with a top-of-the-barrel scope mount and, of course, it made a dandy revolver for Cherie's bid in the Bianchi Cup.

I'll admit that I didn't show up my friends. Fact is, everyone knows a semi-auto is better suited to this kind of game. Well, everybody but Jerry Miculek. What I did accomplish was to have some great fun with a great gun and use less ammunition to hit the same targets. I suspect the reason my accuracy was better than the semi-autos was the little bit of extra time the revolver required for me to run the trigger. I can also say that I didn't experience a single malfunction and every other shooter did. It was really cold and the 1911s were a little pickier than usual. Smith and Wesson's N frame guns have served shooters well since before the late and great Elmer Keith shot the 600-yard deer, and they continue to serve us today.

As I've mentioned before, the first match I ever shot was with a Smith & Wesson Model 19. I still have that gun and I believe that the Model 19 was one of the most perfect revolvers ever made. In 1976, at the time I shot that first match, winning civilian class in my first showing, the Model 19 was considered by many to be the finest revolver available. It was the gun of choice of the legendary Bill Jordan, and though the Colt Python had a faithful following, it held a strong position in the market of premium wheelguns. Smith & Wesson has recently brought the Model 19 back in their Classic line.

My first impression of the Ruger Match Champion was that it strongly resembled those great old Model 19s of the past. True, the Match Champion doesn't have that wonderful S&W adjustable rear sight, but the modern Novak rear and high-vis front are much more the current trend. The Ruger is a six-shooter like the 19, and it's very similar in size and weight. Like the 19, the Match Champion has a smooth and clean trigger pull, both in single and double action.

Of course the new Ruger is a safer gun, using the modern transfer bar system rather than the pinned on firing pin of my old Smith. There's a shrouded ejector rod guide and the grips are Hogue Stippled Hardwood, not quite as elegant as the old Goncalo Alves

The flat-sided barrel, shrouded ejector rod, and high-vis front sight give the Match Champion a feel similar to a competition gun.

The Novak rear sight allows fast sight acquisition, but I'd prefer the newer version with an adjustable rear.

of Model 19s, but still giving a hand-filling traditional feel.

Shooting the Match Champion also brought back memories of great revolvers of the past, with buttery-smooth operation through the loading and unloading sequences, the solid feel of firing a quality double action and none of the mechanical gyrations generated by cycling slides and flying brass.

The sights are easy to see; on my test gun I needed to make an adjustment because the rear sight was too far to the right for point of aim. Shooting Winchester

.38 Special Train, of the Train and Defend line, I managed to get half my shots in a nickel-sized hole with the other five in close proximity. This was standing, deliberate double action from 15 yards, and I felt it was quite reasonable. Recoil with the .38 Special ammunition was downright mild and it was quite comfortable with full-power .357 defensive loads.

My first impression when I received my test Match Champion was that a match gun should have adjustable sights. Apparently, I wasn't the only one who saw this as an oversight because Ruger introduced an ad-

The Ruger Match Champion is a fun-to-shoot, traditional .357 revolver with modern sights and competition features.

justable sighted version of the Match Champion at the 2015 Shot Show, giving it everything it needs to be a great general purpose revolver.

In fact, the term general purpose revolver defines the Match Champion perfectly. The purchaser has the option of a trendy Novak or more traditional adjustable rear sight, and the front sight is a functional fiber optic. While it's traditional in the sense that it's a revolver, it's trendy in looks with a flat-sided outer barrel shroud with a raised top rib around an inner barrel. The grips are traditional in that they're wood, but modern in that they're one-piece with a single mounting screw in the butt.

Lighter and faster and more modern than the GP100 it's spawned from, the Match Champion is sure to find favor as a gun that'll do almost anything you can ask of it, and it'll continue to perform at that level for decades to come.

The checkered walnut grips are reminiscent of the classic revolvers I grew up with and used in matches at the beginning of my shooting career.

CHAPTER 16

FULL-SIZE SEMI-AUTOS

While most will find the full-size duty guns a bit heavy for daily carry, they're still to be considered for some situations. The extra weight and size mean this category of guns isn't handicapped with minor calibers or low magazine capacities. While full-size guns are certainly heavier to carry and hide, they do have virtues smaller guns can only envy. The additional weight and size make them much more accurate for many, and heavier guns are generally more reliable because it's easier for engineers to match the operating spring weight to the ammunition. This is because the slide's weight is part of the resistance in keeping the gun into battery during firing. Light slides mean heavier springs are required to prevent overstressing the mechanism of the firearm.

BERETTA 92

Designed in 1972, with the M9 version adopted by the U.S. Army in 1985, the Beretta 92 is a double/single-action semi-auto with a staggered double-stack magazine. Unlike many semi-autos, the slide on the 92 is open topped, exposing the top of the barrel. The hammer is exposed and the ambidextrous safety is mounted on the slide and de-cocks the hammer. The magazine release is reversible for left-handed users. It uses the familiar three-dot sight system and the rear sight is drift adjustable for windage. Chambered for the 9mm Luger round, magazine capacity is 15+1 and weight is 33.3 ounces with a 4.9" barrel. MSRP is $675.00.

BERETTA PX4

Beretta's full-size pistol offering, the Beretta PX4 in .45 ACP is the most powerful handgun in the Beretta line. The PX4 comes in three calibers 9mm Luger, .40 S&W, and .45 ACP. It has a polymer frame and uses Beretta's locked-breech rotating-barrel system. Like the Beretta 92, this is an exposed-hammer, double/single-action pistol. While I never really liked the double/single system, I do appreciate the fact that it has re-strike capability.

The magazine release can be converted for left-hand use and there are two sizes of larger magazine release buttons available. There's an ambidextrous safety, too, making the PX4 totally suitable for a left-handed shooter. There are three backstrap fillers shipped with the gun to allow fit to any hand and it has three-dot sights. It comes with two magazines. The regular magazine holds nine rounds and the extended magazine holds ten. Weight is just over 28 ounces and MSRP is $575.00.

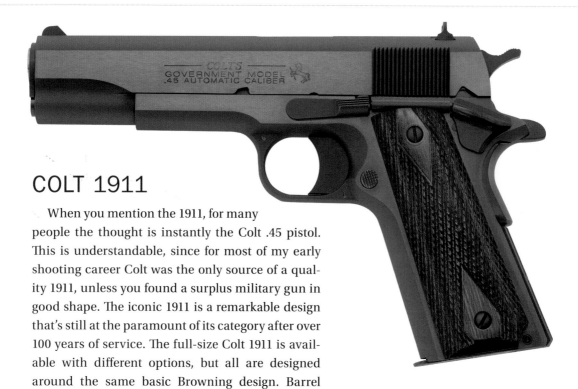

COLT 1911

When you mention the 1911, for many people the thought is instantly the Colt .45 pistol. This is understandable, since for most of my early shooting career Colt was the only source of a quality 1911, unless you found a surplus military gun in good shape. The iconic 1911 is a remarkable design that's still at the paramount of its category after over 100 years of service. The full-size Colt 1911 is available with different options, but all are designed around the same basic Browning design. Barrel length is 5" and weight ranges from 29 ounces to 38 ounces. Available calibers are 9mm, .38 Super, and .45 ACP. Different models can be had, from the basic Series 80 guns that are similar in options to the original service 1911, to upgraded versions with better sights, triggers, grip safeties, hammers, and finishes. MSRPs range from $907.00 for the base 1991 Series to the top-of-the-line Gold Cup at $1,250.00.

CZ 85

The CZ 85 is a steel-frame, double/single-action 9mm semi-auto that uses a double-stack magazine. Capacity is 16 +1, and barrel length is 4.61". It's a traditional exposed-hammer design with a frame-mounted firing pin block safety. The sights are drift adjustable for windage and the safety, magazine release and slide release are ambidextrous. Weight is 34 ounces and MSRP is $628.00. It's also available in the Combat version with an adjustable rear sight for $664.00.

CZ P07

The CZ P07 is a modern polymer-frame double/single-action semi-auto, available in 9mm Luger, .38 Super, and .40 S&W. Magazine capacity in 9mm is 16 + 1. The rear sight is drift adjustable and uses the popular three-dot system. The barrel length is 3.70" and weight is 27.16 ounces. It has an interesting feature in that it can easily be converted from a de-cocker to a manual safety that blocks the hammer, but leaves it cocked. There's a bottom rail for lights and lasers and an extended beavertail. MSRP is $510.00.

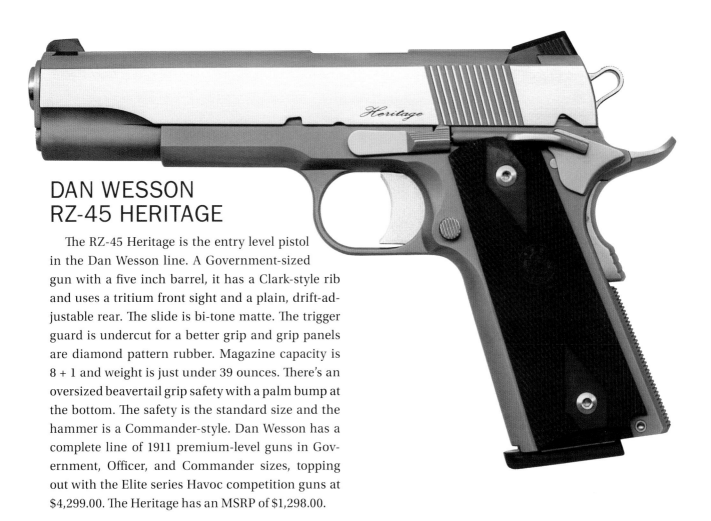

DAN WESSON RZ-45 HERITAGE

The RZ-45 Heritage is the entry level pistol in the Dan Wesson line. A Government-sized gun with a five inch barrel, it has a Clark-style rib and uses a tritium front sight and a plain, drift-adjustable rear. The slide is bi-tone matte. The trigger guard is undercut for a better grip and grip panels are diamond pattern rubber. Magazine capacity is 8 + 1 and weight is just under 39 ounces. There's an oversized beavertail grip safety with a palm bump at the bottom. The safety is the standard size and the hammer is a Commander-style. Dan Wesson has a complete line of 1911 premium-level guns in Government, Officer, and Commander sizes, topping out with the Elite series Havoc competition guns at $4,299.00. The Heritage has an MSRP of $1,298.00.

FNH FIVE-SEVEN

Without a doubt the most unusual gun in this category, the FN 5.7 uses a combination of polymer and steel for the frame and slide. What makes the FN 5.7 unusual is the caliber, a 5.7 x 28mm round that pushes a 31-grain bullet at 2,350 feet per second. The gun is a delayed blowback striker-fired gun with a two-stage striker-fired trigger. The magazine capacity is 20 + 1 and there's an ambidextrous manual safety that's unconventionally located in front of the trigger guard on the frame. With a 4.8" barrel, weight is 20.8 ounces. There's a bottom rail and the rear sight is adjustable. MSRP is $1,349.00.

FNH FNS

The FNH FNS is the first striker-fired pistol from FNH. It's a polymer-frame gun with an ambidextrous safety slide stop and magazine release. There are two interchangeable backstraps to allow a better fit and a bottom rail for mounting lights and lasers. It's available in standard and long slide versions in 9mm and .40. The hammer-forged barrel is stainless steel. There's an external extractor and a loaded chamber indicator. It uses the three-dot sight system and is available without a manual safety. MSRP is $649.00.

GLOCK MODELS 17, 20, 21, 22, 37, AND 31

In the early 80s the Glock Model 17 was introduced and it changed the world of service pistols. The Glock 17 wasn't the first striker-fired pistol, but it was the first to be a commercial success. By combining internal safety features and a long-stroke, two-stage, trigger pull with a center blade safety in the trigger, the Glock provided police departments with a gun featuring large magazine capacity and light weight with a high degree of safety and ease of operation.

Sights are dovetailed and drift adjustable for windage and the trigger is a two-stage striker-fired unit.

The standard-sized Glocks range in weight from about 25 ounces for the 9mm to 29.3 ounces for the .45. Barrel lengths range from 4.48" for the G17 to 4.6" for the .45-caliber G21. Currently available in 9mm, 40 S&W, .45 GAP, .357 SIG, 10mm, and .45 ACP, MSRP ranges from is $599.00.

H&K VP9

H&K released the first striker-fired polymer pistol long before the current generation, but it was before its time and wasn't a commercial success. Now, they're in the striker-fired game again with the VP9, a polymer-frame 9mm with excellent ergonomics and performance. The bore axis is very low, which keeps it flat during recoil. One of the features I really liked was the addition of "charging supports", extra gripping surfaces that appear to be mortised into the rear of the frame behind the normal gripping surfaces. This makes it a very easy pistol to operate, a valuable feature and a big issue with smaller-framed shooters. The VP9 has a magazine capacity of 15 rounds and uses the familiar three-dot sight system with a drift-adjustable rear. It comes with two magazines in a hard case for an MSRP of $719.00.

KIMBER 1911S

Kimber is a highly regarded manufacturer of premium 1911 guns. All Kimber 1911s are single stack with versions with steel or alloy frames. Base gun in the line is the Custom II, a steel-framed gun with a matte black finish, and a flat mainspring housing. It sports a match barrel, front and rear slide serrations, and fixed, low profile sights. MSRP is $871.00. From the base Custom II, there are other lines; Eclipse, Covert, and Gold Match, with dozens of combinations of finishes, grips, serrations, sights, trigger and hammer options, threaded and standard barrels and every other option one might imagine, including rails and laser grips. The top-of-the-line guns are Special Editions, topping out with the Gold Combat with an MSRP of $2,715.00.

MAGNUM RESEARCH 1911

The Magnum Research 1911 line begins with the 1911 G, a .45 ACP with a high-profile drift-adjustable rear sight and a pinned and serrated front. It uses a flat mainspring housing and an extended beavertail grip safety with a palm bump. The hammer and trigger are skeletonized and there's an extended magazine release. MSRP is $831.00. The GR model has a bottom rail for lights and lasers with an MSRP of $1,091.00. There's also a model with a color case-hardened frame for $1,120.00.

REMINGTON 1911 R1

Remington's line of 1911s begins with the R1, a basic 1911 with a flat mainspring housing and double diamond checkered walnut grip panels. The ejection port is flared and lowered, the sights are dovetailed three-dot front and rear. Finish on the carbon steel slide and frame is satin black oxide. It comes in a carry case with two magazines for an MSRP of $729.00 and in stainless for $789.00. Next up in the line is the 1911 R1 Enhanced. It comes in both 9mm and .45 ACP and features an adjustable rear sight and fiber optic front, front and rear slide serrations, and a beavertail grip safety with a checkered memory bump. The trigger is skeletonized and there's a match trigger. The flat mainspring housing is checkered and there are serrations on the front grip strap. It comes with two magazines with bump pads. MSRP is $940.00 in black and $999.00 in stainless. There's also a threaded barrel and Crimson Trace version.

RUGER SR 40/45

Ruger's SR 40 and 45 pistols are polymer-frame, striker-fired pistols using a bladed two-stage, striker-fired trigger. They have an adjustable rear sight with the three-dot sight system. Barrel length is 4.14" and weight is 27.25 ounces in .40 S&W and 30.15 ounces in .45 ACP. Magazine capacity is 15.1 and 10 + 1 respectively. They're available in matte black and bi-tone and have an MSRP of $529.00.

RUGER 1911

When Ruger released the first of their 1911 series, they were the hottest pistols on the want list at gun shops. The combination of Ruger owner brand loyalty and their reputation for building a quality gun, made the guns almost impossible to get. The base gun is the full-size 5" version with a low glare stainless finish. Weight is 39 ounces. Sights are three-dot, drift adjustable with a Novak rear sight and a pinned front sight. The trigger and hammer are skeletonized with a beavertail grip safety with a checkered palm bump. Available in .45 ACP only, the MSRP is $859.00. It's also available in Commander size with a stainless steel frame and a weight of 36.4 ounces, or aluminum alloy at 29.3 ounces. MSRP on stainless is $859.00 and $899.00 for alloy.

SIG P320

SIG has a new striker-fired pistol that's available in both carry and duty sizes. In addition, the new SIG is a modular design that allows the ability to change grip sizes, calibers, frame, and magazine sizes, all on the same serial numbered unit. Because the trigger fire control housing assembly unit carries the serial number, the P320 can be completely modular. In keeping with the modularity, the P320 is available with a standard short reset trigger or a tabbed safety trigger. All controls are ambidextrous and magazine capacity is 17 in 9mm. With SigLite night sights and black nitride finish, MSRP is $669.00.

SIG226

The SIG P226 is a double/single-action, alloy-frame duty pistol that fits the traditional duty gun mold. Chambered in 9mm, .357 SIG, and .40 S&W, it uses a 4.4" barrel and has a lower accessory rail for lights or lasers. The sights are three-dot and the frame finish is hard-anodized matte. The magazine release is in the standard 1911 location and the safety is frame mounted. Magazine capacity in 9mm is 10 or 15 Rounds, .357 SIG 10 or 12 Rornds, .40 S&W 10 or 12 rounds. Weight is 34 ounces and MSRP is $1,015.00 for standard and $1,108.00 for the night sight version.

SMITH & WESSON M&P

The striker-fired polymer-frame M&P was introduced in 2005. It uses a two-stage striker-fired trigger system with a hinged trigger to accomplish the same task as the inner blade trigger on the Glock pistols. Chamberings include 9mm, .40 S&W, and .45 ACP. Unlike many striker-fired pistols, it's available with a manually operated thumb safety. Barrel length is 4.5" and sights are three-dot, drift-adjustable rear. The M&P is available with or without a manual thumb safety. Magazine capacity in 9mm is 17 rounds, 15 rounds in .40 and 10 rounds in .45. Weight is 24 ounces in 9mm and 29 ounces in .45. With an extra magazine and three grip inserts, MSRP is $569.00 in 9mm and .40 and $599.00 in .45.

SPRINGFIELD ARMORY XD

Introduced in 2001 and made in Croatia, the Springfield Armory XD series of polymer-frame, striker-fired pistols have achieved popularity for both defensive carry and competition. They're chambered in 9mm, 40 S&W, .357 Sig, and .45 ACP. They use a bladed two-stage, striker-fired trigger system, have an ambidextrous magazine release, and a rear grip safety that is unique in the modern striker-fired spectrum. All versions feature a lower rail for lights and lasers; sights are dovetailed front and rear, three-dot and the XD comes in both 4" and 5" versions. Weight is 28 ounces for the 4" 9mm and 30 ounces for the .45 with a magazine capacity of 16 and 13 rounds, respectively. The XD series is available in black matte and bi-tone. MSRP is $516.00.

SPRINGFIELD ARMORY XDM

The XDm series comes in 9mm, .40, and .45. It involves some refinements, like interchangeable back straps for a better hand fit, and a longer grip to allow a magazine capacity of 19 rounds in 9mm and 13 in .45. Barrel lengths are 4.5" and weight on the 4.5" being 29 ounces in 9mm and 31 ounces in .45. XDm competition series guns have a 5.25" barrel and feature an adjustable rear and hi-vis front sight. MSRP is $649.00 on the 4.5" and $699.00 on the 5.25".

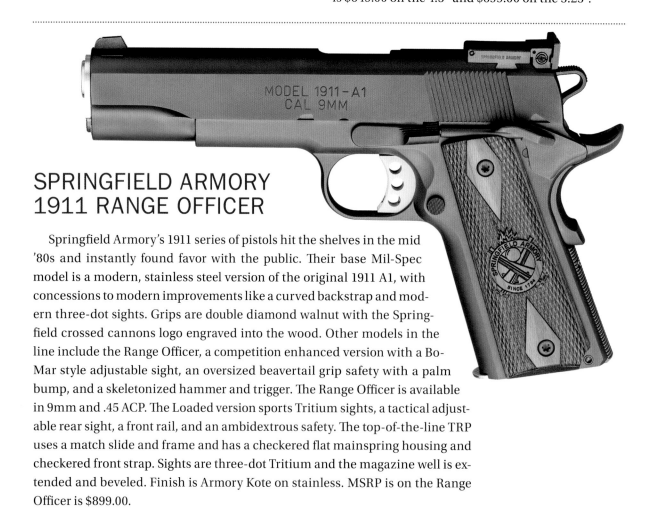

SPRINGFIELD ARMORY 1911 RANGE OFFICER

Springfield Armory's 1911 series of pistols hit the shelves in the mid '80s and instantly found favor with the public. Their base Mil-Spec model is a modern, stainless steel version of the original 1911 A1, with concessions to modern improvements like a curved backstrap and modern three-dot sights. Grips are double diamond walnut with the Springfield crossed cannons logo engraved into the wood. Other models in the line include the Range Officer, a competition enhanced version with a Bo-Mar style adjustable sight, an oversized beavertail grip safety with a palm bump, and a skeletonized hammer and trigger. The Range Officer is available in 9mm and .45 ACP. The Loaded version sports Tritium sights, a tactical adjustable rear sight, a front rail, and an ambidextrous safety. The top-of-the-line TRP uses a match slide and frame and has a checkered flat mainspring housing and checkered front strap. Sights are three-dot Tritium and the magazine well is extended and beveled. Finish is Armory Kote on stainless. MSRP is on the Range Officer is $899.00.

STEYR L40A1 AND L9A1

The striker-fired pistol design has changed the face of modern firearms. Almost every pistol manufacturer now has a striker-fired gun in their line and now, Steyr is expanding their presence in the striker-fired game with the new L9A1 and L40A1. The striker-fired Steyr has the familiar polymer frame and steel slide. It has a low bore axis and a fast trigger reset. An undercut trigger guard and high rear section of the grip allows a very high hand position. Trigger pull is light for the first stage and a typical duty gun break on the second stage. Barrel length is 4.5 inches and weight is 28.5 ounces. The sights are somewhat unusual with a pyramid white outline at the front and corresponding white outlines on the drift-adjustable rear. There's a bottom rail for lights and lasers and a visual and tactile loaded chamber indicator on the rear of the slide. With two magazines, and a hard case, it has an MSRP of $540.00.

TAURUS 24/7

The Taurus 24/7 is a polymer-frame striker-fired pistol using the familiar bladed trigger but working as a double/single action, allowing restrike capability. It's available in 9mm, .40 S&W, and .45 ACP. Barrel length is 4.2" and weight is 28 ounces in all three calibers. All controls are ambidextrous, and there's a bottom rail for lights and/or lasers. Sights are three-dot and with an adjustable rear. There are interchangeable back straps for better hand fit and a loaded chamber indicator. The magazine capacity is 17 +1 in 9mm, 15 + 1 in .40, and 12 + 1 in .45. MSRP is $528.15 in black and $543.41 in bi-tone.

TAURUS 1911

The Taurus 1911 line of pistols are completely loaded with features. The rear sight is adjustable with a dovetailed front. There's an ambidextrous oversized safety, a beavertail grip safety with a generous palm bump, hammer and trigger are skeletonized and grips are checkered black synthetic. There are front and rear grip serrations. MSRP of the blued version is $834.97 and $906.72 for stainless. There's also a stainless version with a bottom rail for an MSRP of $944.88.

WALTHER PPQ M2

Walther's PPQ M2 is a polymer-frame striker-fired gun using the familiar bladed trigger system. Available in 9mm and .40 S&W, it comes with 4" and 5" barrels. Sights are low-profile polymer with three-dots configuration. The slide and magazine release are ambidextrous with the safety located in the 1911 location. There are gripping serrations at the front and rear of the slide and a lower rail. Capacity is 15 + 1 in 9mm and 11 + 1 in .40. Weight in the 4" version is 24 ounces. MSRP is $649.00.

WALTHER PPX

Walther's PPX is a double/single-action, polymer-frame pistol with an unusual trigger system. The trigger is a preset striker-fired trigger that uses energy from the previous round to cock an internal hammer. As a result, the trigger feels like a two-stage, striker-fired trigger, so there's no need for a decocker, or manual safety since the trigger pull is long enough to provide a reasonable margin of safety. The magazine release is ambidextrous, there's a bottom rail and sights are low profile, polymer, three-dot. MSRP is $449.00.

One company always known for reliable and accurate service pistols is SIG. Designed for entry in the XM9 Service Pistol trials in 1984, the SIG P226 is a double/single action. It's similar in design to the SIG P220, but uses a higher-capacity, double-stack magazine. It's available in 9mm, .357 SIG, and .40 S&W. Sights are the usual white dot front and a two-dot, drift-adjustable rear. Magazine capacity is 15 rounds in 9mm and 12 rounds in .357 and .40. There's a lower rail for lights and lasers, and the finish on the Nitron version I tested was a durable looking black nitride.

There are real merits to the double/single-action design because it allows the user to carry the gun with the hammer down and fire the first shot without having to disengage a manual safety. Unlike striker-fired pistols, the hammer-down carry method provides a heavy enough trigger pull that issues like snagged clothing aren't as likely to create an accidental discharge when holstering.

The P226 has a frame mounted de-cocking lever that allows the user to safely de-cock the hammer at the completion of firing. As a result, it's a very safe pistol to operate and that level of safety was probably a factor in it being chosen by the Air Marshal service as their standard duty gun. Air Marshals carried the P226 in the more powerful .357 SIG caliber.

Shooting the 9mm P226 is pleasant, and the gun I tested certainly lived up to accuracy expectations. At 10 yards in deliberate two-handed fire, I managed a one-hole group with an extreme spread of about an inch-and-a-half. My first shot in double action was the highest shot in the group and without it the group would have been close to one inch. Recoil in

9mm is mild due to the steel frame and weight of 34 ounces empty. The sights were easy to see and recover in fast shooting and precise enough for deliberate shots.

The double/single-action system is one that requires some trigger time for best performance. In spite of running more than a hundred rounds through the gun on falling plates before shooting paper, I still pulled the first shot high. The double-action trigger pull is about ten pounds and fairly smooth, though not as smooth as most double-action revolvers. There's no stacking, but there's considerable overtravel once the trigger breaks, making a really precise double-action first shot more difficult than the average revolver. Another issue that makes the trigger a bit hard to manage is the diam-

SIG P226

The P226 isn't a gun that can be converted for left-handed controls. All functions operate as a right-hander. For right-handers the slide release, de-cocker, magazine release, and takedown lever are conveniently located.

eter of the grip. I had to rotate my hand around the grip to get better purchase and get far enough into it for good management in double action.

Single action is crisp and with less noticeable overtravel, but the initial take up and reset are quite long. I suspect that unless I spent quite a bit of time with double/single guns, I'd have problems letting a second shot go unintentionally. I suspect those who chose the system would be better served to stick with it. There's a P226 DAK that's a double-action-only version with a lighter double action pull. My used test gun performed with no malfunctions.

The P226 is a solidly-built and confidence-inspiring pistol, though it's a bit pricy with an MSRP of the base model Nitron at $1,015.00. It has a long and distinguished record of service, including being the choice of Navy Seals. It's rugged, reliable, simple to field strip, durable, and certainly accurate. Other than the somewhat quirky trigger, I can find no fault with it.

At ten yards, two-handed in deliberate fire, I managed nine shots in one ragged hole. The first and highest shot was with the double-action trigger.

The three-dot sights are straightforward and allow fast acquisition and precise shooting.

SPRINGFIELD ARMORY 9MM RANGE OFFICER

I still have my first 1911. I started out with a good one. It's a 1968 pre-Series 70 Gold Cup National Match. Honestly, I probably should have taken better care of it. It has a little holster wear around the muzzle, and it's had a lot of rounds through it. It knocked over bowling pins, shot some steel, and took every stage but one in the only 2700 pistol match I ever fired. (The match was a new shooter only match, we were all newbies.) It's been a great pistol and I'll own it until I die.

When I bought that Gold Cup, Colt was the only company making a quality 1911. There was a 1911 knock off made by Llama but it really wasn't a 1911 because parts weren't interchangeable. Today, it would be almost impossible to keep track of the

Recoil with the 9mm was soft and manageable, perfect for the beginning competitor. It was one of the most pleasant pistols to shoot that I've tested in a long time.

companies that make 1911s and double-stack versions of the 1911.

One of the most noteworthy names in American gun making has been Springfield Armory. Located in Springfield, Massachusetts, the company was a center of manufacture for US military arms from 1777 to 1968. Robert Reese obtained use of the name, changing it to Springfield Armory Inc. in 1974, and developed and marketed the M1A, a civilian version of the M14, under that name. Based in Geneseo, Illinois, the company sold receivers and parts as well as complete M1A rifles. For years, Springfield Armory M1As dominated NRA and DCM Service Rifle competition. I used a Springfield Armory-based gun to win my Distinguished Rifleman badge and President's 100, as did almost every member of my team.

In 1985, Springfield released their 1911, the 1911-A1. Early guns were exact copies of standard-issue 1911s. Other models followed, and the Range Officer was released in 2010. Almost everyone I've talked to who bought a Range Officer has been impressed with the value and quality. Don't forget that it comes with a serviceable holster, a double magazine pouch, an extra magazine, and a really good hard carrying case.

Obviously, there are features that come on more expensive guns that aren't on the Range Officer, but the list of standard features is impressive. With a very affordable MSRP of $977.00 and selling for around $800.00, the Range Officer is designed for competitive shooting and features many of the bells and whistles on guns with a much higher price tag.

Now the company is offering the Range Officer in 9mm Luger, and this really makes sense because

On the Ransom Rest, the Range Officer stayed around the two-inch mark at 25 yards with only two shots outside, and eight in one ragged hole.

so many competitive shooters use 9mm. The cost of shooting 9mm over .45 is considerable, and many matches have round counts somewhere north of 100. Magazine capacities are greater in 9mm and most importantly, recoil is more manageable with a 9mm. Even if the shooter eventually plans to get into serious competition later, beginning with a nine is a good idea. The most serious impediment to fast and accurate shooting is poor trigger management and anticipation of recoil. Beginning with a nine can help a beginning shooter to better manage the trigger while avoiding getting into an issue with flinching.

As a shooting instructor, I see a lot of new shooters who choose to start with a .40 or .45 and then develop serious issues with recoil anticipation. Those issues can have such a disastrous effect on accuracy

as to discourage the new shooter, and sometimes these become habits that are almost impossible to break. The Range Officer in 9mm has everything the beginning competitor needs to get started at a very reasonable cost, and provides more than enough accuracy for all but the more advanced competitors in action shooting.

Of course, the Range Officer as it comes out of the box isn't going to win the Bianchi Cup, but it's a good starting point. Obviously, it could be the basis for a very serious race gun. A fellow named Rob Leatham has had a little more than his share of success using Springfield Armory guns, and he continues to do so.

Everything is there for a performance pistol; in fact, the Range Officer has about everything my first 1911 had, and it was the top-of-the-line Colt Gold Cup. While the exterior finish of the Range Officer

Lots of ergonomic features on the outside, but a basic 1911 on the inside. The Range Officer was well finished inside and out.

is below the level of the Pre-70 Gold Cup, slide and frame fit are as good or better. The barrel bushing fit on the Range Officer is definitely better. I really like the trigger design, and the trigger works well enough for accurate shooting, though a little finesse from a good gunsmith to lighten it and make it a little more crisp would help. The Gold Cup's trigger is a little better, but remember, it was the best 1911 available commercially in 1969.

Shooting the new Springfield was fun. The first thing I noticed was the sights. They're reminiscent of the wonderful Bo-Mar sights that were probably the most popular addition to early 1911s. The front is a Patridge with no adorning dots, something I like. Dot sights are wonderful for novice shooters and defensive work, but they do little for speed and accuracy in competition. The rear sight has solid and tactile clicks and screw heads big enough for regular screwdrivers. While such sights may be a poor choice for concealment, they're a boon on the range.

The Range Officer is loaded with features found on guns twice the price. There's a large, extended beavertail on the grip safety and a healthy bump on the bottom for guys like me with sparse palms.

The Range Officer was fun to shoot and capable of winning matches at a club level, right out of the box.

I sometimes have a problem with the 1911's grip safety, but this one is big enough to ensure engagement. The mainspring housing is the flat pre-A1 style and well-stippled, another feature I like. I would have liked the same stippling on the front of the grip frame as well, but it's smooth. Grips are cocobolo with good checkering and the familiar Springfield Armory logo.

The hammer is skeletonized and large enough to easily disengage, in spite of the big rear sight, and there's an extended safety lever. The trigger is a long one with an Allen screw overtravel adjustment. The magazines are stainless steel and have witness holes. Almost every ergonomic feature you'd ask for on a 1911 target pistol is already there.

Inside, the Ranger Officer is old school. The barrel is stainless steel and is slightly larger at the muzzle end, but otherwise there are no new tricks. The Range Officer is well finished inside and out and I actually like the old-style short recoil spring guide.

Apparently, the old school internals didn't have an adverse effect on accuracy. My first ten-shot string at 25 yards off the Ransom rest produced a right-side flyer, a left-side shot, and seven of the next eight shots were in one hole. I suspect the first shot was the gun settling into the grip adapter. Subsequent groups displayed about the same group size without the flyer but none produced seven shots in one hole. Groups averaged around two inches with Remington 115 Metal Case ammunition, quite respectable for an entry-level-priced pistol.

Standing at ten yards, it was pretty easy to stay within an inch and a half. On plates, the Range Officer was really easy to shoot. I like 1911s and it felt like an old friend in my hand. Recoil was soft, the sights were easy to see and the adjustable sights allowed choosing the sight picture I like to see. I didn't have time to shoot a plate match with it, but I plan to. It's a great little pistol.

I'm not a real competitive pistol shooter. I dabble, but I practice little, and rarely shoot a match with the same gun twice, there are just too many neat guns to try. At my level of competitiveness, I really don't be-

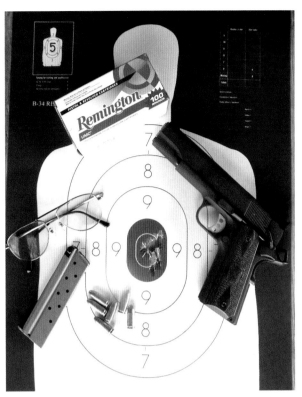

Cleaning the half-scale B34 target at ten yards was easy. The Range Officer is large for concealed carry, but as a recreational and light competition gun, it's a confidence builder because it's so easy to shoot well.

lieve the Range Officer would put me at any real disadvantage over a pistol twice or even three times the price. It's certainly accurate enough to clean all yards on a plate rack and wouldn't give up much on the 50-yard shots in the Practical stage of the Bianchi.

I do have friends who are much better action pistol shooters than I, and they were as impressed with the 9mm Range Officer as I was. After shooting a little over a hundred rounds through it, one of them said, "I like it. I give it a 10."

"A 10?" I said, "That would mean it's as good as your worked-over STI?"

"I give it a 10 when you consider everything, including the price," he said, smiling. "My STI is a 10 when you don't consider the price, and I still had to spend more money to get it there. When you consider the cost, this one's a 10 right out of the box."

IN-DEPTH

Service Striker pistol: The modern striker-fired service guns are reliable, accurate, and easy to learn to operate. Recoil in 9mm was pleasant and all three guns tested represented an excellent choice.

THREE STRIKER-FIRED SERVICE PISTOLS

The introduction of the modern striker-fired service pistol has been the most significant change in service pistol design since the inception of the double-action revolver. Fifty years ago, 95 percent of law enforcement used six-shot double-action revolvers for standard issue. Even the FBI used the 2 ½" Model 19 S&W revolver. In the 70s and 80s the mindset began to change, and departments embarked on a quest for a better service gun in a desire to enhance capacity and reduce reloading times.

A lot of different guns were tried and the results were generally unsatisfactory. Officers who were comfortable with the inherent safety of a double-action revolver began to have issues with the more complicated semi-auto safety systems they needed to deal with. Some departments tried the 1911 as their first attempt to upgrade to a greater magazine capacity and more power. The 1911 isn't an easy gun to shoot, and the safety issues with carrying it cocked and locked created concerns. Also, since the trigger was comparatively light compared to service revolvers, there were issues with accidental discharges when officers forgot to put their guns back on safe before re-holstering. This happened much more frequently when officers were stressed.

In the interest of safety, many departments then tried double-action semi-autos because they could be quickly deployed when carried with the hammer down. While this was probably a better answer, there were still issues of accidental discharges when stressed officers, used to double action revolvers, forgot to put guns on safe before re-holstering. Eventually such designs as double action only semi-autos

were adapted, allowing greater magazine capacity and faster reloading, but suffering with difficult trigger pulls.

In the early 80s Gaston Glock designed the Glock Model 17, a gun that completely changed the face of the service pistol. Using a relatively new design, the Glock 17 circumvented the safety issues of earlier semi-auto designs. By using an inner blade in the trigger and increasing the length of the trigger pull over previous systems, the Glock was able to operate like a double-action revolver, but with over twice the capacity and much faster reloading. While there was original resistance to the polymer frame, the system eventually found its way into its current niche as the most prevalent operating system for service pistols.

Currently, there are three striker fired pistols in primary contention for the service pistol market. There are other notable guns, but for this comparison, I'm covering the guns with the biggest sales numbers. I chose 9mm as the caliber because in recent times, 9mm Luger, with the excellent loadings we now have available, has regained popularity with law enforcement agencies as a good combination of manageability and power. Of the three guns, the Glock was the most compact, the XDm the least, but the differences were fairly minor. All the guns in the test are basic models as would likely be chosen by both civilians and agencies.

First, the similarities: all the guns in the test use a polymer frame. All have non-adjustable rear sights that can be windage adjusted within a dovetail. All have safety triggers that require complete coverage of the trigger before the gun will fire. All use double-stack, high-capacity magazines with witness holes to allow an external round count. The Glock and M&P have 17-round capacities and the XDm holds 19. All three guns have a forward rail for mounting lasers or lights, and all have interchangeable back-straps for better hand fit. All three guns are easy to field strip and clean.

The guns were accuracy tested and several hundred rounds were fired in conducting the tests without a single malfunction. Besides myself, there were two other testers, Ray Owens, president of my gun club and an NRA Rifle, Pistol and Shotgun instruc-

tor, and Mike Byrd, my longtime friend and gun-smith who is a fairly successful action pistol and three-gun competitor.

The Glock certainly deserves first mention because it was the pioneer in the field. The gun tested is the Model 17, the first model in the now-extensive Glock product line. Currently, the latest version is the Generation 4. Other than the recoil spring and extractor designs, the changes in the Glock generations mostly are concerned with ergonomics. While all the guns reviewed have a following, the Glock probably has the most loyal following of any

Field stripping of all three guns was simple. The Springfield Armory XDm is the only gun in the group that can be disassembled without pulling the trigger and the only gun with a single recoil spring.

The more raked grip angle of the Glock was noticed by those who weren't regular Glock shooters. I found myself having to roll the gun forward after every shot to get the front sight down. If you shoot Glocks all the time, this wouldn't be a problem.

handgun in the group. Glock considers its design as a safety action and those safety features are what's propelled the Glock to the forefront of the striker-fired revolution; in fact, those features could be said to have created the popularity of striker-fired pistols. The Glock is affordable, reliable, and safe, all characteristics that make a good service pistol.

Of course, the Glock pistol also has detractors. Glocks use a different grip angle from almost every other semi-auto service type pistol and this generates a fair amount of controversy. The other issue of primary concern is the trigger. Of the three testers who fired these guns, all said the Glock trigger was the worst, and none liked the grip angle in spite of the fact that Ray regularly competes in Glock events.

The sights are a white dot on the front and an outlined U at the rear. One of the testers liked the Glock sight best. The Glock was arguably the hardest of the three to field strip because the takedown tabs must be held down to allow the slide to extend forward.

The Smith and Wesson M&P was introduced in 2005, superseding the Sigma series of pistols with a much better trigger pull and better ergonomics. It's the only of the three guns in the test available with a manual thumb safety. While the Glock partially compresses the striker spring on pulling the trigger, the M&P simply rotates it down.

All the testers felt the M&P had a better feel, even Ray, the Glock shooter. The standard backstrap provides a hand-filling grip that doesn't feel bulky. The M&P was also the winner in the trigger contest, getting two of three votes. Out of the box, it was crisp and had a good feel. All the testers agreed the M&P had the most controllable recoil, though the best time on six plates at ten yards was with the XDm and Mike Byrd, the best shooter in the group. Mike preferred the XDm trigger to the M&P even though the M&P had a better break.

The Springfield Armory XDm and I have a lot of history. I've shot two Bianchi Cups with my 9mm 5.25 with the only modification being a trigger Rob Leatham installed. Mine has been as reliable as any

CAUTION- CAPABLE OF FIRING WITH MAGAZINE REMOVED

SMITH & W
SPRINGFIELD, M

MRM1931

The M&P trigger is hinged rather than bladed. The switchable magazine release makes the M&P completely compatible with left-handed shooters.

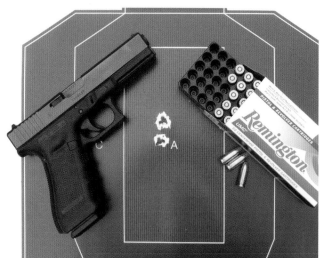

My best 10-yard standing target shot with the Glock resulted in two separate groups but is still remarkably good for ten shots.

I liked the feel of the M&P the best, it also seemed to shoot the flattest. Group size was larger than the other two guns, but shooting unsupported at ten yards isn't a definitive test.

gun I've ever owned, but this is no distinction in this group of guns, they all have the reputation for solid reliability. The XDm has an extra safety feature I really like in the grip safety. For service and duty guns, passive safety systems have proven to have real merit and the grip safety on the XD is a great idea.

The standard XDm we tested had an excellent trigger, and though it was a reasonable trigger for a service gun, it was the lightest. For some reason, the XDm feels tall and a little top-heavy. On recoil, Mike and I observed that it seemed to have the most muzzle flip. I suspect this is because it has the highest center-of-bore over the grip, but again, it shot the fastest times on the plates.

The grip safety on the XDm is a viable safety feature on a service pistol.

The XDm was the easiest gun to field strip and the only one that didn't require a pull of the trigger to remove the slide. I know at least one individual who's shot his hand disassembling a Glock. (Please, no lamentations that he did the wrong thing, this is obvious, but it's something that happens.) The XDm

The XDm had the best trigger, and shot the best target with all ten shots going into one hole. Of course, it's designated as a match version and the other two were straight service guns.

also has the most substantial frame rails, having what looks like twice the contact area as the other two guns.

In summary, all these guns are exceptional firearms with the right blend of accuracy, safety, and reliability that make a great service pistol. What makes a great service pistol doesn't make a great competition or target gun, though all these guns can be modified to do well in competition, and they regularly do. It all boils down to what you like, both in brand loyalty and features. Of the three of us, the M&P came out the winner by a slight margin. We all liked it better, but only a bit better. The Glock ended up at the bottom of our pile but, everyone agreed it's a really good gun. Since all of us have a competitive background, I suspect the trigger hurt the Glock most, but the different grip angle didn't help. I suspect the Glock suffered from being the first in the class. The M&P and XDm both had features like a cocking indicator, grip safety on the XDm and ambidextrous slide release, and simpler take down on the M&P. They're three wonderful guns and all are perfectly suited to the task they're designed for. In the end, it's a matter of your choice, and you can't choose a bad gun among them.

CHAPTER 17

THE HEAVYWEIGHTS

Ok, so maybe a concealed carry citizen doesn't need to carry the most powerful handgun in the world, and this book really is about concealed carry. Still, most who read this are Americans, and in the United States we love a bit of overkill. These guns are the Hemi Cudas of handguns, with enough power to stop anything that walks in the Western Hemisphere. They aren't designed for concealed carry, but they are designed as defensive weapons. I'm sure that the guns in this class that see real duty are almost all employed in Alaska, where it's necessary to work and live around large and dangerous bears.

While none of these guns are pleasant to shoot because they generate copious amounts of recoil and muzzle blast, they are remarkably accurate. As firearms for the concealed carry citizen - even a large citizen who didn't mind a heavy gun - they'd make a poor choice with full-power ammunition because the powerful rounds they employ have far too much penetration to be safe anywhere but the most remote areas. Still, they're fun to think about.

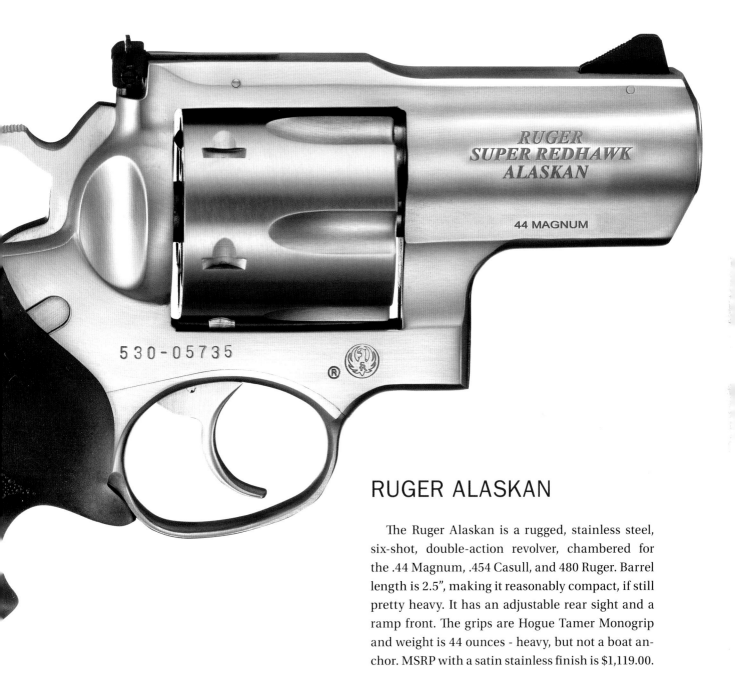

RUGER ALASKAN

The Ruger Alaskan is a rugged, stainless steel, six-shot, double-action revolver, chambered for the .44 Magnum, .454 Casull, and 480 Ruger. Barrel length is 2.5", making it reasonably compact, if still pretty heavy. It has an adjustable rear sight and a ramp front. The grips are Hogue Tamer Monogrip and weight is 44 ounces - heavy, but not a boat anchor. MSRP with a satin stainless finish is $1,119.00.

TAURUS RAGING BULL

The Taurus Raging Bull .454 is a five-shot double action with a 2.250" barrel. It has a fixed rear sight and a fiber optic front. The barrel is shrouded to the muzzle and grips are soft rubber for recoil management. The muzzle is ported on both sides of the front sight. Weight is 44 ounces and finish is matte stainless steel. MSRP is $1,054.78.

SMITH & WESSON .460 V

Smith & Wesson's .460 V might be a really big gun, but it does have a level of versatility that allows it to cover a wide range of ammunition power levels. Chambered for the powerful .460 S&W Magnum, it's also capable of shooting .45 Colt and .454 Casull ammunition. Even with a 3.5" barrel, it's a really big gun, massive in both bulk and weight. Overall length is 10" and weight is 59.5 ounces. Frame and cylinder are stainless steel with a matte finish, grips are synthetic, large, and sport finger grooves. The sights are an adjustable rear and a fiber optic front. The massive barrel has a full-length shroud and the cylinder holds five rounds to provide easier extraction and helps keep the bulk down to massive instead of enormous. I've shot this gun and recoil isn't as punishing as one might think because of the over 60 ounces the gun weighs loaded. It's surprisingly accurate, provided you don't flinch. MSRP is $1,609.00.

SMITH & WESSON 500

The .500 Smith & Wesson is the most powerful production handgun round in the world. The gun that shoots it is a massive five-shot, double-action revolver on the same X frame as the .460. The shortest barrel in the line is the 4" version that has a full-length barrel shroud and is ported at the muzzle to reduce recoil. Sights are adjustable rear and a red fiber optic at the front. Weight in the 4" length is 56.5 ounces and the finish is satin stainless and grips are black synthetic with finger grooves. MSRP is $1,369.00.

CHAPTER 18

THE TRAINERS

While the .22 rimfire might not be the best choice for concealed carry due to its low level of energy and modest power, that very characteristic, along with low price, makes it the most suitable round available for training. All good rifle and pistol trainers have relied on the lowly .22 Long Rifle round for at least a part of the development of their expertise. The .22 is cheap, it has low recoil - which makes learning to shoot accurately easier, and it can be used in locations where other calibers generate too much noise.

Today, we're blessed with trainer versions of so many duty and concealed carry guns that it's not difficult to find one that matches up operationally with your carry gun. To acquire the level of operational training that allows shooting your gun the way you drive your car, there has to be repetition. That level of repetition requires firing of a minimum 2,000 shots. Since rimfire ammunition normally costs about 20% of what centerfire ammunition costs, you can buy a good rimfire trainer and pay for it in ammunition costs. In effect, you get a viable training tool for free.

Of course, the closer your trainer is to your daily carry gun, the better. In some cases, you'll be able to get an exact copy that's almost identical. In some situations,

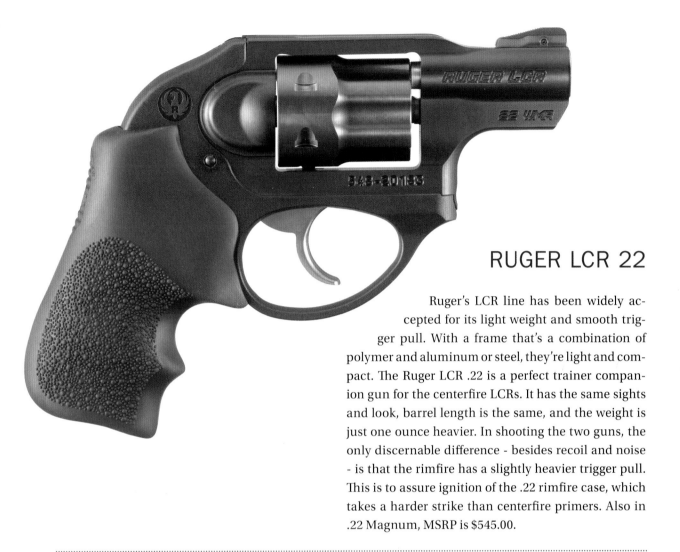

RUGER LCR 22

Ruger's LCR line has been widely accepted for its light weight and smooth trigger pull. With a frame that's a combination of polymer and aluminum or steel, they're light and compact. The Ruger LCR .22 is a perfect trainer companion gun for the centerfire LCRs. It has the same sights and look, barrel length is the same, and the weight is just one ounce heavier. In shooting the two guns, the only discernable difference - besides recoil and noise - is that the rimfire has a slightly heavier trigger pull. This is to assure ignition of the .22 rimfire case, which takes a harder strike than centerfire primers. Also in .22 Magnum, MSRP is $545.00.

SMITH & WESSON 617

The S&W 617 is a full-size K frame ten-shot .22 rimfire revolver. It has a Patridge front and S&W's excellent rear adjustable sight. There are full-size synthetic grips and a stainless steel frame, cylinder, and barrel. It has a full-length barrel shroud that closely resembles the 686 centerfire pistols. While it's considerably larger than the concealed carry versions of the Smith & Wesson line, it has the same quality double and single-action trigger and makes an excellent choice as a training and marksmanship tool. Learning to manage a double-action trigger is

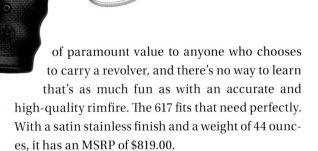

of paramount value to anyone who chooses to carry a revolver, and there's no way to learn that's as much fun as with an accurate and high-quality rimfire. The 617 fits that need perfectly. With a satin stainless finish and a weight of 44 ounces, it has an MSRP of $819.00.

SMITH & WESSON 317

The S&W 317 is an eight-shot .22 rimfire built on the .38 Special five-shot J frame. It uses an aluminum alloy cylinder and frame, putting the weight at 12.5 ounces. With a three-inch barrel it also sports excellent adjustable sights allowing precision accuracy from a tiny package. While it's a great trainer, it's also a wonderful utility/kit gun for camping or general outdoor use. It comes with rubber grips and has an MSRP of $759.00.

CHARTER ARMS PATHFINDER

Charter Arms has been producing small-frame revolvers for a couple generations, and the Pathfinder rimfire version has proven a reliable small-frame trainer and utility gun. It's a six-shot rimfire version of the Undercover centerfire and is all-stainless steel with a matte finish. The grip is rubber and uses the same laser grips as all the other guns in the Charter line. It's available as a 2" fixed-sight gun in both .22 Long Rifle and .22 Magnum. Weight is 19 ounces and MSRP is $363.00 for either caliber.

RUGER 22/45

Ruger's 22/45 is a modified version of the original MK I gun introduced by Ruger when the company began. The frame has been modified to replicate the 1911 grip angle and the magazine release is moved to the 1911 position from the original base of the grip location. The safety is still in the same place and replicates a 1911 safety in location only. As a trainer for accuracy and general firearms handling, it's a great gun. It doesn't really replicate any real duty or carry gun enough to make it a viable cross trainer, but it's just too good as a rimfire in general not to mention. It has excellent sights, a good single-action trigger and is very accurate. MSRP is $369.00.

RUGER SR22

Ruger's SR22 is a small-frame trainer that replicates the modern concealed carry pistol with a double/single-action trigger system. It uses a polymer frame and has an exposed hammer. Sights are adjustable three-dot and the safety and magazine release are switchable for lefties. While almost everything about it replicates the modern double/single carry gun, the frame-mounted safety is a mystery. Instead of sweeping down like almost everything else, it sweeps forward and up. It's also a de-cocker and many concealed carry citizens who use double/single guns don't engage the safety while carrying, instead using it as a de-cocker only and relying on the long trigger pull. It's an excellent trainer with an MSRP of $415.00.

SIG 1911 .22

One of my favorite trainers is a SIG 1911 rimfire that's been hot-rodded into a gun similar to the Para 18/9 I used in the 2011 Bianchi Cup. My friend Mike Byrd, of B&B Machine, replaced many of the standard parts with match gun parts to produce an adjustable-sighted, enhanced rimfire with a wonderful match trigger. I've used this gun for training so much that it's lost probably 20 percent of its original finish. The GSG 1911s use a high percentage of parts that are interchangeable with standard 1911 parts, allowing them to serve as great trainers for competition shooting. GSG, (German Sport Guns) makes another version and also makes the 922, a rimfire that closely replicates the 3" barreled compact 1911s like the Para Executive Carry reviewed in this book. They feature Novak-type sights , skeleton triggers and hammers, a generous beavertail, and a bottom accessory rail. Magazines are metal, extremely solid, and hold 10 rounds. MSRP in the base GSG model is $379.95. The SIG version is $460.00.

SMITH & WESSON M&P COMPACT

Smith & Wessson's M&P Compact is a great little practice gun for the concealed carry citizen. It's a true striker-fired pistol, and everything is configured in a similar manner to 90 percent of striker-fired guns. As an M&P, it uses a hinged trigger instead of the bladed system of most striker-fired guns, but this isn't a tactile difference that's noticed for training purposes. There's a manual thumb safety, but training for a gun that doesn't use a safety simply means not using the thumb safety on the M&P. It's accurate and reliable and has an adjustable rear sight. With a magazine capacity of 10 + 1, it has an MSRP of $389.00.

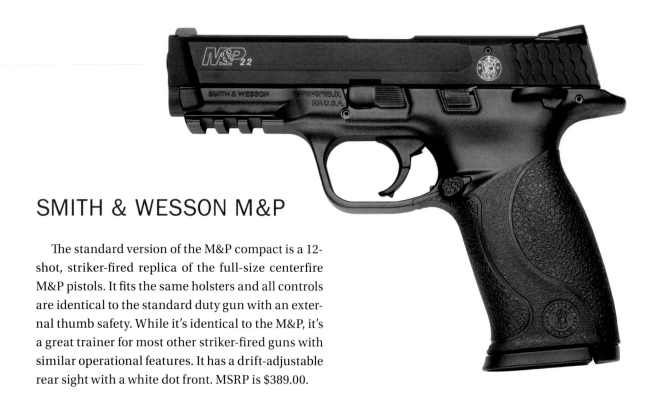

SMITH & WESSON M&P

The standard version of the M&P compact is a 12-shot, striker-fired replica of the full-size centerfire M&P pistols. It fits the same holsters and all controls are identical to the standard duty gun with an external thumb safety. While it's identical to the M&P, it's a great trainer for most other striker-fired guns with similar operational features. It has a drift-adjustable rear sight with a white dot front. MSRP is $389.00.

WALTHER PPQ 22

Walter's PPQ is similar to the M&P 22 in full size, in that it completely copies its companion centerfire, the PPQ M2. Everything about the PPW replicates the centerfire gun in operation, size, and shape. It weighs just three ounces less but has the same controls and trigger style as its big brother. It comes as a four-inch or five-inch model and has a 12-round magazine. There's also a tactical version with a threaded barrel. MSRP is $429.00.

TACTICAL SOLUTIONS
GLOCK CONVERSION KIT

Another alternative is the Tactical Solutions Glock 22 conversion kit. Consisting of a slide/barrel/spring assembly and a magazine, you can convert your Glock 17 or 19 into a semi-automatic .22. The conversion takes seconds to complete. You remove the magazine, check the gun for clear, and remove the slide assembly. You then install the Tactical Solutions 22 slide assembly and insert the .22 magazine and the conversion is complete. MSRP for the conversion is $345.00.

IVER JOHNSON 22 CONVERSION
FOR THE 1911

Iver Johnson makes a .22 rimfire kit for the 1911 in a standard version with fixed sights, and deluxe model with adjustable sights. The kit consists of a slide, barrel, and spring assembly and a 15 shot magazine. To convert to .22 you simply switch slides and magazines and it's ready to run. Available in bright or black, the basic model is $199.00, and the deluxe with adjustable sights, is $249.00.

THE CHOICE IS YOURS

The decision of which gun makes the best choice for concealed carry for you and your lifestyle doesn't come down to a simple equation. Every gun listed in this book might very well offer the perfect choice for a specific need. Where you live, where you go during the course of a normal day, how committed you are to practice and preparation, and of course your personal preferences, all create a profile for you that few other people share.

To best make this choice, realistically assess your needs and take into consideration the things you feel you need in a gun. In the editorial parts of this book, I have expressed opinions based on my own experience and preferences. Those opinions are just that – opinions, and there's no intention on my part to override the ideas of the reader, but instead to add additional insight. While I don't consider a full-size, high-capacity gun viable for concealed carry, I don't lead your life and if you want to carry such a gun, it's your decision. Ultimately, if you decide your first choice wasn't what you really need, you can always buy another gun, and today we're blessed with a lot of options for you to test without having to buy them.

In my classes as an instructor, I make different guns available for my clients to test. Most indoor ranges have rental guns, and spending a session with a rental gun before purchase is a great way to find out if it's really what you want. However, don't forget that concealed carry guns are carried much more than they're used, although if you wind up having to use your gun in self-defense, it must be capable of stopping the aggressor reliably. Life would be simpler if that were the only issue, but that isn't the case. The gun you carry must be a gun you can handle properly and operate under pressure.

If your gun malfunctions, you must be able to get it running again in a tiny amount of time, and your success in doing this could potentially mean your life.

Not only this, but the gun you choose has to be a gun you can shoot accurately enough to hit your target in a vital area. As noted elsewhere in these pages, in many cases the appearance of a firearm is enough to stop the threat, and firing the gun that results in a near miss will stop many aggressors. The problem is you're not firing that shot on a shooting range. In many cases, you're firing that shot in a public location with a chance of an errant shot hitting an innocent person. If you shoot, you must hit your target or face the possibility of injuring or killing an uninvolved bystander. Besides the legal ramifications, imagine living the rest of your life knowing your bad decision cost the life of another innocent person.

Also of consequence is the fact that your choice of firearm has to have safety features that are compatible with your lifestyle. If there are never children around you and your firearms, you might make a different choice than if there are small children present in your life.

Finally, the gun you choose must be a gun you can comfortably conceal and carry on a daily basis without getting slack and leaving it at home because of inconvenience. For a defensive firearm to serve its purpose, it has to be within easy reach when you need it. If we took this final consideration off the table, the choice would be an easy one; I'd carry a large and powerful, high-capacity, full-size pistol or perhaps even a shotgun. Most of us have trouble when it comes to measuring our own level of discipline. If this weren't the case, everyone who wants to lose weight would simply lose their excess weight by eating less. Humans by nature overestimate their ability to commit to a plan, and choosing a gun that you'll leave behind will quickly soften your resolve for daily carry. For you to fulfill your commitment to be a daily concealed carry citizen, you must choose a gun that will be comfortable enough to go with you every day and in every situation. In level of importance, this is the most important criteria for daily defensive carry. The best gun

THE GUN YOU CARRY MUST BE A GUN YOU CAN HANDLE PROPERLY AND OPERATE UNDER PRESSURE.

FOR YOU TO FULFILL YOUR COMMITMENT TO BE A DAILY CONCEALED CARRY CITIZEN, YOU MUST CHOOSE A GUN THAT WILL BE COMFORTABLE ENOUGH TO GO WITH YOU EVERY DAY AND IN EVERY SITUATION. IN LEVEL OF IMPORTANCE, THIS IS THE MOST IMPORTANT CRITERIA FOR DAILY DEFENSIVE CARRY. THE BEST GUN IN THE WORLD WILL DO NOTHING FOR YOU IF YOU DON'T HAVE IT WHEN YOU NEED IT.

in the world will do nothing for you if you don't have it when you need it.

Ultimately, the choice is yours. There are so many excellent choices in every one of the categories listed in this book. None of them are bad guns and I've only scratched the surface of all the individual choices. We're currently blessed with the ability to buy the best defensive firearms in the history of the firearms industry. Ammunition for personal defense is the best it's ever been as well. Closely examine your needs and try a few guns that fit. Pick the best for you and learn to use it without having to think about what it takes to operate it and shoot accurately. By doing your homework, your chances of prevailing when faced with a dangerous situation are greatly enhanced.

WHAT I CARRY

Of course, my ultimate endorsement of what I believe is the very best gun for daily concealed carry is the gun I actually carry every day. I suspect some who read this book wonder exactly what I carry on an everyday basis. While many of my friends carry several different guns for different occasions, I carry the same gun every day no matter what I'm doing. When I was contacted about writing this book, the same gun I carry today was in my appendix holster. I chose it because it does everything I think a concealed carry gun should do. It's reliable as a rock, reasonably accurate in both normal and extremely low light, and compact and light enough for me to carry it every single day without discomfort or the temptation to leave it home.

I might be better served by carrying a smaller gun when required by weather and the tasks of the day,

and a larger gun with more capacity during winter when concealment is easier, but I see the value of continuity. My carry gun is always in the same place on my body, my draw is always the same and I use it enough in my teaching events that shooting it is both natural and effective. During concealed carry classes when the opportunity arises for demonstration, I use my daily carry gun which is always in place in my daily carry holster.

My Smith and Wesson 637 isn't as light as some guns and it isn't as powerful as others, but I have complete confidence in it based on the fact that I've often shot flies with it at close range during classes and range sessions. At 13.8 ounces, it's not as light as other guns I've tested, but it shoots one-hole groups exactly where the sights are looking at close range. The trigger is smooth and the Crimson Trace grip laser provides pinpoint accuracy in low light. I've shot a three-inch group with it at 25 yards in low light using the laser.

After doing all the research involved in writing this book, I've decided that .38 Special +P is adequate for stopping, though I sometimes wish my little 637 was a .357 just because you can never have too much stopping power, though you can have too much penetration.

Certainly, there are other guns that will perform as well, but this is the one I carry. Other guns are slimmer, more powerful, lighter in weight, have greater capacity, more accuracy, and lower recoil. For me the gun I carry is a good compromise for the way I live, and concealed carry guns are as much about compromise as anything I can think of.

I may change to another gun next week, but I doubt it.

CHAPTER 20

QUICK REFERENCE GUIDE

Model	Trigger	Calibers	Weight Oz.	Barrel Length	Capacity	MSRP
SUBCOMPACT SEMI-AUTOS						
Beretta 21A Bobcat	D/SA	.22 LR, .25 ACP	11.8	2.4"	7 + 1	$410.00
Beretta Pico	DAO	.380 ACP	11.5	2.7"	6 + 1	$398.00
Colt Mustang	SA	.380 ACP	11.8	2.75"	6 + 1	$672.00
Diamondback 380	SFDA	.380 ACP	8.8	2.8"	6 + 1	$394.00
Diamondback DB9	SFDA	9mm	11	3"	6 + 1	$431.00
Glock 42	SFDA	.380 ACP	13.75	3.25"	6 + 1	$449.00
Kahr P380	SFDA	.380 ACP	9.9	2.5"	6 + 1	$667.00
Kahr CW380	SFDA	.380 ACP	10.2	2.58"	6 + !	$419.00
Keltec P3AT	SFDA	.380 ACP	8.3	2.7"	6 + 1	$318.00
Kimber Micro Carry	SA	.380 ACP	13.4	2,75	6 + !	$651.00
Ruger LCP	SFDA	.380 ACP	9.4	2.75"	6 + 1	$389.00
Smith and Wesson Bodyguard	DAO	.380 ACP	12	2.75"	6 + 1	$379.00
Taurus 738 TCP	DAO	.380 ACP	10.2	2.84"	6 + 1	$254.02
Taurus PT25	DAO	.25ACP	12.3	2.75"	9 + 1	$276.28

Model	Trigger	Calibers	Weight Oz.	Barrel Length	Capacity	MSRP
COMPACT SEMI-AUTOS						
Beretta Nano	SF2S	9mm	19.8	3.07"	6 + 1	$475.00
Bersa Thunder	D/SA	.380 ACP	20	3.54"	8 + 1	$569.00
Glock 36	SF2S	.45 ACP	22.4	3.77"	6 + 1	$637.00
Glock 26	SF2S	9mm	21.8	3.42"	10 + 1	$599.00
Kahr CM9 CM40	DAO	9mm	15.9	3"	6 + 1	$460.00
Keltech P-11	DAO	9mm	14	3.1"	10 + 1	$333.00
Keltech PF9	DAO	9mm	12.7	3.1"	7 + 1	$333.00
Kimber Solo	SF2s	9mm	17.1	2.7"	6 + 1	$765.00
Magnum Research Micro Desert Eagle	SA	.380 ACP	14	2.2"	6 + !	$467.00
North American Arms Guardian	DAO	.380 ACP	18.7	2.5"	6 + 1	$449.00
Ruger LC9s	SF2S	9mm	17.2	3.12"	7 + 1	$449.00
Ruger LC 380	SF2S	.380 ACP	17.2	3.12'	7 +1	$449.00
Ruger SR9C	SF2S	9mm	23.4	3.4"	17 + 1	$529.00
SCCY CPX	DAO	9mm	15	3.1'	10 + 1	$319.00-$599.00
SIG P238	SA	.380ACP	15.2	2.7"	6 + 1	$679.00
Sig P938	SA	9mm	16	2.7"	6 + 1	$750.00
Smith and Wesson Shield	SF2S	9mm	19	3.1"	7 + 1	$449.00
Smith and Wesson M&P Compact	SF2S	9mm	21.9	3.5"	12 + 1	$569.00
Springfield Armory XDs	SF2S	9mm	23	3.3"	7 + 1	$599.00
Springfield Armory XD Compact	SF2S	9mm	26	3"	13 + 1	$599.00
Taurus Millennium G2	SF2S	9mm	22	3,2'	12 + 1	$434.59
Taurus 709 SLIM	SF2S	9mm	19	3"	7 + 1	$503.73
Walther PPK	D/SA	.380 ACP	20	3.3"	6 + 1	$695.00
Walther PK 380	D/SA	.380	18	3.66"	8 + 1	$399.00
Walther PPS	SF2S	9mm	19	3.2"	8 + 1	$599.00
Remington R51	D/SA	9mm	22	3.4"	7 + 1	NA

Model	Trigger	Calibers	Weight Oz.	Barrel Length	Capacity	MSRP
MID-SIZED SEMI-AUTOS						
Beretta PX4 Sub Compact	D/SA	9mm	26.1	3"	15 + 1	$575.00
Beretta 92 Compact	D/SA	9mm	31	4.25"	13 + 1	$745.00
Bersa Thunder	D/SA	.380 ACP	18.9	3.5"	10 + 1	$569.00
Bersa BP9CC	SF2S	9mm	21.5	3.3"	8 + 1	$429.00
Colt New Agent	SA	.45 ACP	22.5	3"	7 + 1	$1,078.00
Colt Defender	SA	.45 ACP	24	3"	7 + 1	$973.00
CZ P O1	D/SA	9mm	28	3.8"	14 + 1	$627.00
CZ P 07	D/SA	9mm	26	3.8"	15 + 1	$510.00
CZ SDP	D/SA	9mm	28	3"	14 + 1	$1,420.00
Guncrafters CCO	SA	.45 ACP	33/27	4.25"	7 + 1	$2,899.00
FNH FNX9	D/SA	9mm	21	4"	17 + 1	$799.00
FNH FNs	SF2S	9mm	23.4	3.6"	17 + 1	$649.00
Glock 19	SF2S	9mm	23.6	4"	15 + 1	$599.00
HK P30	D/SA	9mm	23	3.86"	15 + 1	$1,023.00
Kahr T 9	D/SA	9mm	26	3.9"	8 + 1	$857.00
Keltec PMR 30	SF2S	.22 Magnum	13.6	4.3"	30 + 1	$415.00
Kimber Pro Carry II	SA	.45 ACP	28	4"	7 + 1	$919.00
Para Executive Carry	SA	.45 ACP	30	3"	8 + 1	$1,399.00
Remington R1 Carry	SA	.45ACP	38.5	4.25"	7 + 1	$729.00
Ruger SR9	SF2S	9mm	27.25	4.14"	17 + 1	$429.00
SIG P220 Compact	D/SA	.45 ACP	29.6	3.9"	6 + 1	$1,166.00
Smith and Wesson 1911 SW1911 Sub Compact	SA	.45 ACP	26.5	3"	7 + 1	$1,229.00
Springfield Armory RO Compact	SA	.45 ACP	28.5	4"	6 + 1	$899.00
Springfield Armory XD 4"	SF2S	9mm	28	4"	16 + 1	$599.00
Taurus 840	D/SA	.40 S&W	29.6	3.625"	17 + 1	$486.93

Model	Trigger	Calibers	Weight Oz.	Barrel Length	Capacity	MSRP
FULL SIZED SEMI-AUTOS						
Beretta 92	D/SA	9mm	33.3	4.9"	15 + 1	$675.00
Beretta PX4	D/SA	9mm	28	4"	17 + 1	$650.00
Colt 1911	SA	.45 ACP	38	5"	8 + 1	$907.00
CZ 85	D/SA	9mm	34	4.61'	16 + 1	$664.00
CZ P07	D/SA	9mm	27.16	3.7"	16 + 1	$449.00
Dan Wesson RZ 45 Heritage	SA	.45 ACP	39	5"	8 + 1	$1,298.00
FNH FNs	SF2S	9mm	25,2	4"	17 + 1	$649.00
FNH Five-seveN	SA	5.7 x 28	20.8	4.8"	20 + 1	$1,349.00
Glock 17	SF2S	9mm	25	4.48"	17 + 1	$599.00
HK VP9	SF2S	9mm	25.56	4.09"	15 + 1	$719.00
Kimber 1911 Custom II	SA	.45 ACP	38	5"	8 + 1	$871.00
Magnum Research 1911	SA	.45 ACP	38	5"	8 + 1	$831.00
Remington 1911 R1	SA	.45 ACP	38	5"	7 + 1	$729.00
Ruger SR 40/45	SF2S	.40 S&W	27.25	4.14'	15 + 1	$529.00
Ruger 1911	SA	.45 ACP	39	5"	8 + 1	$859.00
SIG P320	SF2S	9mm	25.8	3.9"	17 + 1	$669.00
SIG 226	D/SA	9mm	34	4.4"	15 + 1	$1,015.00
Smith and Wesson M&P	SF2S	9mm	24	4.5"	17 + 1	$569.00
Springfield Armory XDm	SF2S	9mm	29	4.5"	19 + 1	$649.00
Springfield Armory XD	SF2S	9mm	28	4"	16 + 1	$599.00
Springfield Armory 1911 Range Officer	SA	.45 ACP	38	5"	8 + 1	$899.00
Styer L40A1and L9A1	SF2S	9mm	28.5	4.5"	17 + 1	$540.00
Taurus 24/7	D/SA	9mm	28	4.2"	17 + 1	$528.15
Taurus 1911	SA	.45 ACP	38	5"	8 + 1	$834.97
Walther PPQ M2	SF2S	9mm	24	4"	15 + 1	$649.00
Walther PPX	SF2S	9mm	26	4"	16 + 1	$449.00

Model	Trigger	Calibers	Weight Oz.	Barrel Length	Capacity	MSRP
SUBCOMPACT REVOLVERS						
Charter Arms Undercover, Off Duty	D/SA	.38 Special	12	2"	5	$383.00
North American Sidewinder	SA	.22 LR, .22 Manunum	6.7	1"	5	$349.00
Ruger LCR	DAO	.38 Special	13.5	1.875"	5	$545.00
Smith and Wesson 642	D/SA	.38 Special	13.7	1.875"	5	$469.00
Smith and Wesson Bodyguard	DAO	.38 Special	14.4	1.9"	5	$539.00
Smith and Wesson 340 PD	DAO	.357 Magnum	11.4	1.875"	5	$1,019.00
Smith and Wesson W 351 PD	D/SA	.22 Magnum	10.8	1.875"		$759.00
Taurus 85 Ultralite	D/SA	.38 Special	17	2"	5	$413.17
Taurus Vue/Novue	DAO	.38 Special	9.4	1.5"	5	$599.00

Model	Trigger	Calibers	Weight Oz.	Barrel Length	Capacity	MSRP
COMPACT REVOLVERS						
Chiappa Rhino DS 2" Alloy	D/SA	.357 Magnum	22	2"	5	$405.00
Charter Arms Bulldog	D/SA	.44 Special	21	2.5"	5	$429.00
Ruger's LCR .357	DAO	.357 Magnum	17.2	1.875"	5	$619.00
Ruger LCR 9mm	DAO	.357 Magnum	17.2	1.875"	5	$619.00
Ruger LCRx 3"	D/SA	.38 Special	15.7	3"	5	$545.00
Ruger SP 101	D/SA	.357 Magnum	25	2"	6	$719.00
Ruger GP100 3"	D/SA	.357 Magnum	36	3"	6	$749.00
Smith and Wesson Model 60	D/SA	.357 Magnum	22.6	2.125"	5	$729.00
Smith and Wesson Model 36	D/SA	.38 Special	19.5	1.875"	5	$749.00
Smith and Wesson Model 60 3"	D/SA	.357 Magnum	23.2	3"	5	$799.00
Smith and Wesson Model 327	D/SA	.357 Magnum	21	2"	8	$1,309.00
Smith and Wesson Model 627	D/SA	.357 Magnum	37.6	2.625"	8	$1,079.00
Smith & Wesson 686 Plus	D/SA	.357 Magnum	34.1	2.5"	8	$849.00
Rossi 38 Special and .357 Magnum	D/SA	.357 Magnum	26	2"	6	$454.89
Taurus 605 Polymer	D/SA	.357 Magnum	19.75	2"	5	$471.32
Taurus Judge 4510 Polymer	D/SA	.45 LC/.410	23	2"	5	$653.32
Taurus Judge Public Defender	D/SA	.45 LC/.410	28.2	2.5"	5	$653.32

Model	Trigger	Calibers	Weight Oz.	Barrel Length	Capacity	MSRP
FULL SIZED REVOLVERS						
Chiappa Rhino	D/SA	.357 Magnum	30	4"	6	$795.00
S&W M&P R8	D/SA	.357 Magnum	36.3	5"	8	$1,329.00
Smith and Wesson Model 69	D/SA	.44 Magnum	39	4.25"	5	$849.00
Smith and Wesson 686	D/SA	.357 Magnum	40	4"	7	$829.00
Smith and Wesson 686 SSR	D/SA	.357 Magnum	38.3	4"	7	$999.00
Smith and Wesson 625	D/SA	.45 ACP	42	4"	6	$979.00
Smith and Wesson 29	D/SA	.44 Magnum	42	4"	6	$999.00
Smith and Wesson 27 and 627	D/SA	.357 Magnum	41.2	4"	8	$1,059.00
Smith and Wesson 627 V Comp	D/SA	.357Magnum	47	5"		$1,559.00
Smith and Wesson 986	D/SA	9mm	34.9	5"	8	$1,550.00
Smith and Wesson Governor	D/SA	.45 LC, .45 ACP, .410	29.6	2.75"	6	$1,119.00
Ruger GP100	D/SA	,357 Magnum	42	4"	6	$725.00
Ruger Redhawk	D/SA	.44 Magnum	47	4"	6	$1,029.00
Ruger Super Redhawk	D/SA	.44 Magnum	53	7.7"	6	$1,079.00
Taurus 65	D/SA	.357 Magnum	38	4"	6	$488.46
Taurus Judge	D/SA	.45 IC, .410	28.2	2.5"	5	$607.53
Taurus 44	D/SA	.44 Magnum	45	4"	6	$726.49
Taurus 608	D/SA	.357 Magnum	52	4"	8	$688.43

Model	Trigger	Calibers	Weight Oz.	Barrel Length	Capacity	MSRP
THE HEAVYWEIGHTS						
Taurus Raging Bull 454	D/SA	.454 Casull	44	2.250"	6	$1,054.78
Ruger Alaskan	D/SA	.480 Ruger	44	2.5"	6	$1,119.00
Smith and Wesson 460 VXR	D/SA	.460 S&W	59.5	3.5"	5	$1,609.00
Smith and Wesson 500	D/SA	.500 S&W	56.5	4"	5	$1,369.00

Model	Trigger	Calibers	Weight Oz.	Barrel Length	Capacity	MSRP
THE TRAINERS						
Ruger LCR 22	D/SA	.22 LR	14	1.875"	8	$545.00
Smith and Wesson 317	D/SA	.22 LR	12.5	3"	8	$759.00
Smith and Wesson 617	D/SA	.22 LR	44	6"	10	$819.00
Charter Pathfinder	D/SA	.22 LR	19	2"	6	$363.00
Ruger 22/45	SA	.22 LR	32	5.5"	10 + 1	$369.00
SIG 1911 22	SA	.22 LR	31	5"	10 + 1	$460.00
Ruger SR22	D/SA	.22 LR	17.5	3.5"	10 + 1	$415.00
Smith and Wesson M&P 22 Compact	SF2S	.22 LR	15.3	3.56"	10 + 1	$389.00
Smith and Wesson M&P	SF2S	.22 LR	24	4.1"	12 + 1	$389.00
Walther PPQ	SF2S	.22 LR	20	5"	12 + 1	$429.00
Tactical Solutions Glock Rimfire Conversion	SF2S	.22 LR	N/A	4.5"	12 + 1	$345.00
Iver Johnson 1911 Rimfire Conversion	SA	.22 LR	N/A	5"	15 + 1	$249.00

Model	Trigger	Calibers	Weight Oz.	Barrel Length	Capacity	MSRP
TRIGGER LEGEND						

Single Action	SA
Striker Fired, two stage	SF2s
Double/single Action	D/SA
Double action only	DAO